Embodying American Slavery
in Contemporary Culture

Embodying American Slavery in Contemporary Culture

LISA WOOLFORK

University of Illinois Press

URBANA AND CHICAGO

Library of Congress Cataloging-in-Publication Data
Woolfork, Lisa
Embodying American slavery in contemporary culture /
Lisa Woolfork.
p. cm.
Includes bibliographical references and index.
ISBN 978-0-252-03390-2 (cloth : alk. paper)
1. Slavery—Social aspects—United States. 2. Slavery—
United States—Psychological aspects. 3. Psychic trauma—
Social aspects—United States. 4. Popular culture—United
States. 5. Body, Human, in popular culture. 6. Slavery
in literature. 7. Slavery in motion pictures. 8. Historical
reenactments—United States. 9. United States—Intellectual
life. 10. United States—Social conditions—1980–
I. Title.
E441.W89   2008
306.3'62—dc22   2008019217

To Ianthia Woolfork
and Nellie McKay
with eternal thanks
for everything

Contents

Acknowledgments

I am grateful to a number of people and institutions for helping bring this project to its current state. Funding for research and development was generously provided by many sources. The University of Virginia awarded me several Summer Grants, a Small Grant, the Humanities and Social Sciences Research Award, as well as the crucial third-year sabbatical fellowship. I am also grateful to the Woodrow Wilson Foundation and its Career Enhancement Fellowship that not only allowed me time to research and write but also hosted a wonderful conference for fellows and mentors to share their work and to interact. I also acknowledge the English Department at the University of Virginia, a supportive institutional environment that respects its junior colleagues and is invested in their success. I am grateful to the Reference Department at the University of Virginia Law School Library for offering support and a peaceful climate in which to work during my sabbatical. I also thank Joan Catapano and the University of Illinois Press, including Dawn McIlvain, Cope Cumpston, and Annette Wenda. I am also grateful for the readers whose insightful comments shaped this book.

I am thankful for the guidance offered at many stages of researching and writing this project. Professors in the Departments of English and Afro-American Studies at the University of Wisconsin–Madison remained in touch with me well after I graduated and continued to offer advice and read drafts. Chief among these was my graduate mentor, adviser, director, and "academic mother," Nellie Y. McKay. Her gifts of patience, guidance, praise, cajoling, recognition, and belief that I could do it (even when I doubted) will never be forgotten. I also thank Dale Bauer, Michael Bernard-Donals, Susan Stanford Friedman, Jeffery Steele, William L. Van de Burg, and Craig

Werner for their sage, timely, and prompt advice. Colleagues and cohorts from graduate school also pushed my work in different directions. For this I thank Kim Blockett, Keisha Bowman, Maya Gibson, David Ikard, Cherene Sherrard-Johnson, Alicia Kent, and Greg Rutledge. Colleagues at the University of Virginia's English Department have been generously supportive of my work. I am particularly grateful to my colleague and faculty mentor Deborah McDowell for her generous critical insights and willingness to read early painful drafts. I also thank Rita Felski, Caroline Rody, and Marlon Ross for reading sections and offering valuable comments that shaped this work. Other University of Virginia colleagues in the English Department and beyond offered insights into the writing process, words of support, and general goodwill; these include Steve Arata, Aniko Bodroghkozy, Alison Booth, Gordon Braden, Karen Chase, Sylvia Chong, Steve Cushman, Joanna Drucker, Elizabeth Fowler, Susan Fraiman, Ian Grandison, Grace Hale, Eleanor Kaufman, Michael Levenson, LaTaSha Levy, Lotta Lofgren, Eric Lott, Franny Nudelman, Vicki Olwell, Steve Railton, Jahan Ramazani, Marion Rust, Lisa Russ Spaar, Chip Tucker, David VanderMulen, Corey Walker, Jennifer Wicke, and others. I also appreciate the English Department staff—including Cheryll Lewis, Pam Marcantel, Lois Payne, Randy Swift, and June Webb—for making Bryan Hall such a "workable" space. I thank the graduate students who provided valuable research assistance: Schuyler Esprit, Ann Kirschman, Elizabeth Pittman, Tainika Taylor, and Elizabeth White. I also thank my students in the fall 2005 semester of Trauma Theory and African American Literature for enduring repeated screenings and spirited discussions of several *Chappelle's Show* episodes, especially Z'etoile Imma for sharing her grade school experience of *Roots*.

I would also like to recognize those who generously tolerated my many questions about reenactment and performance. Regarding Colonial Williamsburg, Harvey Bakari, Emily James, Richard Josey, Harriot Lomax, Hope Smith, Robert Watson, and Henry Wiencek were very gracious and helpful. I thank Erin Krutko, whose research converged with mine, for talking with me. Dylan Pritchett, who works as a freelance storyteller and reenactor, has been extraordinarily patient and forthcoming. I thank Kim D. Jones, administrative coordinator for *The Maafa Suite* program at St. Paul's Community Baptist Church in Brooklyn, New York, for helping me secure tickets for the performance. I also thank Tony Browder, founder of the Institute for Karmic Guidance, who spoke with me about his Middle Passage program.

I thank my family for their patience and encouragement during this process. I am grateful to and for my husband, Ben Doherty, who supports my life and work. I thank my two sons, Riley and Ryan Doherty, for giving me balance, keeping me centered, and making me laugh. I also thank my parents, Norman and Ianthia Woolfork; my sisters, Sybil and Stephanie Woolfork; my nephew, Devin Riley Wilson; my grandmother Edna Walker; my mother-in-law, Mary Doherty; my sister-in-law, Molly Doherty; and all my other family members. I thank my running buddy, Selena Cozart, and my quilting and sewing friends in the Charlottesville Area Quilting Guild. All of these good people (and countless others) have patiently tolerated me going on and on about "my book."

Introduction

Go There to Know There

During a recent Juneteenth commemorative weekend at our local community college, the program coordinator issued a provocative invitation. Describing the many events of the day—which included an art workshop for children, exhibit of slavery artifacts, and quilting demonstrations—she announced a small series of re-created moments from slavery that had been set up in the areas outside the building. "We're going to take you back there," she said of the reenactments that included simulations of Goree Island and an auction block. Participants, most of them black, would drift through the simulated scenes in an effort to temporarily and imaginatively locate themselves in slavery. The purpose of the program was to offer the opportunity to get close to the concepts and experiences of captivity and slavery. By several accounts from participants and coordinators, the event was a success.

What separates the books, films, exhibitions, reenactments in *Embodying American Slavery in Contemporary Culture* from other representations and interpretations of slavery are the ways in which they use the contemporary body as an invitation for the reader, viewer, or patron to locate themselves in the past; readers, viewers, and visitors are prompted to ask themselves, "What would I do?" in the context of American slavery. There is a range of response to these simulated scenes: some people willingly invest themselves by projecting and imagining themselves in these positions; others take the offer as an opportunity to consider history in a light other than the distant text-based position; still others find the notion either preposterous in its audacity (the past is not a place to visit) or as yet another example of black self-defeatism (dwelling on a past that cannot be changed) or even self-abuse (Isn't the present bad enough? Do you really need a return to slavery?).

This book seeks to extend the work of African American literary scholars such as Claudia Tate and Hortense Spillers who have engaged psychoanalysis in their work. My project concentrates specifically on trauma theory, a subset of psychoanalytic theory and cultural analysis. I examine representations of slavery that expose the racial and cultural particularity of trauma theory. This undertaking is complicated. Although few would deny that slavery was a traumatic experience, slavery is rarely mentioned in discussions of literary trauma theory. Rather than force precepts of trauma theory to fit American slavery, my arguments are based on a select group of contemporary African American novels, films, and performances based on slavery that have long been engaged in a trauma theory of its own.

In this book, I present a mode of bodily reference that I call "bodily epistemology." This concept challenges prevailing trauma theory by proposing a way to consider the corporeal dimensions of traumatic experience. Appearing primarily in works that question the temporal boundaries between the past and the present, bodily epistemology is a representational strategy that uses the body of a present-day protagonist to register the traumatic slave past. The impetus of this theory can be explained by the unlikely combination of two observations from two great American writers, Zora Neale Hurston and Gertrude Stein. At the close of Hurston's *Their Eyes Were Watching God,* the protagonist, after relating her adventures to her friend, says, "It's a known fact. . . . You got to go there to know there." Stein's famous claim about Oakland is the rejoinder, "When you get there there is no there there." These phrases provide a context in which to consider the representational strategies discussed in this book. I use these claims to critique and propose an alternative to trauma theory as usually understood. The plots of the literature and films in this study can be summarized as follows: the protagonist suffers from a form of amnesia about the slave past (they do not know their ancestors, they know little and care less about slavery, they are unaware of the meaning of their contemporary "freedom"). The protagonist then finds her- or himself unwittingly transported to the slave past where she or he is confronted with a living, traumatic history that becomes a personal priority. In this way, characters are forced physically to "go" to the slave past to better "know" it. And when they "get there" they discover that (counter to their previous attitude about slavery) there *is* a "there there," a slave past that is, in the words of *Beloved*'s Sethe, "waiting there" to be recognized, remembered, or even reexperienced. Bodily epistemology, rooted in speculative fiction and several touring venues, combines the time-travel convention of fantasy fiction with the imperatives of realism to pose an alternative to the predominant antirepresentational ethos of much current literary trauma theory.

Embodying American Slavery Contemporaneously: Go There to Know There

The historical complexity of African American slavery demands a new approach to trauma. Whereas trauma is clinically viewed as private, slavery was a highly visible, public, self-reproducing system where the sentience of the enslaved was used to further implicate them in bondage. The current designation of trauma as ephemeral or unapproachable does not take into account the public and private, nationally and internationally, contested meanings of African American slavery, a traumatic event that was represented even as it was happening. Although fugitive, emancipated, and freeborn blacks in the eighteenth and nineteenth centuries produced a voluminous amount of poetry, prose, fiction, autobiography, and oral accounts indicting slavery, until relatively recently few of these documents have been viewed as authoritative historical texts. As Ira Berlin explains, "The memory of slavery in the United States was too important to be left to the black men and women who experienced it directly" (Berlin, Favreau, and Miller, *Remembering Slavery* xiii). For more than a quarter century, many contemporary black authors and critics have aimed to remedy that erasure. As early as Margaret Walker's *Jubilee* (1965), contemporary representations of slavery by African American writers imagine the slave past in an attempt to remember and reauthorize the enslaved. Literary representation matters to African American writers who believe, as Deborah E. McDowell observes of novelist Sherley Anne Williams, that "history's lies can be corrected and its omissions, restored" by the production of counternarratives ("Negotiating between Tenses" 145).

Through the lens of bodily epistemology, I concentrate on books, films, and reenactments of slavery that might be classified as speculative fiction. In Octavia Butler's novel *Kindred* (1979), Haile Gerima's film *Sankofa* (1993), and Phyllis Alesia Perry's novel *Stigmata* (1998), a contemporary black woman "returns" to the slave past, where she is confronted with a previously unknown part of her personal or racial history. The made-for-teen films *Brother Future* (1991) and *The Quest for Freedom* (1992) follow the same plotline, but with black male teen protagonists. For them, the slave past serves as a rehabilitative and disciplinary location, much as a school field trip to jail might work in a prison aversion program. In living-history reenactments and museum exhibitions, like the National Great Blacks in Wax Museum, visitors come face-to-face with a corporeal rather than a textual or cinematic representation of the slave past. These works offer implausible, yet stylistically realistic, interactions between characters in the slave past and those of the "free" present. This representational strategy references the slave past by imagining and addressing the lived experience of slavery in bodily terms.

Bodily epistemology points to a mode of trauma theory that addresses the corporeal meanings of slavery. To borrow from Lindon Barrett, "The primary and recurring location marking crisis within or reaffirmation of the instituted relations and ideologies of master and slave remains the African American body" ("African American Slave Narratives" 421). By resorting to bodily strategies to represent the slave past, these novels bear what Caroline Rody describes as "the burden of communicating an authentic truth" about slavery's traumatic effects. Although these texts are literary representations and thus necessarily mediated, invented, and clearly not real, Rody suggests that for these writers, "the inherited conviction of slavery's evil renders the word of fictional slaves true in a sense not solely epistemological or even political, but moral" (*The Daughter's Return* 21). By deploying living bodily referents to evoke, signal, or revisit slavery, the literary representations and cultural practices in my study both address the slave past and, in Saidiya Hartman's terms, "redress" the pained black body by "counterinvesting in the body as a site of possibility" (*Scenes of Subjection* 51).

Despite the troubling position the black body has been forced to occupy in the mind-body dichotomy, the writers, filmmakers, and living-history proponents in my study resort to the bodily metaphor as a compelling representational strategy due, in part, to what Dennis Patrick Slattery considers the body's usefulness as "a visual aid, a vision that aids our imagination in order to deepen the texture of our lives" (*The Wounded Body* 15). The body, in my theory of bodily epistemology, is used to mediate multiple forms of knowing the past. The works in this book use the bodily metaphor to suggest that the bodies of blacks in the present share a degree of corporeal resonance with (and a bit of spiritual obligation to) those enslaved in the past. Janie's words—"go there to know there"—are part of a conversation carried on by writers like Butler and Perry whose speculative neo-slave narratives depict the past and the present as mutually constitutive spheres allowing for travel in between. These novels suggest that to know the "there" of the traumatic past, one must go there. This insistence on a view of the traumatic past as "accessible" by fantastic or paranormal means is a way to remember the slave past, to keep the event alive for the protagonist. The dangers of not referencing the past, these works imply, include the risk that slavery will be forgotten or misinterpreted. To guard against this possibility, some writers posit the body as a viable means to know the past, whereas others emphasize the cultural practices that seek to bridge the gaps between past and present, unknown and known. It is this dual attention to keeping the past and present as mutually significant spheres of experience, to always consider the past not just through the mental techniques of memory but also through a physical connection, that makes bodily epistemology a promising approach to conceptualizing the trauma of slavery.

Encountering Trauma (Theory)

This book is built, in part, on a reexamination of trauma theory, especially the way it relates to the "mind-body split." Though *trauma* in its Greek origin signified a physical wound, in Freud's usage trauma refers exclusively to the mind. This shift, which for Freud is marked by his "repudiation" of the seduction theory, is crucial to the development of psychoanalysis, as it permits an unprecedented, imaginative, and detailed approach to the inner workings of the psyche. However, separating the concept of trauma from the body has unintended implications and, when placed in the context of the trauma of slavery, signals the mind-body dialectic that has adversely informed attitudes toward the black body since the Enlightenment.

An early example that represents the distinction between mental and bodily trauma in the context of African American slavery is suggestive. Though there are many accounts of physical and emotional abuse in slavery, an eighteenth-century account by Janet Schaw, "a Scottish lady of quality," suggests the implications of unraveling the physical and mental components of trauma. In her travel narrative, Schaw reports on whipping as a form of punishment for slaves: "When one comes to be better acquainted with the nature of the negroes, the horrour of it must wear off. It is the suffering of the human mind that constitutes the greater misery of punishment, but with them it is merely corporeal. As to the brutes it inflicts no wound on their mind, whose natures are made to bear it, and whose sufferings are not attended with shame or pain beyond the present moment" (quoted in Montag, "The Universalization of Whiteness" 286). In her analysis of eighteenth- and nineteenth-century representations of violence against slaves, Saidiya Hartman characterizes beating scenes often found in antislavery literature as forging "identification between those free and those enslaved" through the use of pain as "the common language of humanity [that] extends humanity to the dispossessed and, in turn, remedies the indifference of the callous" (*Scenes of Subjection* 18). Schaw's report fractures the possibility of sympathetic or empathic connection between white readers and black sufferers, however, by deploying a mind-body dichotomy that implicitly separates the idea of white mental trauma ("suffering of the human mind") from black physical trauma ("with them it is merely corporeal"). Schaw uses black pain and its temporality (its limit to "the present moment") to characterize physical trauma as an impermanent wound that does not produce mental trauma. Hartman pinpoints the implications of this approach: "If this pain has been largely unspoken and unrecognized, it is due to the sheer denial of black sentience rather than the inexpressibility of pain. The purported immunity of blacks to pain is absolutely essential to the spectacle of contented subjection or, at the very least, to discrediting the claims of pain" (51).

Current trauma theory, though neither overtly nor intentionally racist, implicitly reinforces the mind-body split in its elaboration of the paradox of trauma. The implicit division is effectively expressed in Cathy Caruth's analysis of latency when she writes, "If a life threat to the body and the survival of this threat are experienced as the direct infliction and healing of a wound, trauma is suffered in the psyche precisely, it would seem, because it is *not* directly available to experience" (*Unclaimed Experience* 31–32). In this analogy, wound is to flesh as trauma is to mind, implying that, in these separate spheres, physical wounds, because they are *directly inflicted,* do not embody or harbor trauma. Bodily injury can be experienced, registered, and resolved on a material level, thus making healing possible. However, injuries to the psyche are elusive, leaving no marks to be eradicated. In this way, physical pain is interpreted as tangible and accessible, thus making recovery from its deleterious effects more likely. This formulation, grounded in the body, assumes that the body is a fixed and easily codified variable. This analysis reflects the prevailing view of the corporeal in literary trauma theory: the body is tangible, already known; the mind is more complex. Physical pain is facile or obvious, whereas mental injury is more difficult to assess. This conception of mental injury as intangible informs trauma theory, which in turn runs the risk of reinforcing the mind-body dichotomy and invoking its racial dimension.

The intangible quality of trauma informs much of literary trauma theory, which is embedded in a set of specific discursive practices that define the traumatic event as fleeting, ephemeral, and referenced only by the most oblique strategies. According to Freud's theory of the accident neurosis (in which a train accident survivor walks away from the wreckage apparently unharmed only to relive the accident in dreams or flashbacks weeks later), the traumatic event is virtually a nonevent, characterized by Freud as a "trifling" provocation less relevant to the survivor's neurosis and less interesting to psychoanalysis than the effects it produces. This scenario constructs the traumatic moment as a missed experience, harmless in its initial occurrence but damaging only later when the event is replayed indirectly through symptoms of psychic distress. In Freud's formulation, trauma is not rooted in the site of its initial impact; it resides in the consciousness by means of a fundamental temporal dislocation known as latency. A cursory sampling of the leading scholarship in trauma theory illustrates the endurance of Freud's position that the traumatic event is neither assimilated nor fully experienced as it occurs but is instead known only belatedly. Shoshana Felman examines the effects of belated trauma in poetic language, and Dori Laub in his work with Holocaust testimonies asserts that massive trauma is neither witnessed nor registered in its initial impact (Felman and Laub, *Testimony*). Geoffrey H. Hartman implies that, given trauma's elusiveness, the notion of "traumatic knowledge" is contradictory ("On Traumatic Knowledge").

Latency, many theorists claim, is a metonym for the ways trauma works in history. As Cathy Caruth observes, "For history to be a history of trauma means that it is referential precisely to the extent that it is not fully perceived as it occurs; or to put it somewhat differently, that a history can be grasped only in the very inaccessibility of its occurrence" (*Unclaimed Experience* 187). This extension of trauma's inherent latency into the processes of history has unanticipated effects when used to understand the history of African American slavery. It is true that for twenty-first-century readers, scholars, and historians, African American slavery is a fundamentally inaccessible experience, one that was never seen (by us) as it occurred. Today, slavery can be known only through histories, testimonies, narratives, and other cultural artifacts. What would it mean, however, to suggest that slavery was a "trifling" provocation, not "fully perceived" by those who lived it? What does the interpretation of trauma as ephemeral yield for slavery?

The antirepresentational position of much literary trauma theory suggests that to understand traumatic experience is inevitably to misunderstand it, for as Walter Benn Michaels claims, "The attempt to explain it can only be an attempt to reduce it" ("'You Who Never Was There'" 11). This perspective is most clearly expressed by Claude Lanzmann, for whom efforts to directly represent the Holocaust are obscene because "is it not visible. You cannot look at this" (Lanzmann, Larson, and Rodowick, "Seminar" 99). His nine-hour film *Shoah* aims to transmit the Holocaust rather than represent it. Michael Rothberg describes this approach as "antirealist"—a position that removes the event from "standard historical, cultural, or autobiographical narratives and situates it as a sublime, unapproachable object beyond discourse and knowledge" (*Traumatic Realism* 4). Rothberg criticizes trauma theory's claim that trauma is known only in its absence, its force "marked by its lack of registration" (quoted in Caruth, *Trauma* 6). The paradox of trauma's elusiveness generates a corollary aesthetic paradox for literary analysis: the more legible a representation, the less suitable it is as a site for trauma. As Walter Benn

Michaels remarks, "If to understand is, inevitably to misunderstand," then "it is only the 'mere noise' one 'does not understand' that makes it possible to bear true witness" ("'You Who Never Was There'" 11). My project intervenes in this formulation by presenting a group of texts and cultural practices that eschew incomprehensibility as a constitutive element of trauma.

Literary Imagination: Embodied Representations

There is a vast amount of compelling contemporary fiction, nonfiction, film, and museum work (much of it by African Americans) on American slavery. Historical accounts, such as Nell Irvin Painter's *Sojourner Truth: A Life, a Symbol* and Walter Johnson's *Soul by Soul: Life in the Antebellum Slave Market,* endeavor to bring parts of the slave past into better focus and offer a more sophisticated understanding. There are novels that make the legacy of slavery more resonant for contemporary blacks by showing the prolonged and profound psychology of bondage and captivity, such as Toni Morrison's *Beloved,* Gayl Jones's *Corregidora,* and David Bradley's *The Chaneysville Incident.* Historical novels such as Sherley Anne Williams's *Dessa Rose,* Lorene Cary's *The Price of a Child,* Charles Johnson's *Middle Passage,* and Edward P. Jones's *The Known World* concentrate energy on imaginatively reanimating and repopulating the slave past while re-creating its attendant feelings and experiences. Parodies such as Ishmael Reed's *Flight to Canada* and Alice Randall's *Wind Done Gone* satirize and revise previous representations of slavery and their racist generic codes. Television and film productions such as *Roots* and *Amistad,* or documentaries such as *Africans in America: America's Journey through Slavery,* make slavery more visible for audiences, filling in gaps that may reside between the written word and its reader.

This book examines a specific form of reenactment, one that uses a present-day body to interrogate the conditions in the slave past. For this reason, I turn to more speculative fiction, a literary form that generally has a broader field of play, where time travel (even space travel), immortality, spirit possession, or vampires are accepted as reasonable. I take these texts seriously for the approach they use to gain access to the slave past. Through bodily epistemology, these protagonists execute a rationally impossible yet believably and realistically depicted interpretation of Janie's injunction to Pheoby: go there to know there. In this way, a twentieth- or twenty-first-century protagonist is placed in conditions of nineteenth-century slavery. I am interested in the interface created by this representation, the direct confrontation between the free present and the slave past, for it is here that a distinctly African American trauma theory emerges, a formulation that is equally interested in the body and the mind, a concept suitable for realist and speculative literature.

Popular Imagination: Embodied Reenactments

In addition to acting as a representational strategy in literature and film, bodily epistemology is also a mode of slavery remembrance in museum exhibits and commemorative practices. These literary and popular imaginative spheres share an interest in bodily epistemology because of a belief in the present-day African American body's potential (and responsibility) to reference the life experiences of enslaved blacks. Contemporary racism against blacks is frequently cited as evidence of slavery's enduring legacy. As such, the social costs of black life in the present prove the persistence of similar, if more ardently held, racist views of the nineteenth century.

Within the popular sphere, black visitors to certain slavery exhibits or programs find themselves framed by images that urge them to consider the slave past in a more personal or confrontational way. Talking with a slave character at a living-history museum, pouring a libation at a Middle Passage program, standing shoulder to shoulder with other blacks in a simulated slavehold during a Juneteenth commemoration, or being assigned the role of a fugitive slave during an immersion reenactment are all examples of bodily epistemology at work. These gestures are based on the premise that forcing visitors to imagine themselves into the perspective of slaves—to temporarily locate themselves in a simulated position of bondage—may offer a more proximate and more complex interpretation of the slave past. Living-history proponents frequently claim that it is better to learn by "doing." I take this claim seriously, reading it as more than an instance of anti-intellectualism. It is more accurately a *different* form of intellectual activity, which Grant Farred calls vernacular intellectualism (see *What's My Name?*). Bodily epistemology can be considered a form of black vernacular trauma theory.

Slavery reenactments are the clearest sign and source of vernacular trauma theory. Heavily invested in bodily epistemology, creators and actors (as well as some spectators) perceive this performance of slave life as a site of memory, a space in which present-day viewers are invited to (perhaps required to) suspend their disbelief, their twentieth- or twenty-first-century perspective, and gaze upon or participate in a scene from the slave past. It is useful to consider briefly this work in relation to the estimated one million Civil War reenactors in the United States. Though many of these men and women are motivated by different reasons (a fascination with the military campaigns, maneuvers, or troop movements or an interest in historic uniforms and munitions), there are comparatively few black Civil War reenactors, save for the all-black groups such as those who reenact scenes from the Fifty-fourth Massachusetts Regiment. Many blacks, it appears, distrust Civil War reenacting, perhaps because of the predominant view among white reenactors that slavery had little or nothing to do with the war. For this reason, one man noted that whereas many whites reenact Confederate and Union battles, "you won't find slavery reenactors" (Webb, letter to the editor). This man is not the only person who finds the idea of slavery reenactors objectionable or ridiculous. Consider the black teenager who asked a Colonial Williamsburg slave reenactor if he was "retarded," concluding that the reenactor "must be" to dress up as a slave for a living.

Although their numbers are not even close to one million, there are more slavery reenactors and reenactments than one might initially imagine. Throughout the United States, varying in genres, frequency, and degree of sophistication, slavery reenactments can be divided into three generic modes—ritual, historic, and immersion—each with its own conventions. Ritual reenactments usually take place in a church setting or have distinctly spiritual activities like naming of ancestors or more familiar rituals of Holy Communion, sweat lodges, and fire walks. For example, two walking pilgrimages—Lifeline Expedition in 2005 and Interfaith Pilgrimage of the Middle Passage in 1998—share the priorities of ritual reenactments to pay tribute to lost ancestors, to atone for or remember slavery, and to acknowledge the persistent legacy of slavery. Many ritual reenactments promote bodily epistemology in asking audience members (sometimes called "celebrants") to participate in ritual activities like pouring libations to lost ancestors, reciting special prayers specific to the Middle Passage, or learning techniques for cultivating memory (for instance, an African Holocaust Day in Chicago advised participants on how to erect an ancestral shrine in their homes). The purpose of these ritual reenactments is to foster memory of slavery through its simulation. This version of embodied representation promotes mourning and encourages recognition of slavery's trauma in an effort to resolve and address its legacy in contemporary black life.

In historical reenactments, living-history museums feature black men and women who regularly reenact scenes or tasks from slavery (Colonial Williamsburg is a premier example). Slavery reenactors also arrange to perform during special programs at sites that do not regularly include reenactment (among them Monticello, Historic Brattonsville, and Latta Plantation). Unlike books or movies that depict a contemporary black person becoming located in the slave past, these reenactors both embody and enable a representation of that temporal shift for museum patrons. The reenactors are museum professionals, many of whom (like Hope Smith, who, though at the time of this writing is only in her late twenties, has worked at Colonial Williamsburg for twenty years) began reenacting scenes from slavery at Colonial Williamsburg as children. This museum's corporate structure, coupled with its educational mission, prompts interpretive staff to consider themselves as both teachers and performers. Detailed research goes into the drafted representations. Although it may prevent gross inaccuracies, such research does little to ensure how reenactments will be received. A controversy at Historic Brattonsville in South Carolina—where a cadre of black slavery reenactors quit over a dispute regarding "happy" slave scripts—is but one example of the vexed nature of this form of reembodying American slavery.

Immersion experiences are even more controversial than slavery reenactments, in part, perhaps, for their presumption in incorporating people—tourists, campers, and museum visitors—into an unpredictable experience for which they are unprepared. The procedures for an immersion reenactment are diverse. Some, held indoors, involve being blindfolded and asked to imagine oneself as an African captive. Others take place outdoors in wooded areas (complete with dogs and slave patrols) where individuals or groups are assigned identities as fugitive slaves needing a safe harbor. Many dismiss the notion of slavery immersion reenactments out-of-hand: slavery should not be a tourist diversion, nor can the original experience of slavery be fully replicated. The most common objection concerns the current black experience: isn't contemporary life sufficiently challenging without returning to slavery, even in simulation? Despite these and other objections, slavery immersion reenactments have been offered since the late 1980s. Usually promoted as Underground Railroad learning experiences, camps such as 4–H Camp Ohio and YMCA Camp Cosby in Alabama take middle school students on a simulated journey from slavery to freedom. And the numbers are significant: approximately five to seven hundred students participate in Camp Ohio's experience annually. Those figures are even higher for the "Follow the North Star" program at Conner Prairie, a living-history farm and museum in Indiana, where nearly thirteen thousand have participated since the late 1990s. Though I do not address this form of reenactment in this study, these projects share the same goals as the other works in this book: that knowledge about the slave past can be better acquired and understood when the learner participates bodily in a version of that past.

How to Get There

I begin my project with a consideration of trauma and time travel, using Octavia Butler's *Kindred* (1979) and Haile Gerima's *Sankofa* (1993). I read these two works together because of their remarkably similar premise: a contemporary black American woman is remanded to serve time in the slave past. Both works offer a significant critique of and alternative to the ways in which traumatic knowledge is usually revealed in fiction. Their means, however, differ greatly. Whereas Gerima deprives his contemporary protagonist of any twentieth-century consciousness during her stint in the slave past where she becomes a "vessel," or receptor, for a slave woman's story, Butler's protagonist is fully aware of her new temporal circumstances. Butler composes a historical novel of slavery set in two time periods (the nineteenth and twentieth centuries) and locations (Maryland and California), a compelling tale of generational conflict, personal responsibility, and black progress. As several scholars have noted, the novel is deeply concerned with familial contracts and obligations. Dana, the twentieth-century black female protagonist, and her white husband, Kevin, marry despite family objections and social conventions. Still, their deliberate forgetting of their ancestral pasts troubles their relationship, as they are literally forced to confront a version of that past through time travel. Butler, in part, directs her time-travel gaze toward those of her generation who have an eclipsed, impatient, or intolerant view of the life choices of their predecessors. For instance, Butler recalls overhearing a young black radical activist in the 1970s complaining about the accommodationist stance of the previous generation of blacks, saying, "I'd like to kill all these old people who have been holding us back for so long. But I can't because I'd have to start with my own parents" (interview with Rowell 51). Butler says that she wanted to take that young man back to the past, to show him the difficulty of those choices, to force him to see the ethical complexity of those conditions in greater clarity. Butler's reversal of the linear space-time continuum and of the notion of chronological as well as ideological progress is more than a staple of science fiction. Butler uses the time-travel technique to raise moral dilemmas of interracial love and sex, gender equality, and racism. In this way, she elevates a trope of fantasy fiction into a meditation on the means and meanings of traumatic knowledge. Because of its representational strategy of time travel, I claim *Kindred* as the inaugural example of bodily epistemology.

In an aggressive rendition of Butler's paradigm, Haile Gerima depicts a black woman in need of schooling by the slave past. *Sankofa* explicitly deploys the time-travel paradigm when Mona protests her captivity in the slave dungeons by shouting, "I'm not an African! I'm an American!" Both Gerima and Butler use the physical body to transcend normative modes of being and knowing. In relation to trauma theory, *Kindred* and *Sankofa* enact a scenario in which traumatic pasts may lapse but remain unfinished. Butler's and Gerima's use of time travel as a representational strategy serves as a potential, if speculative, restorative technique—proposing to restore the lost or forgotten traumatic elements of slavery for their twentieth-century protagonists, in addition to restoring the body and its experience to a trauma theory that privileges obliquity.

Phyllis Alesia Perry's 1998 novel *Stigmata* invokes the complex issues of the body and its capacity for transmitting traumatic knowledge. In Chapter 2, "Touching Scars, Touching Slavery: Quilts, Trauma, and Bodily Epistemology," I consider her use of the controversial phenomenon of Christian stigmata, where the bleeding wounds of Christ's crucifixion appear on the hands and feet of a modern-day believer. Perry's novel uses ancestral spirit possession and reincarnation to posit the physical body as a site for knowledge of the slave past. The novel's present-day protagonist, Lizzie, shares consciousness with two female ancestors, each of whom is preoccupied with the traumatic history of her ancestor who survived the Middle Passage to be enslaved in America.

Like Butler and Gerima, Perry uses a nontraditional representational strategy (reincarnation and spirit possession) to emphasize the traumatic dimension of a lost past and to embody the legacy of the slave past in contemporary African American life. In addition, she probes the limitations of bodily epistemology by subjecting her protagonist's mystical experience to the rational scrutiny of psychiatrists and other physicians. Whereas Butler's time travelers keep their journeys secret, Lizzie's visible scars and painful wounds continually reveal themselves, marking her not only as a physical witness to a brutal slave past but also, in the novel's rational universe, as a potential suicide case with self-inflicted wounds. Applique quilts emerge as a significant parallel and interpretive approach to Lizzie's wounded body when she inherits a quilt from her grandmother. The appliqués (figures applied on the surface of a quilt top) illustrate the story of her ancestor's captivity and enslavement. Unlike the geometric symmetry and squares of patchwork quilts, appliqué relies on a less structured visual field, telling a story through slightly raised figures on a smooth terrain. Likewise, Lizzie's scars—raised circular areas of flesh around her wrists and ankles and a textured smattering of lash marks on her back—signify on her otherwise whole body, bearing witness to the trauma of her captive and enslaved foremother.

In the work of Butler, Perry, and Gerima, black women find themselves unwillingly and unwittingly cast into a traumatic history where their participation becomes a significant part of a nineteenth-century story and of their twentieth-century present. Dana and Lizzie learn something from their exposure to the slave past. Mona, in particular, learns to change her irreverent ways. These works do not depict the traumatic slave past as an ephemeral and resistant moment. Instead, the slave past is presented as a concrete and necessary reminder of unacknowledged trauma, one that can be used as a form of moral instruction or correction.

This disciplinary element, however, is far more overt when directed toward the wayward black male teenager in the late 1980s and early 1990s, whose condition (some would say "endangerment") preoccupied those in the social sciences, law enforcement, television, and film. In Chapter 3, "Teach You a Lesson, Boy: Endangered Black Male Teens Meet the Slave Past," I turn to two films geared for young audiences, *Brother Future* (1991) and *The Quest for Freedom: The Harriet Tubman Story* (1992). These films reflect America's cultural anxiety about the state and place of black masculinity in the Reagan-Bush era. Both films depict the slave past as a rehabilitative location, and their narratives expose the protagonists to a combination of prison aversion program tactics (like those of Scared Straight) and zero-tolerance discipline. In both cases, the cosmic strategy of time-travel immersion effectively, thoroughly, and inexpensively reforms the boys. The films imagine a universe in which moments of the slave past are resurrected to function as a jail or prison would in a crime-deterrence program, but without questioning the parallels between the two institutions (incarceration and slavery) in the past or the present. The institution of slavery is evoked here as a panacea and made to serve as an uncomplicated disciplinary tool for twentieth-century black male teens.

In Chapter 4, "Slave Tourism and Rememory," I turn from novels and film to consider the ways in which bodily epistemology emerges in the popular spheres of museum spectatorship and reenactment. What are the implications of encountering a representation of a traumatic element of the slave past in a museum, a venue usually reserved for pleasure or edification? In what ways do such depictions of a traumatic past transcend, confront, or resist the commodification process necessary to produce the conventions of museum spectatorship? What is the relationship between the black public sphere and those institutions that depict slavery through embodied performance? Who is authorized to depict the slave past? This chapter considers the possibilities and limitations of reembodying American slavery by returning to the tourist elements of Haile Gerima's film *Sankofa,* reading the Middle Passage and slave ship re-creation at Baltimore's National Great Blacks in Wax Museum, and exploring the controversy prompted by Colonial Williamsburg's 1994 slave-auction reenactment. These apparently disparate expressions share an underlying commitment to bringing lost horrors forward, to hold them in the faces of viewers, to shock and startle. The re-created ship's hold locates visitors aboard a slave ship, turning spectators into witnesses of the traumatic scenes formed in wax. This small wax museum and independent film reference slavery as a real and meaningful aspect of American history, national memory, and African American identity. The Great Blacks in Wax exhibit implicitly invokes bodily epistemology in its attempt to locate visitors in the past context of Middle Passage captivity. Visitors walk down a simulated gangplank to the exhibit, while a recorded voice snarls, "Here comes a new batch of slaves." Through such urgently physical referential strategies, these works present slavery as a literal, embodied event. Colonial Williamsburg sparked a national discussion of slave history when its African American Interpretive Program department announced a slave-auction reenactment. Although the National Great Blacks in Wax Museum is less critically sophisticated than America's largest living-history museum, its exhibit of the Middle Passage is located in a broader narrative of black progress. I explore the lesser-known elements of Colonial Williamsburg's slave-auction controversy, paying particular attention to the gender dimensions that characterized the tension between black protesters and the museum's black program creator. Some of the controversy surrounding the reenactment, I believe, stemmed from the way the program, unlike the wax slave ship, isolated a painful moment from the slave past without the consolation of emancipatory resolution.

Building on the tensions of the slave-auction controversy, I move to a more detailed discussion of two forms of slavery reenactment: ritual and historical. In Chapter 5, "Ritual Reenactments," I begin with a consideration of vernacular trauma theory as it appears in the use of the term *Maafa*. A Kiswahili word meaning disaster, catastrophe, or calamity, the term *Maafa* first appeared in the Afrocentric lexicon of slavery in Mariba Ani's 1981 study of African retentions in black American culture. Since then, *Maafa* (usually capitalized) has gained wide use in black vernacular expression and theorization about slavery and its aftermath. Academic journals, major newspapers, and popular magazines yield few instances of the term, but it is frequently used within the black popular sphere, a sign of grassroots theorizing about slavery. This term is a way that self-defined black communities and their constituents describe the event in a language rooted in the cultural particularity deeply shaped by the event. The shift to the term *Maafa* from terms such as *Middle Passage, transatlantic slave trade,* or, more problematically, *black* or *African Holocaust,* is an act of cultural possession that strives to emphasize the singularity or uniqueness of the historical event and its psychological cost. In this vernacular theoretical frame, *Maafa* is akin to the word *Shoah* (the Hebrew word for the Holocaust), an effort to linguistically claim a specific set of events for a specific racial or cultural group.

This vernacular theory of trauma relies on forging a connection between the slave past and contemporary moment. In Chapter 5, I discuss the ritual reenactment *The Maafa Suite: A Healing Journey,* a psychodrama performed since 1995 at a black Baptist church in New York. The church has taken on this elaborate performance (which also features lectures, seminar, libations, and seaside closing ceremony) as part of its theological practice. In Chapter 6, I analyze historical reenactments of daily slave life at Colonial Williamsburg as a site for vernacular theorization in the interactions between tourists ("guests," in museum parlance) and museum employees portraying slaves. These conversations provide a space in which to consider the multiple meanings of slavery, especially the ways the experience is constructed and contested.

These six chapters explore the many ways and implications of bodily representing an encounter between the slave past and a free present. The books, films, and cultural events imply that to remember slavery from a physical and emotional distance is not the most suitable memorial. Instead novels like *Kindred* force a black protagonist to occupy a more proximate connection. The National Great Blacks in Wax Museum confronts its visitors with its interpretation of slave ship captivity; African American historical interpreters at Colonial Williamsburg interact with guests in the character of slaves, or, as a Colonial Williamsburg staff supervisor claimed, "in the skins of the ancestors." These literary and cultural works offer themselves as incentives to memory, as a way to speak to and for the lost, forgotten, or erased slaves, to keep the legacy of slavery ever present.

But slavery is not the province of academic or vernacular intellectuals alone. Today, theories, mythologies, jokes, and anecdotes about slavery continue to flourish in black communities. Consider the following incidents:

> One dark night, a young black woman finds herself alone in a seedy part of town. Shadows lurk in doorways as she heads to her car and speeds away. Later, when telling friends about the incident, someone asks her if she was afraid. She replies: "as a runaway slave." They all laugh.
>
>   I'm heading in to pick up my precocious six-year old from summer day camp. One of the camp's coordinators, a black woman whose now-adult children were educated in our city's public schools, advises me to watch out for my son as he starts public school. She urges me to be vigilant and active, because when it comes to our children's education, she claims that many black parents behave like "dumb darkies on the plantation."

The concluding chapter, "A Soul Baby Talks Back," is grounded in the sacred and profane expressions that abound as black folks make meaning about the event and memory of slavery. To close my study, I consider the representations of slavery in *Chappelle's Show,* a Comedy Central skit and stand-up program produced by Dave Chappelle. In addition to sketches about bloopers and outtakes from the miniseries *Roots* and a time-travel skit featuring "players" (as in "player haters") on a slave plantation, Chappelle's company insignia is an image of a bald, shirtless Chappelle with iron-shackled wrists. The quick sound bite accompanying the image is "I'm ree-aa-ch, bee-aa-ch" (I'm rich, bitch), which is actually sampled from a sketch on slavery reparations. *Chappelle's Show* offers the space in which to consider comedy and laughter as a strategy to rethink the complexity of slavery representation and a black vernacular approach to traumatic knowledge.

African American slavery can illuminate meaningful gaps and fissures in the structure of trauma and its literary and cultural mode of analysis. In its interrogation of trauma theory, my project is congruent with the larger contested question of the relevance of psychoanalytic theory to African American life and cultural expression. In this book, I try to address the serious concerns that Hortense J. Spillers identifies as troubling the connections between race and psychoanalysis: "Little or nothing in the intellectual history of African Americans within the social and political context of the United States suggests the effectiveness of a psychoanalytic discourse, revised or classical, in illuminating the problematic of 'race' on an intersubjective field of play, nor do we yet know how to historicize the psychoanalytic object and objective, invade its heredity premises and insulations, and open its insights to cultural and social forms that are disjunctive to its originary imperatives" ("'All the Things'" 76). In this declaration and elsewhere, Spillers herself does this important work. The psychoanalytic modes of African American literary analysis performed by Claudia Tate, Mae Henderson, and others address psychoanalysis in its historical moment and extend its insights into a meaningful critique of African American literature (Tate, "Freud and His 'Negro'" and *Psychoanalysis and Black Novels;* Henderson, "Toni Morrison's *Beloved*"). I hope that this book, in its offering of bodily epistemology, can also make the considerable insights of trauma theory available and relevant to the contemporary representations and performances of African American slavery.

1. Trauma and Time Travel

In her important essay on the role of psychology in the history of slavery, Nell Irvin Painter notes the difficulty of applying twentieth-century methodologies to eighteenth- and nineteenth-century circumstances. "When used carefully, perhaps gingerly," she argues, psychology "provides a valuable means of understanding people and families who cannot be brought to the analyst's couch." She considers science fiction the perfect gateway to such analysis: "Ideally, historians could enter a kind of 'Star Trek' realm of virtual reality in which we could hold intelligent conversations with the dead, then remand them to their various hells, purgatories, and heavens and return to our computers. Lacking this facility, we can only read twentieth-century practitioners and enter the archives with our eyes wide open" ("Soul Murder and Slavery" 128–29). It is significant that Painter invokes science fiction as a possible means to create rich and accurate historiography, for *Kindred* and *Sankofa,* in their use of time travel, hold such conversations with the dead, bringing the past and the present face-to-face.

In addition to serving as an impossible, yet highly effective, form of historiography, these two nontraditional creative works provide the opportunity to reconsider fundamental elements of trauma theory. As speculative fictions, Octavia Butler's 1979 time-travel novel *Kindred* and Haile Gerima's 1993 film *Sankofa* are compelling sites in which to explore the possible meanings of slavery and trauma theory. Though time travel is a fixture in fantasy and speculative fiction, a genre considered by some to lack literary complexity, Butler and Gerima effectively renovate this device, bringing it to bear on the issues of history and traumatic knowledge. Butler's bridge between the past and present generates a series of doubles and oppositions in and beyond the plot; I use two sets of these oppositions to read the body of (and in) the novel and to illuminate its implicit critique of trauma theory. Gerima's similarly themed film uses the slave past for behavioral modification cum history lesson. Though his film eschews many of Hollywood's generic conventions, he adopts those of the slave narrative to create a vision of slavery that presses upon the current boundaries of traumatic knowledge. In their staging of a present-day protagonist's supernatural return to the slave era, *Kindred* and *Sankofa* are instances of bodily epistemology that implicitly critique the mind-body dialectic that informs trauma theory.

I begin this discussion with *Kindred,* a novel unique to Butler's oeuvre and an inaugural text for the project of bodily epistemology. Introduced to readers in 1979, Dana Franklin, Butler's time-traveling protagonist, was the first to "go there to know there" regarding the slave past. Nearly fifteen years later, Mona, a fashion model, would pursue a comparable—but more aggressively represented—return to the slave past. *Kindred* is partly the result of a mediation on Butler's own family history and partly a product of her impulse to have those in the present learn from those in the past. Haile Gerima is also invested in representing ancestral voices, creating a scenario that urges, even forces, blacks in the diaspora to recognize and reconnect with their unknown slave past. Their representations of time travel differ in each woman's awareness of the time shift: Dana retains her twentieth-century perspective; Mona, though cognizant of her capture and branding (the two events that mark her reembodiment of slavery), has her consciousness replaced by Shola, the slave woman for whom she acts as a vessel. Despite these differences, Butler and Gerima remain linked in their use of speculative representational strategies to place their contemporary female protagonist in a position to identify the slave past and ultimately use that past to better understand her present.

Set in 1976, *Kindred* is the story of Dana Franklin, a young black woman, and her mysterious journeys to the nineteenth-century Maryland plantation of her ancestors; Alice Greenwood, a black female slave; and Rufus Weylin, her white master. In order to ensure her family's twentieth-century existence, Dana believes she must protect the accident-prone Weylin, her white ancestor with whom she shares a mystical connection: he can abduct her (unconsciously) from the twentieth century when his life is endangered, and Dana can return to her present when her life is threatened. In this way, Dana protects Rufus from various childhood mishaps and later serves him when he becomes an adult. The most conflicted "service" she provides Rufus is to encourage Alice to submit to Rufus's unwanted sexual advances. Alice eventually but reluctantly "succumbs" to Rufus's demands, gives birth to several children (one of whom engenders Dana's family line), and commits suicide. Though her future existence is secure, Dana cannot leave the past unscathed. When Rufus seeks to replace Alice with Dana by attempting to rape her, she kills him but not before he seizes her arm, part of which is torn from her body by the cosmic pull of the past.

In its crossing of the temporal boundary, *Kindred* constructs a range of oppositional categories that parallel the divide between the past and present, the most central of which is slavery and freedom. These include physical immediacy and nostalgic distance, presence and absence, and, in Christine Levecq's terms, "event and memory, raw encounters and retelling, reality and textuality" ("Power and Repetition" 527). I suggest here that the novel presents two additional sets of categories that provide a context in which to address the discursive practice of trauma theory: observer and participant, book learning and lived experience. As part of a representational strategy invested in emphasizing the traumatic event of slavery, the novel also critiques two essential elements of trauma theory: the principle of latency as essential to traumatic experience (by forcing Dana to not only observe slavery but also actively participate in it) and the indirect referencing of the traumatic event (by eschewing "reference" in favor of direct exposure). Using these categories, I read *Kindred* as a tale of two stories: a time-travel narrative engaged in a bodily mode of referencing the traumatic slave past and an allegorical critique of a Freudian, or accident-based, definition of trauma.

The bodily mode of reference is a way to focus on the traumatic event and Dana's exposure to it. By placing Dana in the past so that she might develop an appreciation for the various meanings of slavery, Butler participates in a trend, new in the 1970s, to reform the historical study of slavery. Paying closer attention to the words, feelings, customs, and other ways slaves made meaning about their lives, historians, as Ashraf H. A. Rushdy remarks, "began for the first time to draw on the slaves' own testimonies" (*Remembering Generations* 14). Butler's project is also informed by this historiographic desire to listen to the experience of slaves. Though Butler concedes that her representation of slavery is not mimetic, the novel demonstrates what Dennis Patrick Slattery has described as "the essence of mimesis [which] is somatic, visceral, a shared psychic element wherein we feel the action, the wounding, the marking of the body, in our own being" (*The Wounded Body* 13).[1] The novel stages Dana's interface with the traumatic past as such a process: a visceral, shared, and wounding exposure. The past, for Dana, is a site of increased sensation and vividness, which at times becomes more "real" to Dana than her present. Butler's bodily imaginings of slavery reshape elements of trauma theory by suggesting a new way to reference trauma across temporal lines.

This return to the past permits a reconsideration of the temporal delay of latency, a factor that makes the mind "miss" the trauma and permits it to be known only in flashbacks or other forms of indirect reference. Rather than represent the traumatic event as elusive, Butler uses the time-travel device to explore the notion that the slave past can be referenced directly.

In many fantasy and science fiction novels, time travel is a form of entertainment and spectatorship. As the following comments from speculative-fiction expert Monte Cook imply, time travel is similar to any other journey: "The trick is to get as much information as possible about the time and place that you want to visit (and your route if you have a Wellsian time machine) and then to plan your trip based on that information. Once you have the information, you can estimate the probability of various courses of action and pick the one that shows the best chance of success" ("Tips for Time Travel" 54). Cook's advice for would-be time travelers represents the traditional view presented in many science- and speculative-fiction works: time travel is a controllable form of movement, and one can decide whether (and where) to travel. The idea of individual agency is not called into question; rather, time travel is at the service of the individual. The fantastic and mundane elements of time travel are further suggested by the time machine as a transportation device that is subject to human control.

The absence of a time machine is one way that *Kindred* revises these accepted representations of time travel. Whereas some science fiction critics find *Kindred*'s version of time travel unconvincing, I suggest that using an invisible yet strong emotional force to pull characters back through time is a strategy that questions the instrumental focus in some science fiction narratives in which time travel relies on technological innovation. It is also a comment on the idea of inviolate individualism. Rather than have Dana invent or find a time machine, she is abducted into the past by a white man. The random nature of Dana's abductions not only undermines her individual will but also makes her twentieth-century freedom suspect.

Kindred also challenges the entertainment value of time travel. Unlike the scenario Cook describes, Butler's characters do not return to the past of their own will or for amusement. Although they do try to prepare themselves for their time in the past, that preparation is a reactive (rather than proactive) gesture. Once Dana and Kevin, her white husband who returns with her on one occasion, discover the unpredictability of their time travel, their only defense is to acquire relevant but largely inadequate information. The entertainment value of time travel is completely eradicated, as seen in Kevin's early attitude about antebellum Maryland and the repercussions of his beliefs. Kevin, who upon first arriving in the nineteenth century tells Dana,

"This could be a great time to live in. . . . I keep thinking what an experience it would be to stay in it" (97), is inadvertently left behind. Stranded in the nineteenth century for five years, Kevin finds himself caught in the brutality of slaveholding ideology. By replacing Kevin's romantic notions of the past with grim reality, *Kindred* subverts the impulse to look nostalgically at the historical past.

Eschewing a nostalgic approach to history, representations of time travel can also be used to reenvision the past. Arguing that time travel is a way to reconsider the flexibility of time, Barbara Puschmann-Nalenz observes that many speculative-fiction writers abandon "the generally accepted idea that history is irreversible as time is irreversible" (*Science Fiction* 103). Some science fiction, she argues, engages the time-travel device to offer a different version of reality by changing the outcome of historical conflicts. Such novels depict reversals of cataclysmic moments in world history, telling stories of the Allies losing in World War II, the Union's defeat by the Confederacy, and Europeans expelled by Native American troops. These reconfigurations depend on a premise that history is as flexible as time. Events that are considered fixed, in the present, are represented as entities capable of change.

Kindred, however, represents a different view of history, for whereas the space-time continuum is fluid (allowing Dana and Kevin to travel from twentieth-century California to nineteenth-century Maryland), history is not. As Kevin tells Dana, "We're in the middle of history. We surely can't change it" (100). This representation of history as static is not accidental. Butler could have chosen to make the past as flexible and fluid as her depiction of space and time. However, such a malleable history would not permit *Kindred* to stage a return to the traumatic past. As Butler remarks, "I don't use a time machine or anything like that. Time travel is just a device for getting the character back to confront where she came from" (interview with Kenan 496).

This confrontation with one's origins suggests the use of time travel as a vehicle for the therapeutic scene. Though the psychoanalytic aspects of time-travel fictions remain largely unexamined, a notable and important exception comes from feminist film critic Constance Penley, whose essay "Time Travel, Primal Scene, and the Critical Dystopia," analyzes time travel in the 1984 action film *The Terminator.* The blockbuster movie starring Arnold Schwartzenegger engages time-travel paradoxes and Freud's ideas of originary fantasy. Penley accurately summarizes the film's plot as follows: "In 2010, a killer cyborg is sent back to the present day with the mission of exterminating Sarah Conner, a part-time waitress and student, the future mother of John Conner, the man who will lead the last remnant of humanity to victory over the machines which are trying to rid the world of humans. John Conner chooses Kyle Reese, a young and hardened fighter, to travel back in time to save Sarah from the Terminator" (reprinted in Kuhn, *Alien Zone* 119). Penley argues that the film is driven by a particular form of desire—the primal-scene fantasy—arguing that *The Terminator* demonstrates the fantasy of overhearing or observing parental intercourse, of being at the scene, so to speak, of one's own conception. John Conner enacts the primal scene by sending Kyle Reese to protect his mother, and ensures his own birth on two levels. First, John sends Kyle to protect Sarah from elimination. Second, Kyle, who has become enraptured by Sarah's photograph, makes love with Sarah, who has become attracted to Kyle's heroism. Their sex act leads to John's conception.

At first glance, it seems far-fetched to compare *Kindred* with *The Terminator*. The dissimilarities are obvious. *The Terminator* is a dystopic speculation on the dangers of technology featuring human annihilation at the hands of menacing cyborgs. Yet Penley's analysis locates an element that the novel and film share: the primal-scene fantasy. Penley writes, "The idea of returning to the past to generate an event that has made an impact on one's identity, lies at the core of the time-loop paradox story" (73). I argue that the primal scene is addressed in *Kindred* on two levels. First, as an individual, Dana is forced to confront the traumatic nature of her family heritage. Second, on a broader plane, *Kindred* uses time travel to recapture a different primal scene: the peritraumatic, or impact, phase of American slavery.[2] In *Kindred,* the return to slavery is an opportunity to consider the institution as an originary trauma for African Americans.

The generative desire represented by the primal-scene fantasy is played out in the novel's present-day and past settings. Dana knows her roots are based in nineteenth-century Maryland, thanks to a detailed genealogy written in her family's Bible. Though the genealogy lists who begat whom, it provides little else. So when Dana returns to the past and encounters Rufus and Alice as children, she wonders how they will marry ("or would it be marriage?" [28]) and engender her family line. Dana also wonders about the flexibility of time and her role in history. She considers, "[Rufus's] life could not depend on the actions of his unconcieved descendant. No matter what I did, he would have to survive to father Hagar, or I could not exist. That made sense. . . . But this child needed special care. If I was to live, if others were to live, he must live. I didn't dare test the paradox" (29). To protect herself, she must also protect Rufus.

Thus, like John Conner in *The Terminator,* Dana finds herself facilitating a primal scene. Yet, unlike Conner, Dana's generative moment is based on rape, not mutual affection. Dana says, "It was so hard to watch him hurting her—to know that he had to go on hurting her if my family was to exist at all"

(180). This line reveals Dana's almost pornographic relation to her generative moment, that she must *watch* Rufus "hurting" Alice not only refers to the frequent beatings Alice receives but also implies the pain of a forced sex act. In this way, Dana's primal scene can be called a traumatic primal scene. Not only is repeated rape a trauma for Alice, who must endure it bodily and emotionally, but Dana must also live with the traumatic knowledge that her family line was generated by coerced sex. In addition, acting partly on a survival impulse and partly forced by Rufus, Dana must participate in her traumatic primal scene by encouraging Alice to submit to Rufus's sexual demands. Dana does not have the option to dissuade Rufus from raping Alice. She needs this sexual violation to happen if she is to exist. Critic Diana Paulin puts the matter this way: "In order to put history back 'in place,' she must enable Rufus to rape Alice. Her responsibility leads to several questions: what would happen if she let Rufus die? Why are her actions limited to repeating the past and what are the implications of these limited choices (in the past and in the present)?" ("De-essentializing Interracial Representations" 192n13). One implication is that white male privilege transcends time and space, hence Rufus's ability to summon Dana to him. This privilege ironically coincides with Dana's need for self-preservation. Dana's desire to protect her present and future family line, even at the expense of her past family, is paramount.

Given this priority, history is represented as a stable entity in *Kindred*. Unlike Paulin's suggestion that the past must be put back "in place," I argue that history is represented as inflexible. Other time-travel stories present a malleable view of history. For example, in Ray Bradbury's short story "A Sound of Thunder" (1952), a time traveler to the dinosaur era kills a butterfly and thus alters all aspects of the future. The past is also flexible in the film *Back to the Future* (1985), which features a teenager who time-travels back to his parents' teen years. While there, he encourages his extremely shy father to ask his (would-be) mother to the prom, thus ensuring his own birth and improving his family's financial status and, curiously, their physical appearance in the future. Unlike these imaginative ventures, *Kindred* relies on a static view of the past. History as stasis is necessary here, I believe, to allow the characters access to a past significantly marked by trauma. If history were presented as flexible, then Dana (and Kevin) would never know the physical, mental, and emotional complexity of life in slavery.

Kindred depicts history as intransitive to freeze the context to which Dana and Kevin return. In that moment, Dana is faced with similarly limited choices of slave women. She is also subject to physical abuse and forced to modify all aspects of her behavior and visage to comply with slaveholding ideology.

As part of its exploration of the slave past, *Kindred* calls into question the divide between an observer who watches an event and a participant who actively engages in it. These categories matter, because they parallel the essential tension between the traumatic moment and its recognition as trauma. Dana's exchange of the observer role for that of the participant signals her physical and moral immersion in the slave past and permits a closer look at latency and the timing of trauma.

In her article about trauma as an "unclaimed experience," Cathy Caruth demonstrates the connection between latency and history when she observes, "For history to be a history of trauma means that it is referential precisely to the extent that it is not fully perceived as it occurs; or to put it somewhat differently, that a history can be grasped only in the very inaccessibility of its occurrence." She further suggests, "The historical power of trauma is not just that the experience is repeated after its forgetting, but that it is only in and through its inherent forgetting that it is first experienced at all" ("Unclaimed Experience" 187).

Kindred critiques the idea that a history of trauma is "not fully perceived as it occurs" by placing Dana in the midst of the traumatic slave past. While there, she casts herself as an observer, one who watches rather than participates. But when the barrier is breached, she becomes a participant actively invested in the past. This move is a significant one, for in erecting the shield of distance only to erase it, Butler provides a space in which to consider the interval between trauma's initial impact and its subsequent references.

Dana and Kevin are observers when they first establish places for themselves on the Weylin plantation. As Dana assumes the role of Kevin's slave and Kevin that of private tutor, they work to fit into their roles as much as possible, but are bothered by their easy adjustment to plantation life. As Dana puts it, "It seemed as though we should have had a harder time adjusting to this particular segment of history—adjusting to our places in the household of a slaveholder" (97). She believes that their move to a more chronologically and ideologically regressive time should have created more tension, and Dana questions the facility with which the two adjust to and even comply with racist attitudes so antithetical to their own.

As observers, Dana and Kevin achieve only partial understanding of the nineteenth-century world in their choice to keep the traumatic past or, in their case, present at bay. However, Dana is unable to adapt to the observer position as completely as Kevin, who finds a reasonably comfortable place in the nineteenth century. Dana's moral discomfort suggests her proximity to, but not immersion in, the traumatic past, for she is both there (in the nineteenth century) and not there, in the sense that she has not yet forged a meaningful emotional connection to it. *Kindred* stages this gap between trauma and its registration in the mind and in history as parallel to the distance between the observer and the participant. Dana's return to the slave past as an observer who will become a participant represents a process not possible in trauma theory: to experience the event as it occurred and to recognize it as trauma while it is happening.

Dana crosses the boundary between observer and participant when she overhears a game in which slave children place themselves on an imaginary auction block, complete with an auctioneer describing the skills of the children, who are then sold to the highest bidder. Moved by the sight of children promoting their value on an imaginary auction block, Dana confronts Kevin about their positions on the Weylin plantation, telling him, "You might be able to go through this whole experience as an observer. . . . I can understand that because most of the time, I'm still an observer. It's protection. It's nineteen seventy-six shielding and cushioning eighteen nineteen for me" (101). The words *shielding* and *cushioning* are important here as a point of reference for understanding the temporal delay of trauma. Some analyses of trauma attribute the inherent latency of trauma to the stimulus barrier, a shield in the mind that automatically rises when exposed to an overwhelming experience. Here, the children's game shatters both Dana's stimulus barrier and the boundary between observer and participant. Dana's admission that she "can't maintain the distance" and is "drawn all the way into eighteen nineteen" places her squarely in the midst of the traumatic past. Dana's participation and emotional connection to the past signal, in Alison Landsberg's terms, an "experiential involvement" ("America" 76).

In addition to locating Dana in the traumatic past, the novel also provides a context in which to consider how Dana addresses herself to that past. By this I mean that Dana's ways of learning about the past seem restricted to two forms: she can read about it or immerse herself physically and emotionally in the experience. I want to draw attention to the ways in which the novel's construction of the relationship between book learning and primary experience critiques the element of indirect reference inherent to trauma theory. The novel, in its use of the time-travel device, seems to drive a conceptual wedge between the ability to know the past through books and to know the past by experience. It is this virtually impossible scenario (since no one can time-travel to the past) that I wish to consider as it refers to the representational mode in trauma theory. Whereas in trauma theory the traumatic event can be referenced only indirectly, *Kindred*'s improbable fantasy offers a scenario that claims it is only through direct experience that it can be fully appreciated.

Kindred is a book that stands in almost ironic relation to textual represen-tation. Generally speaking, the novel values literacy and the act of writing as both vocation and avocation. It acknowledges that fiction and nonfiction books are the only real way to peer into the past and the only source of information on circumstances that are long dead. The novel itself is such a book. At the same time, the novel deploys a scenario that resurrects the past and forces two present-day people to know it. It seems crucial to the novel's approach that this return to the past not be mediated by books. As the story of Dana's abductions grows more complicated, *Kindred*'s early reliance on textual knowledge begins to wane. At the beginning of the novel, textual knowledge—texts of fiction, history, genealogy, cultural artifact—is held in high regard. But as Dana's frequent journeys erode the boundaries between past and present, so does the novel's faith in the belief that books are the only way to reference a traumatic experience.

Let me rush to clarify that I am not suggesting that the only way to know the slave past (or any past) is to time-travel there firsthand. Nor is my ex-ploration of the relationship between book learning and primary experi-ence a capitulation to an anti-intellectualist position that book learning is less valuable, practical, and relevant to knowing the world (past or present) than firsthand experience. Indeed, both reading and experience are mutu-ally constitutive modes of learning. I acknowledge the deep significance of literacy for blacks in the past and present. Instead, I suggest that *Kindred*'s representation of these two modes of knowledge is part of an attempt to "de-center the cognitive," to borrow from Alison Landsberg, and "experience history in a personal, bodily way" ("America" 76). It also permits a rethinking of the ways to reference the historical past and the ways of representing the traumatic past in trauma theory: whereas the prominent mode of trauma theory insists that trauma can be referenced in only the most indirect ways, *Kindred* goes for the direct approach.

In trauma theory, the elusive structure of trauma (in the mind and in history) is also a crucial part of its literary analysis and critical practice that view the traumatic event as beyond direct reference. The antirepresentational position of trauma theory suggests that to understand traumatic experience is to inevitably misunderstand it, for, as Walter Benn Michaels claims, "the attempt to explain it can only be an attempt to reduce it" ("'You Who Never Was There'" 11). This perspective is most clearly expressed by Claude Lan-zmann, for whom efforts to directly represent the Holocaust are obscene. His nine-hour film *Shoah* does not aim to represent the Holocaust but instead depicts, according to Shoshana Felman, a "refusal of psychological under-standing, and in a vaster sense, a refusal of understanding as such" (Felman and Laub, *Testimony* 203). Lanzmann's work resonates with trauma theory in its tracing of trauma as an indirect experience that resists reference or representation. Michael Rothberg's description of this approach as an "antirealist" one—which removes the event from "standard historical, cultural, or autobiographical narratives and situates it as a sublime, unapproachable object beyond discourse and knowledge"—is also consonant with trauma theory's discursive practice that claims trauma is known only in its absence, its force "marked by its lack of registration" (*Traumatic Realism* 4).

The paradox of trauma's elusiveness generates a corollary aesthetic paradox for literary analysis: the more realist or legible a representation, the less effectively it renders trauma. As Walter Benn Michaels remarks, "If to understand is, inevitably to misunderstand," then "it is only the 'mere noise' one 'does not understand' that makes it possible to bear true witness" ("'You Who Never Was There'" 11). Within the aesthetic paradigms of trauma theory, realism, as Alison Landsberg suggests, "tends to fall on the side of transmissibility, while more abstract, elusive modes of representation fall on the side of truth" ("America" 68). *Kindred* in its navigation of book learning (indirect reference) and primary experience (direct reference) intervenes in this formulation by presenting, through a highly speculative representational mode, the idea that incomprehensibility does not have to be the constitutive element of trauma. Reading *Kindred*'s unadorned prose as a critique of indirect reference, I suggest that close attention to the novel's surface and simple premises shows the ways it places itself against the dominant forms of knowing and referencing trauma.

Initially, the written word occupies an unchallenged place of high value in *Kindred*. Yet as Dana is transported through time and space, this privileged place becomes unsteady. Butler both claims and critiques textual representation, retaining its important value as a repository of memory and experience while rejecting the impulse to completely substitute these depictions for empathic forms of connection with the past. Thus, she sends Dana, who has "a linguistically sophisticated consciousness," back to a "world whose impact is less textual than physical" (Levecq, "Power and Repetition" 529). Rather than abandoning book knowledge in favor of primary experience, *Kindred* concludes with a modulated vision that combines text-based knowledge with primary experience. Since the past can be known today only through texts, it is significant that Butler *textually* stages a return to the days of slavery that is not dependent on texts. Though she does not reject written modes of understanding slavery, Butler's use of time travel paradoxically promotes the impossible option of knowing the past directly.

For Dana, who, like Kevin, is a burgeoning writer, books are significant markers of her twentieth-century life. In Dana's present, text-based knowledge is an adequate means to understand the world and the only way to know the past. *Kindred* critiques this dependence on books by staging Dana's first abduction into the slave past from her home library. This location among books sets the context for the tension between textual representation and primary experience as ways of "knowing" the traumatic past. This epistemological conflict increases as the novel progresses and is staged in several pivotal scenes, mainly centered on the six trips Dana makes to the past in order to understand her family origins and the traumatic conditions that engendered it. Through these trips, the novel presents a progression of ideas: At first, text-based knowledge is presented as a reliable means of understanding the past. Then, faith in text-based knowledge recedes in favor of primary experience as the best way to understand the past. At the novel's close, *Kindred* presents a balanced approach that combines text-based knowledge with primary experience.

In the beginning of her returns to the past, Dana relies on her cursory readings of black history books to acquire important information about slavery. From her books, she learns that white people "won't kill [her]. Not unless [she's] silly enough to resist the other things they'd rather do—like raping [her], throwing [her] in jail as a runaway, and then selling [her] to the highest bidder when they see that [her] owner isn't coming to claim [her]." Given this dismal reality, she admits, "I almost wish I hadn't read about it." But Dana continues to supplement her knowledge of her genealogy with texts of African American history because she believes this information is vital to her survival in the antebellum period. Dana and Kevin try to create a foundation of knowledge that will prepare Dana for her ordeals in the past by consulting books, only to find "nothing. I hadn't really thought there would be anything in these books" (48). Dana returns for her third trip to the past equipped with little information from these texts. She carries this scant knowledge with her just as she carries a denim gym bag filled with twentieth-century provisions.

To some extent, the information Dana gleans from the history books is useful. When she meets Rufus's father, she adjusts her behavior to fit the context: "At first, I stared back. Then I looked away, remembering that I was supposed to be a slave. Slaves lowered their eyes respectfully. To stare back was insolent. Or at least, that was what my books said" (66). The addition of the phrase "that was what my books said" emphasizes Dana's dependence on books as the scripts for her performance of slavery, and illustrates the social and behavioral constructions of slavery: Dana does not "naturally" modify her gaze but does so because she has read about this socially prescribed behavior. Though Dana's text-based knowledge has helped her navigate different subject positions, she does not (or rather cannot) rely exclusively on this knowledge. Significantly, she learns much about her new role from listening to slaves and is, as Missy Dehn Kubitschek observes, able to augment her limited knowledge with their help. When Dana does try to depend on the information she has derived largely from books, the results are disastrous.

We see an example of this failure on Dana's fourth trip. Motivated by Rufus's unfulfilled promise to send her letters to Kevin, who has been left behind, Dana runs away to locate Kevin herself. Her escape is foiled when another slave woman, jealous of Dana's role on the plantation, betrays her to the Weylins. But Dana also blames herself and the failure of books to adequately prepare her. Comparing her escape attempt with the one Alice made earlier, Dana remarks, "We were both failures, she and I. We'd both run and been brought back, she in days, I in only hours. . . . I probably knew more than she did about the general layout of the Eastern Shore. She knew only the area she'd been born and raised in, and she couldn't read a map. I knew about towns and rivers miles away—and it hadn't done me a damned bit of good!" (177). Dana's comparison of her approach to emancipation with Alice's approach is also a commentary on the difference between text-based knowledge and primary experience. Alice has no book learning, whereas Dana has read about local geography. Alice's limited success, however, was based on the knowledge she had gleaned from lived experience. Dana's fiasco is a comment on the twentieth century's reliance on texts as a way to master knowledge of the past. Dana's failure to escape nineteenth-century slavery then can be viewed as a failure of texts to fully prepare one for the vagaries of the past and as a critique of textual representation as mastery of the historical past. In addition, Dana's complaint can be seen as a critique of the indirect referential of trauma theory. Whereas trauma theory avoids looking at the traumatic moment, Dana's predicament suggests that the past must not only be seen but also be actively engaged.

Recalling that Rufus's father once described her as an "educated nigger," Dana muses, "What had Weylin said? That educated didn't mean smart. He had a point. Nothing in my education or knowledge of the future had helped me to escape." Dana realizes that her book learning has been relatively useless in the nineteenth century, particularly as it relates to procuring her own freedom. As these questions race through her mind, her body answers, "I moaned and tried not to think about it. The pain of my body was enough for me to contend with" (177). Dana is forced to suppress thoughts of self-reproach because her pained body is a more immediate concern. As Kubitschek observes of this scene, "The thoughts, the analysis, are perceived as something separate from, almost hostile to, her beaten body. Dana prefers even the physical pain to the psychic humiliation of feeling a slave's fear" (*Claiming the Heritage*

38). Although I recognize a mind-body split in this scene, I disagree with Kubitschek's view that Dana prefers pain to "psychic humiliation." Pain is not a substitution for analysis; rather, the scene links these two ideas to further the critique of book knowledge and primary experience, for it is here that Dana's "intellectual, distanced appreciation of slavery" is transformed "into an emotional, visceral understanding" (*Kindred* 35). The device of time travel decreases the "distance" (critiquing book knowledge and indirect reference) and provides a "visceral" understanding (endorsing primary experience and direct reference). But although this scene privileges primary experience, the novel does not end on this note.

Kindred concludes with a balanced view of book knowledge and primary experience as ways to know the past. In the epilogue, a nuanced reconceptualization emerges when Dana and Kevin drive cross-country from California to Maryland to search for remnants of their nineteenth-century experience with slavery. Their search, however, is less than satisfactory: Rufus's house is gone, "its site . . . now covered by a broad field of corn. The house was dust, like Rufus" (263). The absence of Rufus's house shows that primary experience can also be suspect. In a way, the field of corn that covers the site is a palimpsest: the organic nature of primary knowledge hides the means of its production and even its existence. In other words, living things perish, homes eventually crumble to dust, and physical evidence can be impermanent.

Frustrated by their unsuccessful search for the Weylin plantation, Dana and Kevin turn to the next best thing: text-based documentation of the time. They search the archives of the Maryland State Historical Society, and Dana describes the place as one of their "old haunts" (263), though "haunt" takes on another meaning here, since Dana and Kevin are like ghosts. The other people who shared their nineteenth-century experiences are dead. They have knowledge of events that other researchers in the archives have only read about. In their time travels, Kubitschek argues, Dana and Kevin "have acquired understanding of the past, not as some procession of abstracts like 'slavery' and 'westward expansion,' but as a collection of known individuals' experiences." Yet in spite of their firsthand experience, they too must rely on books to get more information, to supplement and complete their brief experience. As Kubitschek writes of Dana and Kevin's time in the archives, "The records of history cannot satisfy emotional cravings to trace the individual lives of those not valued" (*Claiming the Heritage* 26). Although text-based knowledge may pale in comparison to primary experience, *Kindred* ultimately decides that both are necessary to know the past. Part of Dana and Kevin's final conversation of the novel verifies this:

"You've looked," he said. "And you've found no records. You'll probably never know."

I touched the scar Tom Weylin's boot had left on my face, touched my empty left sleeve. "I know," I repeated. "Why did I even want to come here. You'd think I would have had enough of the past." (264)

Dana's need to "touch solid evidence" (as Kevin later puts it) is partially satisfied by the combination of text-based knowledge and primary experience. The archival records give her some indication of what happened after the house was set on fire to disguise Rufus's murder, but not completely. This representation of Dana touching her scars is also a metonym for the importance of accessing traumatic knowledge using both symbolic gestures and physical evidence. Dana represents the need to know trauma on literal and figurative levels, to acknowledge the meanings of trauma in the body and in narrative representation. In its extreme and improbable narrative scheme, *Kindred* shows, to borrow from Alison Landsberg, the ways in which the "experiential mode complements the cognitive with affect, sensuousness, and tactility" ("America" 76). The novel also makes the simple yet important point that corporeality was an essential part of slavery. Butler's use of a present-day black body to reference the slave past reiterates the meanings of the black body in slavery, which Lindon Barrett describes as "the primary and recurring location marking crisis within or reaffirmation of the instituted relations and ideologies of master and slave" ("African American Slave Narratives" 421). *Kindred*'s representation of a bodily reference to the slave past also provides an opportunity to introduce the notion of corporeality to trauma theory. In its balanced conclusion that blends multiple ways of knowing the traumatic past, the novel suggests new ways to think about the definition and referential possibilities of trauma. To supplement the cognitive model of indirect reference, *Kindred* introduces the concept of bodily engagement to the discursive practice of trauma theory to produce a representation of traumatic knowledge that combines the literal and the figurative, and equally values soma and sema (body and mind).

The return to the past staged in *Kindred* reflects a strategy to illustrate the deleterious emotional and physical consequences of slavery, to move its readers by offering them a contemporary character through which to relate to the now more proximate slave past. Dana's responses to the past are meant to serve as a mirror for contemporary readers; her concerns with hygiene, for instance, might well reflect those of a promiscuously identifying reader. Using Dana as a lens through which to make slavery's complex horror more clear, however, is not without distractions from the mission to know slavery more intimately. Does Dana's character make slavery more real for readers, or does her presence as a prism obfuscate our vision of the actual slave characters in the novel? Why must Dana's character be present to tell what is (or should be) at its heart Alice's story? In a way, Dana's return as a sympathetic twentieth-century woman who can bring the past into greater relief is not unlike the position of white reporter John Howard Griffin, whose 1961 book *Black Like Me* took the mainstream (white) reading audience on a journey through the segregated South to reveal the deep injustices against black people. The acclaim for this book overshadowed the bitter irony that, among the broad (white) reading public, sympathetic attention to the plight of blacks could be roused only by a white man. Haile Gerima circumvents this empathic difficulty by using his time-traveling protagonist as a receptor for a female slave character's story.

Haile Gerima's 1993 film *Sankofa* shares similar motivations as *Kindred*. Fundamentally, both are driven to collapse the boundaries between slavery and freedom, the living and the dead, using a contemporary black woman to connect the present and the past. In addition, both engage and revise the conventions of their field. Octavia Butler broadens the science fiction genre by crafting racially relevant scenarios and, in *Kindred*, deploying the convention of time travel to critique both contemporary and historical race relations. Trained in film at the University of California at Los Angeles, Gerima is part of the 1970s L.A. film school, a collective of independent filmmakers of color (including Charles Burnett) that rejects Hollywood cinematic convention, style, and visual technique.[3] *Sankofa* is an independent film that couples complex cinematic language with realistic representation of slavery based on nineteenth-century slave-narrative conventions. *Sankofa*, in its realist representation of slavery, challenges traditional notions of trauma theory, specifically the idea that the past is unknowable and the traumatic moment elusive. Like *Kindred*, *Sankofa* uses time travel to get to the traumatic past. Unlike Dana, however, once she returns to the past, Mona, the film's protagonist, is deprived of her preslavery consciousness or existence. Instead, she becomes a vessel or what the film describes as a "bird of passage" through which the spirits of the dead tell their story. Part of this revelation is dependent, then, on the collapse of the boundary between the past and the present as well as the living and the dead. Gerima achieves this proximity through the use of tourism as an interpretive framing device for the film (which I discuss in Chapter 4) as well as by deploying and revising several slave-narrative techniques in the body of the story. The result is a film that reproduces fundamental slave-narrative conventions to represent the slave experience in the hopes of transmitting some part of the traumatic past.

Sankofa opens with the voice-over of Gerima's poem "Spirits of the Dead," a virtual roll call of the African diaspora that emphasizes the physical abuse, demanding labor, and liminal ontological condition of slaves who hover between the worlds of the living and the dead, waiting for a channel through which to express their story:

> Those tied, bound, and whipped
> from Brazil to Mississippi,
> step out and tell your story
>
> Those in Jamaica, in the fields of Cuba,
> in the swamps of Florida,
> the rice fields of South Carolina
> you Waiting Africans,
> step out and tell your story!
>
> Spirit of the dead, rise up!
> Lingering spirit of the dead, rise up
> and possess your bird of passage!
>
> From Alabama to Surinam,
> up to the caves of Louisiana,
> Come out you African spirits!
> Step out and claim your stories!
>
> (82)

The voicing of the poem is Gerima's first gesture toward a cinematic interpretation of a slave-narrative convention: the authenticating document. Usually written by white abolitionists, authenticating documents are brief endorsements of slave narratives that serve as letters of introduction to white readers. These documents frame the narrative by verifying the author's identity and veracity. Gerima's inclusion of the poem authenticates the film by invoking and encouraging the spirits of slaves to rise up and claim their story. In the first moments of the film, framed in the sound of the voice-over, the camera revolves around several bronze statues: a mother and child, a sankofa bird, and a man pulling at chains around his neck. The sound of the relentless, insistent, and ritualistic drums and the call of the drummer underpins the dominant narrative of reclamation expressed in "Spirits of the Dead." The tension between the swirling camera work and the stillness of the statuary suggests the conflation of past and present. The camera's action around the statues coupled with the call-and-response impulse of the poem emphasize a different form of historical knowledge. If bronze work is considered to be a more elevated art form than wax and "reinforce[s] traditional social barriers and prompt[s] a sense of detached reverence for the depicted individual" (Kendrick, "'The Things Down Stairs'" 12), then Gerima removes these barriers by making the bronze figure more active with the revolving shooting technique, insistent drumming, and poetry recitation.

The introductory elements of the film are important because they establish the diction of Gerima's cinematic language, which is essential to his reconceptualization of slavery in film and its representation of rememory. The transition from the statues to the sugar cane fields and eventually to the layered images of Mona listening to the Sankofa drummer presents a tableau that is at once prologue and authenticating documentation. The poem's roll call of the African slave trade also reflects the telescopic quality of the film's setting. Although the film was shot at several locations (Jamaica, Louisiana, and Ghana), the plantation setting of the story refuses to be firmly located in any specific historical or geographic place. This ambiguity might frustrate those viewers and critics who interpret it as a sign of Gerima's ahistoricity. I, however, view the lack of concretization not as a denial of the specificity of the African diaspora but as an attribute of its powerful influence: he constructs the setting for slavery as one that could have happened anywhere. The opening sequence is a self-authenticating gesture that frames a narrative film that attempts to cinematographically re-create and symbolically resurrect the slave past.

The story begins with Mona—a supermodel—frolicking on the beach at the encouragement of a white photographer. Dressed in a leopard-skin swimsuit, orange wig, and matching fingernails, Mona responds to her photographer's sexually charged prompts ("Let the camera do it to you, Mona"). Sankofa, the name given to the castle's self-appointed guardian who communes with the spirits of slaves, interrupts the photo shoot and tells Mona to go back to her roots. Later, when she curiously follows a tour group into the slave dungeons, she is inadvertently left behind and locked in the dungeon. While there, she experiences the tortures of African captivity and is possessed or transformed into Shola, a house slave on a sugar plantation who takes over Mona's consciousness. Through her perspective, we see slave life in both its exceptional and its mundane forms, culminating in a rebellion that ends Shola's story. Mona emerges from the castle naked and crying. An old woman embraces her, wrapping her hair in white fabric and her body in African cloth. The photographer appears and asks where she has been, but Mona seems not to hear him and runs in the direction of Sankofa's drums. There she sits on the floor with other black people who look similarly dazed. The group, which includes Gerima, stares vacantly yet resolutely at the sea. The film closes with a refrain from the opening poem "Spirits of the Dead."

At this point, I would be remiss if I did not admit that the film has several ideological shortcomings. Like other critics, I concede that this film over-simplifies and reduces important issues. Consider bell hooks, who, after hearing high praise for the film, was disappointed to find that "this script of slavery comes right out of *Gone With the Wind*. It has moments where it affirms Black self-determination, but it's so sentimental when it comes to gender." The ambitious film fails for hooks, who admits that "it's kind of sad that this is our vision of a film that begins to address our issues be-cause, once again, it's on such a banal level" ("Challenging Capitalism" n.p.). Sylvie Kande charges Gerima with reducing the multiple meanings of the sankofa bird to a "simple formula" and in a heavy-handed way "indicating the obligatory direction and necessary steps of an 'authentic' personal and political awakening" ("Look Homeward, Angel" 129). In her estimation, the film manipulates the emotions and anxieties of African Americans, who are "vulnerable to anyone who can assert, as does the Ethiopian filmmaker, his unmistakable African roots" (141).

Though I acknowledge these critiques, I suggest that these remarks may be insufficiently attentive to what the film achieves. Its combination of super-natural return (through rememory) and realist adaptation of slave-narrative conventions suggests its importance for my reconsideration of trauma theory in light of African American culture. The thinly veiled allegory of Mona as a typical American provides her experience as an object lesson. Does Gerima propose that there is a right way and a wrong way to tour a slave dungeon? Is the black visitors' stunned silence at the end of the film a representation of a traumatic effect? Does this mean that the right way for blacks to visit a slave dungeon would result in trauma? If there is a right way to visit a slave dungeon, Mona does not know what it is. Her transgressions, which include recapitulating the primitivist images of black female sexuality, commodifying black subjectivity, hiding behind her white photographer when challenged by the castle's spiritual guardian, and then laughing at him, all remand her to the traumatic past where she learns why her behavior is transgressive.

Mona's loss of innocence about the slave trade is one of the most important slave-narrative conventions that Gerima expresses in cinematic language. Traditionally, this convention describes slaves' dawning awareness that they are not free individuals but property. A key example of this occurs in the beginning of Harriet Jacobs's 1861 narrative: "I was born a slave; but I never knew it till six years of happy childhood had passed away" (Jacobs, McKay, and Foster, *Incidents* 9). Unlike Jacobs, Mona is willfully ignorant rather than innocent, and though she could be a point of identification for twentieth-century viewers, any possible connection to Mona is thwarted by camera work that portrays her very unsympathetically. For example, Mona's job as a supermodel could engender sympathy for her, as it does for Diana Ross's character in *Mahogany* (1975), where the camera is equated with a deadly weapon and the photographic act equals "humiliation and violation" (Gaines, "White Privilege" 71). Rather than being captured in a freeze-frame of the photographer's lens, which might generate sympathy for a woman frozen in time and space, Mona is not confined in that way. We instead see her as if we are looking over the photographer's shoulder, or looking at her from a wide angle with the other tourists. Mona actively participates in her sexual objectification. Writhing on the ground beneath the white photographer's camera in feigned sexual ecstasy, Mona is portrayed as self-indulgent, inappropriate, and in active opposition to the sacred space of the slave castle.

When Mona's curiosity gets the best of her, prompting a visit to a slave dungeon, she is entering what Pierre Nora has described as a *lieu de mem-oire* (site of memory). For Mona, the slave dungeon becomes a place "where memory crystallizes and secretes itself . . . at a particular historical moment." Such sites then become "a turning point where consciousness of a break with the past is bound up with the sense that memory has been torn—but torn in such a way as to pose the problem of the embodiment of memory in certain sites where a sense of historical continuity persists" ("Between Memory and History" 284). In the film, the slave castles concretize memory by preserving the history of the slave trade so that when Mona stumbles into it, even though it is long past, it is (in Toni Morrison's terms) still waiting for her. Mona trails so far behind the tour group that she is alone in the camera's frame, but the tour guide's voice contextualizes the moment, explaining how long captives would wait in the dungeons: "Some of them would be here over a year, and most of the time this would take place at night. Yes, they were taken out of here at night. The shouts, the cries of desperation, [are] still remembered along this coast line." Mona overhears this explanation, but when she is inadvertently left behind, the tour guide's words literally come to life. The dungeon grows dark, and she sees Africans in chains reaching toward her. As she bangs on the door for help, several white men enter and drag her kicking and screaming back to the past. Mona stands on the line between the past and the present, protesting her immunity, "I'm not an African! Don't you recognize me? I'm Mona! I'm an American!"

Mona's transition from the past to the present is marked by violence against her body. Two men hold each of her arms while another rips the shirt from her back and brands her with a hot iron. Gerima has remarked that this scene "allows an exploration of the past. It unleashes the collective memory of people who had certain identities and characters and beliefs. I mean, this is not my wish, but I think sometimes when we are in crisis or a tragedy occurs, we get awakened to a certain memory bin. It's the mind that is branded when Mona is branded" (Woolford, "Filming Slavery" 100). The cinematic language here emphasizes Mona's physical transformation and the beginnings of redemption. Curiously, the camera is not positioned at eye level, which would "approximate . . . our natural position in the world." Instead, the scene is shot from above, a camera angle that emphasizes "political or social comment" and shows "dominance and power relations between the oppressed and oppressing classes" (Gabriel, "Towards a Critical Theory" 86). Also, the Foley work (a film-editing technique used to fill in sound for footsteps or closing doors) plays a significant role: when she is branded, the sound of sizzling flesh dominates the scene. This is the traumatic moment for Mona, marking the fundamental break in her epistemology and her consciousness. To parallel this transition, the sound track changes from the percussive African chanting to Thomas A. Dorsey's well-known gospel song "Take My Hand, Precious Lord," performed by Aretha Franklin. Dorsey's classic song, composed out of a personal tragedy, encompasses and transcends its individual elegiac quality to become a definitive gospel song. Its tone reflects Dorsey's distinctive gospel-blues style, while its story of a weary, embattled soul seeking divine intervention is reminiscent of slavery's sorrow songs. Considering this and the song's own inaugural invocation as seen in the lines that follow, it is fitting that this song accompanies Mona's birth as Shola:

> At the river I stand
> Guide my feet, hold my hand
> Take my hand Precious Lord
> lead me home.

Using this song and Mona's searing flesh to mark the end of her "innocence," Gerima renders an important slave-narrative convention in cinematic language.

Another slave-narrative convention crucial to Gerima's rememory of slavery is the representation of punishment. When Shola first introduces herself and goes through her daily routine, tensions on the plantation are high because a group of runaways has been recaptured. As a chained group of men and one very pregnant woman is herded back to the plantation, Shola explains that Kuta, the pregnant woman, ran to the hills in the hopes of "having her baby in a free place." The return of the runaways also suggests the interrelation between trouble in the fields and trouble in the big house. As Shola explains, while the runaways were still free, she was made to bear the brunt of the master's frustrations. This leads her to flash back to the times when she "caught hell" from him; specifically, we are transported to Shola's rape, the first punishment scene. Filmed in excruciating detail, the rape scenes are nearly pornographic, not for the nudity, since both are mostly clothed, but for the camera angles used to portray the scene. When the master pushes Shola to the ground, where she braces herself on her hands and knees, the camera is not positioned squarely on the side to see both equally, but rather it is aligned more closely with the master's body, putting the viewer in a position to witness his violent thrusts and look down on Shola. The image then switches to a close-up of Shola's head and shoulders: the master grabbing handfuls of her hair, her face contorted in pain and mouthing silent screams.

In this proximate pornography, the film exploits a conventional element of male slave narratives: the sexual abuse of black women. Frances Smith Foster has observed that whereas female slave narrators did not dwell on sexual abuse as the defining aspect of their existence, male slave narrators often depicted the sexualized violence against black women as a way to address their own lost masculinity (*Witnessing Slavery* xxxiii). As Deborah E. McDowell notes in her important essay about Frederick Douglass's frequent representation of violence against black women: "Douglass's repetition of the sexualized scene of whipping projects him into a voyeuristic relation to the violence against slave women, which he watches, and thus he enters into a symbolic complicity with the sexual crime he witnesses" ("In the First Place" 203). In the coercive medium of film, viewers are also forced into a more modulated complicity. The first camera angle, which aligns itself with the master's point of view, establishes a position of dominance, whereas the second camera angle privileges Shola's pain. The result of this scene is not identification with the master (which is frustrated by the simple conditions of the film as a slave narrative) but identification with Shola. As Gerima remarks when confronted with complaints about gender stereotyping, "People kept seeing themselves in this character, and [men] didn't have this separation 'because I'm a man.' They didn't say to me, 'You didn't show a man.' They told me they went through what she went [through]" (Woolford, "Filming Slavery" 96). Still, the repeated rape scenes suggest that the film has the same gender problems as Douglass's narrative, leaving it similarly vulnerable to McDowell's cogent critique: "It can be said both to imitate and articulate the pornographic scene, which starkly represents and reproduces the cultural and oppositional relation of the masculine to the feminine, the relation between seer and seen, agent and victim, dominant and dominated, powerful and powerless" ("In the First Place" 204).

If Gerima's depiction of Shola's rapes (unconsciously) adopts the gender stereotyping and pornographic gaze of Douglass's narrative, he also (unconsciously) revises the conventional scene of a female slave being beaten in his depiction of Kuta, the pregnant runaway. To contextualize this representation, I turn to one of the most emblematic female whipping scenes in the slave-narrative genre, that of Douglass's Aunt Hester. In the 1845 *Narrative,* Douglass's master, jealous of Aunt Hester's attention to another male slave, punishes her for disobeying his orders to stay at home. Douglass, hiding in a closet, sees the entire transaction, which he describes in great detail as his passage through the "blood-stained gate of slavery." After the master stripped Aunt Hester from the waist up, "he made her get upon the stool, and tied her hands to the hook. She now stood fair for his infernal purpose. Her arms were stretched up at their full length, so that she stood upon the ends of her toes," Douglass continues, "And after rolling up his sleeves, he commenced to lay on the heavy cowskin, and soon the warm red blood (amid heart-rending shrieks from her, and horrid oaths from him) came dripping to the floor" (259). This is Douglass's inauguration into slavery.

Kuta's beating, coupled with Mona's rape scene, is a crucial element of Gerima's realist approach to slavery's representation. He presents images and scenes in a complex format that serve as the viewer's inauguration into slavery. Though the physical arrangement is similar to Douglass's description (Kuta is tied by her hands from a scaffold), Gerima revises this scene. Kuta is depicted not as a helpless victim but as a rebel whose gaze challenges her oppression until the moment of her death. Whereas a white man beats Aunt Hester, Gerima places the whip in the hands of a black man. In fact, the white man, an overseer named James, takes a background role and forces the slaves to execute the punishment. In a perversity of self-governance, James tells the head slaves, Noble Ali and Joe, "Ya'll know what to do," and the men dig postholes and erect scaffolds. Though several scaffolds are erected on a lush, expansive plantation hillside, only three are shown in the whipping scene (perhaps as an allusion to Christ's crucifixion and three crosses on Calvary). Shot from above, the scene is fraught with tension as James tries to get first Joe and then Noble to beat the runaways. Sitting on horseback, James summons Joe, who declines, saying that he "can't count and whip at the same time, though, suh." James then hands Noble the whip, telling him, "Here. Let's have some fun. Draw me some blood from them black hides." In the following conversation, when Noble claims that he is too tired to beat the runaways, James replies,

I got me a tired nigger.
Noble: Yes, suh.

James: Well, I guess you'd better count.
Noble: Massa James, you know I can't count.

Both Noble and Joe are masking, trying to resist in the face of an impossible situation. Though they both accept James's racist definition of themselves, they both fail to avoid punishing Kuta: Joe is forced to count the blows while Noble beats Kuta. In its wide-angle vision that emphasizes the stalking, pacing overseer in the background and the close-up shots that shift between Joe (the counting slave), Noble Ali (the beating slave), Kuta (the beaten slave), and the other slave witnesses, this scene suggests that Gerima is attempting in cinematic language to render this most powerful slave-narrative convention.

The whipping scene resembles in part a conversation between Kuta and Noble, though the larger slave community is implicated. The camera scans the field and includes the other slaves in this scenario: Shango, Shola's lover, races through the fields, trying to get other slaves to help rescue Kuta and the others. Nunu, who is also Joe's mother, watches Noble and Joe with intensity. Other slaves peer through the cane to see what is happening but to also remain hidden from the overseer's view. The camera oscillates between close-up shots of Noble, Joe, and Kuta. With each blow he delivers to the pregnant woman, Noble grows more remorseful. Joe, who is counting the lashes, is also visibly shaken by the role he is forced to play. Kuta, who is hanging by her wrists, turns her face to look Noble directly in the eye as he beats her. She does not scream or cry out as the first blows are delivered. Instead, she returns every whiplash with a steady gaze at Noble. Kuta remains silent; or, rather, her screams are muted by drumming and the sound of whiplashes that dominate the scene. Kuta's voice is muted until the fortieth lash; only then are her screams articulated on-screen, after which she dies. In response to Kuta's death, Nunu calls the field slaves to come and surround the body. Nunu takes her machete and performs a postmortem cesarean section on Kuta's body. While the baby is removed, the camera focuses on Kuta's still profile, which rocks from side to side with the motion of Nunu's machete and the removal of the baby. The baby's first cries are then jump-cut with another bird's-eye view of Mona's branding back in the slave dungeon, suggesting the parallel between the two birth scenes. In this version, we notice that in her agony, Mona cries out the name "Shola."

The slave-narrative convention that brings Shola's story to a close is the resistance motif. Though various forms of resistance are depicted throughout the film (including running away, avoiding odious tasks, and attending forbidden meetings), the film's energy leads to the climactic rebellion. For Gerima, who defines his work in opposition to what he calls the "plantation school of cinema," resistance is a key ingredient to his representation, permitting him to bring "the individual identities and motives of the characters, transforming the 'happy slaves' into an African race opposed to this whole idea, by making the history of slavery full of resistance, full of rebellion" (Woolford, "Filming Slavery" 92). In his estimation, his film is a form of corrective history: "Whites wrote a history of whites having freed Black people, which makes Black people people who never freed themselves" (93). Gerima conflates Shola's personal liberation from rape with the general slave uprising. In her final act, Shola, who has been demoted to field labor following a thwarted escape attempt, frees herself, in part, by killing her rapist master. Having found Shola on a secluded part of the field, her master dismounts his horse. At the same time, the film crosscuts to scenes of armed slaves storming the hillside (the same hillside where Kuta was killed) and James reclining in a hammock. The master circles Shola, trying to get behind her and push her down, but Shola keeps herself in front of him. Eventually, he trips into a patch of cane, and Shola descends on him with her machete. Two head slaves spot and pursue her. She hears gunshots close by, but instead of feeling pain, she is lifted into the air by a giant bird and flown over the water, where her story ends. At this point, Shola and her story recede, and Mona emerges naked from the castle a stunned and chastened woman.

For some viewers, Mona's stark transformation is the film's greatest achievement: the reeducation of a black woman so corrupted by Western or European ideas that she cannot properly respect the sacred ground of the slave castle. Gerima declares that "many of us [blacks] have disconnected our antennae. But those people in shackles who crossed the ocean are trying to speak to us"—a statement that implies that he, for one, has his antennae turned on (Rickey, "Labor of Love" E2).

Kindred and *Sankofa* are representations that depict hearing, if not always heeding, the ancestral voices of "those people in shackles who crossed the ocean." Still, the "antenna" required to connect to the slave past is complicated technology. If the implied goal of this empathic connection is to achieve perspective by "standing in the shoes" of someone else, how is that accomplished without depriving that person of their shoes? Is empathy possible or doomed to be frustrated? What does it mean that some readers connect to Dana (as they are meant to) as a focal point to understand the physical and emotional brutalities of slavery? Where does this leave Alice, the real slave (not the time-traveling impostor), as represented in the novel? Gerima takes the opposite position, using Mona to time-travel from the dungeon (after she is branded) to the slave past, where her consciousness is replaced by Shola's. Though this relocation privileges Shola, the actual slave character, it does not show Mona coming to grips with what the slave past means for her personal and racial history. *Stigmata,* a novel by Phyllis Alesia Perry, represents a balance between Gerima's and Butler's protagonists and their methods of empathy.

2. Touching Scars, Touching Slavery

Trauma, Quilting, and Bodily Epistemology

Here, put yo' han' on my face—right here on
dis lef' cheek—dat's what slave days was like.
—Henrietta King, former slave

The body is at once a question and an answer. Yet despite the inherent paradox of the body's interpretational complexity, African American fictional and autobiographical narratives of slavery continue to engage corporeality as a representational strategy. In the early twentieth century, former slave Henrietta King uses her body's markings to reference her slave experience (Berlin, Favreau, and Miller, *Remembering Slavery* 21). Interviewed as part of the federal Writers' Project to collect memories and stories about slave life from the last generation of blacks who had been enslaved, King recounts a tale of slavery that centers on her marked body. King, who was permanently scarred as a child by a severe beating in which many of her facial bones were broken, supplements the detailed description of her abuse by citing her body as a form of evidence. Inviting the interviewer to touch her scarred face, King offers her body as proof of slavery's brutality, using her body to document her narrative and vice versa.[1] King's narrative engages bodily epistemology: positing the body as a site of "knowing" the traumatic slave past. Her use of bodily referents provides a way to intervene in prevailing views of literary trauma theory by considering a representation of trauma that registers on both the discursive and the physical levels.

Phyllis Alesia Perry's 1998 novel, *Stigmata*, also uses the body to address the slave past. The representational strategy of bodily epistemology—the idea that the traumatic slave past can be referenced in the body after the event itself—operates in at least two ways in contemporary stories of slavery. As I discussed in the previous chapter, one method is exemplified by Octavia Butler's novel *Kindred* and Haile Gerima's film *Sankofa*, in which a present-day person can be returned to the past to better understand the experience and legacy of enslavement. The second, present in Gayl Jones's *Corregidora*, features a person in the present who experiences the slave past via bodily symptoms while remaining physically in the present. *Stigmata* uses the second method. A paranormal neo-slave narrative that is equal parts family saga, captivity narrative, and mental illness memoir, *Stigmata* deploys ideas of bodily reincarnation and supernatural wounding to resurrect the lost slave past and its meaning for one family.

My primary concern here is to illuminate the ways in which the novel's bodily references open up a space to rethink the antirepresentational impulse in contemporary trauma theory. This impulse has been influenced largely by Freud's theory of latency and the accident neurosis, which defines trauma as an elusive experience absent from the moment of its initial impact. Congruent with this elusive depiction of traumatic experience, many trauma theorists claim that trauma cannot be adequately expressed in a realist narrative mode but is instead best revealed by obliquely suggestive and esoteric narrative inferences. Henrietta King would disagree. Her invitation, nay demand, that her interlocutor touch her face depends on her body and its realist, referential ability to communicate a lost past. This encounter, like the work of Butler, Jones, and Gerima—to name only three—implies that American slavery urges a reconsideration of trauma theory's definition of the traumatic event.

Perry's novel stages interplay between the initial impact of slavery's trauma and the need to recognize or remember that trauma. Using the body as a locus of memory, the novel both adapts and revises Lindon Barrett's interpretation of the black body as "symbolizing a mythical distance from the mind and mythical entrapment in corporeality" ("African American Slave Narratives" 425). Reincarnation, bodily referents, and quilting aesthetics work together in *Stigmata* to challenge the mind-body dichotomy implicit in prevailing trauma theory and posit an alternative for coming to physical and emotional terms with traumatic knowledge.

Though the novel emphasizes the necessity of embodiment and its pivotal role in reclaiming and resurrecting a traumatic legacy, Perry's representation also acknowledges the paradox of corporeality, the body's status as both evidence and suspicion, as Lizzie's wounds remain open to interpretation. When Lizzie DuBose inherits a trunk from her grandmother Grace, the psychological and physical legacy of the bequest has dire consequences for her. Like Grace before her, Lizzie soon manifests spontaneous painful wounds on her wrists, ankles, and back, marks originally made on the body of her great-great-grandmother Ayo during her capture, Middle Passage, and enslavement. In addition to inheriting Ayo's stigmatic wounds, Lizzie's multilayered consciousness shares space with Ayo's and Grace's memories and life experiences. To explicate the connection among Ayo, Grace, and Lizzie, the novel covers a variety of issues—abduction and abandonment, reincarnation and stigmata, mental illness and psychiatric diagnosis—at a sometimes dizzying pace. Whereas her friends and relatives who accept the paranormal may view Lizzie's wounds as a mysterious replaying of her great-great-grandmother's trauma, in the novel's rational world her wounds are viewed as self-inflicted signs of a serious mental disturbance, for which she is institutionalized. Because Lizzie's wounds alone cannot convey the meaning of her reincarnation experience, Perry supplements Lizzie's body by using it as the basis for a recovery effort. To fully narrate Lizzie's stigmatic experience, Perry brings together the seemingly disparate elements of quilting aesthetics and trauma theory to know the slave past.

Stigmata incorporates an already heavy burden of meanings about the black female body. Vanessa D. Dickerson reflects prevailing black feminist thought when she locates the discourses of black women's corporeality at "the ugly end of a wearisome Western dialectic: not sacred but profane, not angelic but demonic, not fair lady but ugly darky," more animal than human ("Summoning Somebody" 196). *Stigmata* takes this dialectic into account yet alters its parameters by adapting the established mystical phenomenon of stigmata—where the wounds of Christ's Crucifixion appear in the body of a present-day believer—and refiguring it within a black female body. Ayo's wounds do not correspond to those of Christ's Crucifixion but are instead the marks of her capture, Middle Passage, and enslavement: circular raised scars on her wrists and ankles, a maze of whip scars on her back. This substitution suggests new conceptions of the black female body, trauma, and history. Perry's revision of the stigmatic concept explores one way to redeem the black female body and its historical experience. As I will suggest later, this sanctification of the black body is part of a broader effort to remember slavery and its legacy. The novel also speculates on the ability of trauma to imprint itself on the body beyond the initial impact on the mind. Ayo's capture, Middle Passage, and enslavement constitute a trauma so severe that it takes several generations to work through it. Each inheritor of Ayo's traumatic legacy (a female child from every other generation) experiences physical manifestations of her original trauma and creates an appliqué quilt to address it.[2] These quilts play an important role in moving Ayo's trauma from a literal level to a figurative one and reflect the therapeutic process of transforming traumatic memory into narrative memory.

According to trauma theorists Bessel Van der Kolk and Onno Van der Hart, narrative memory is an interactive process composed of mental structures that "people use to make sense out of experience" ("The Intrusive Past"

160). In contrast, traumatic memory is isolated, "inflexible," and "invariable." Lacking a social component, traumatic memory "is not addressed to anybody, the patient does not respond to anybody; it is a solitary activity" (163). Thus, recovery requires that traumatic memory be transformed into narrative memory in order to communicate the traumatic experience. Perry stages the change between traumatic memory and narrative memory by deploying bodily references that require additional intervention to make sense. Because Grace's and Lizzie's scars (and layered consciousness) are open to interpretation in the rational world, few people will take seriously their claim of being the reincarnation of a traumatized slave. Their wounds doubly stigmatize them (fleshly imprinting and social rejection) and could generate a form of despair similar to traumatic memory. Aware that Grace and Lizzie run the risk of becoming completely self-referential and isolated, Perry imagines the quilt as therapy and narrative release. Specifically, the appliqué quilt becomes a form of narrative memory. The quilt is part of a transformative process that takes traumatic memory, which is interior and addressed to no one, and brings it to a social level, where it is then addressed to an external audience. Lizzie and Grace create appliquéd quilts that actively resist the fragmentary element of patchwork or pieced quilts. Their rejection of the pieced quilt is a refusal of linear processes and the acceptance of a new iconographic form of narrative memory, one that would recuperate the traumatic memory (which resides only as pain and scarring in their physical body) into a communicable form. Forced to attend and expunge Ayo's traumatic past, Grace and Lizzie create appliqué quilts that narrate a painful family legacy. Using Grace's and Lizzie's bodies to refer to Ayo's trauma and their quilts to produce its narrative, Perry acknowledges the need for addressing trauma at the literal and figurative levels. Because scars reference Ayo's pain but do not transmit the narrative behind it, Grace and Lizzie use appliquéd quilts to tell Ayo's wounded (and wounding) story in a material way.[3]

Set in the small town of Johnson Creek, Alabama, and prefaced by a genealogy chart, *Stigmata* is a circular, paranormal narrative with three protagonists: Ayo, her granddaughter Grace, and her great-great-granddaughter Lizzie. The family's traumatic legacy begins with Ayo's abduction, Middle Passage, and enslavement. These physically and emotionally damaging events permanently imprint themselves on Ayo's sense of self and transcend her body after her death. The physical manifestations of Ayo's trauma recur as her granddaughter Grace and her great-great-granddaughter Lizzie each relive pivotal moments in Ayo's life in the diaspora and are physically marked with her wounds. The novel is set in three distinct time periods. The years 1846 to 1900 cover Ayo's life in Africa, her capture at age fourteen, Middle Passage, slavery, and freedom; she dictates these events in her declining years to her daughter, Joy, who writes them in a journal. From 1914 to 1958, Joy's daughter, Grace, unsuccessfully struggles to understand Ayo's physical and emotional presence in her body, eventually abandoning her three small children, including her daughter, Sarah. Much of the narrative occurs between 1974 and the late 1990s, beginning when Sarah's daughter, Lizzie, inherits Grace's trunk, which contains an exquisitely appliquéd story quilt, a small square of indigo fabric, a fraying straw doll, and the handwritten story of Ayo's abduction as transcribed by her daughter.[4]

Ayo's mother, a fabric dyer and seller, taught her daughter a cyclic West African cosmology based on a form of reincarnation that affects a girl child every other generation. As Ayo tells her daughter, "I come from a long line of forever people. We are forever. Here at the bottom of heaven, we live in the circle. We back and gone and back again" (17). Perry might be grounding this idea of perpetual return on the beliefs of the Akan in Ghana who, according to W. E. Abraham, "did not conceive the world in terms of the supposition of an unbridgeable distance between the two worlds, the temporal and the non-temporal" (*The Mind of Africa* 52). Perry articulates a philosophy of reincarnation that is as dependent on the eternal spirit or consciousness as it is on the body or the flesh. This interdependency of mind and body allows an elderly Ayo to predict that her daughter, who has recently given birth to twin boys, will eventually give birth to a daughter but only after Ayo has died, since "she cant get here cause Im in the way" (33).

Grace is the daughter who becomes the vehicle for Ayo's painful story to be remembered. Unfortunately, Grace not only embodies Ayo's traumatic past but also precipitates another trauma for her own daughter, Sarah, when she leaves her family, fearing that her "madness" will cause her to be institutionalized. This anxiety becomes a self-fulfilling prophecy for Sarah's daughter, Lizzie, who spends more than ten years in various mental health care facilities, after she inherits the wounds.

Stigmata focuses primarily on Lizzie's return from rehab; her efforts to adjust to her new freedom, reacquaint herself with relatives, reestablish trust with her parents, and perhaps have a sex life. The novel opens with Lizzie's exit interview from a mental institution. As she answers the doctor's questions, Lizzie reflects that she is merely giving the requisite answers in order to be released. Though she believes herself to be a conduit for her grandmother Grace and her great-great-grandmother Ayo, Lizzie has learned not to tell anyone about it. This deception is necessary for her return to the outside world. After many years of residential treatment facilities, Lizzie is chagrined that her release took "fourteen years and some well-acted moments of sanity"

(6). Lizzie's reentry project is complicated. Not only must she restore confidence between her and her parents, but she must also convince them that she was never crazy in the first place, that in fact she shares consciousness with Grace and Ayo. Only then can she heal Sarah's pain of abandonment. To heal these wounds, Lizzie embarks on an appliqué quilt project, one that will visually narrate the story of Grace's forced departure from Johnson Creek. Lizzie hopes that the quilt will communicate Grace's reasons for leaving and the ironic fact that, given Lizzie's stigmata, she never really left.

In the same way that nineteenth-century American women writers of sentimental fiction hoped their representations would make social change, Perry uses the sensate black female body in *Stigmata* to refer to the traumatic past and revise some forms of thinking about the black body in general. In *Stigmata*, Lizzie tries to deploy her wounds as a narrative, or perhaps counternarrative, to verify the truth of her reincarnation claim. Janet Beizer's analysis of the hysteric female body in nineteenth-century France is instructive on this point. Beizer considers the medical practice of dermographism, where doctors wrote on a patient's anesthetized skin with a stylus or nail to produce raised marks on the "impressionable" hysteric's flesh.[5] Doctors used the hysteric patient's body as a writing surface to compress women's voices into an "inarticulate body language" to be spoken, ventriloquized, by a male narrator *(Ventriloquized Bodies)*. Lizzie's scars constitute a different form of dermography. Instead of having her flesh inscribed by doctors who want to reify their authority, she is marked from within by Ayo, an ancestral presence who was rarely permitted authority.

Perry's use of the body is part of a way to refer to Ayo's trauma and commemorate its initial inscription. Because the novel works to counter cultural apathy regarding slavery, Perry's use of the supernatural (figured here as stigmata and reincarnation) is necessary for the story she needs to tell. The story of Ayo's capture and enslavement is part of what Nancy J. Peterson calls a "wounded history" that "requires the capacity to exceed normative narrative expectations." For Peterson, such stories are written "as literature, or fiction, and not as history, for only literature in our culture is allowed the narrative flexibility and the willing suspension of disbelief that are crucial to the telling of these histories" (*Against Amnesia* 7). This interpretation helps to explain the novel's governing principle—"she's not crazy, just reincarnated"— as a method of speaking the unspeakable. Perry's use of the supernatural is consonant with what Kathleen Brogan has identified as fictions of cultural haunting, where ghosts reference "group histories that have in some way been threatened, erased, or fragmented." The paranormal mode of representation emphasizes "the difficulty of gaining access to a lost or denied past, as well as the degree to which any such historical reconstruction is essentially an imaginative act" (*Cultural Haunting* 6). Perry engages these important questions of access and historical reconstruction through the image of the quilt. In the close attention it pays to the metaphorical meanings of quilts, *Stigmata* provides a space to consider the constructed nature of its production and strategies for representing trauma.

Like many quilt shows, museum exhibitions, artists, teachers, books, and magazines, Perry distinguishes between a pieced or patchwork quilt and an appliqué one. Her choice of appliqué rather than patchwork as a mode of transforming traumatic memory into narrative memory reflects the symbolic and metaphoric differences between the two forms. The process of patchwork quilting involves cutting small pieces of fabric sometimes (though less frequently today) from used clothing or household textiles and sewing them together to make a new, larger, more useful product. Patchwork quilts are a textile allegory to jazz or the blues: improvising with the scraps of life to create something new, powerful, and emotionally resonant. However, one must take care not to fetishize the fragment.[6] Though a patchwork quilt improvises with materials, it remains aesthetically limited to a grid framework (see Figure 1). By this I mean that patchwork literally works in patches: squares, rectangles, triangles, and other geometric forms are sewn side by side to create a larger geometric form, usually a square or rectangle (see Figure 2). Appliqué quilts are not limited to this geometry; instead, fabric is cut into shapes representing people, animals, flowers, or objects and then applied to a whole-cloth foundation . This technique is more ornamental than functional, requiring more fabric to maintain consistency in color and design. The meticulous attention to iconographic detail, when successful, results in an appliqué quilt that tells a story, expresses a scene, or documents an event or social moment, usually in a nonlinear narrative, in the images that it presents (see book jacket image, Viola Burley Leak's "The Middle Passage," for an example of such an appliqué quilt).

In *Stigmata*, Grace and Lizzie's appliqué quilts are based on Ayo's abduction, Middle Passage, enslavement, and its subsequent legacy. By eschewing the fragmented yet geometrically structured requirements of a pieced quilt, Perry positions the appliqué quilt as a strategy for traumatic recovery. When Lizzie proposes a quilt project to her mother (who is also her daughter), Sarah balks, "I really hoped you would change your mind and do a pieced quilt. I don't know anything about appliqué. Are you sure you want me to help you with it?" Lizzie replies, "Oh yes. I'm not going to do it without you and it's not hard" (66–67). Whereas Sarah would prefer to make a pieced quilt, Lizzie insists on appliqué. Each woman's choice of quilt modality reflects the way they conceptualize time and history. For example, when Sarah complains to Lizzie that the quilt's imagery is confusing and would be more discernable "if the pictures were in a row," the following conversation ensues:

> "Life," I say, "is nonlinear, Mother."
> "Depends on how you look at it. You may see it as a circle. But it always seems like a line to me. . . . The past is past."
> "Well, I like circles," I say nonchalantly. "The world seems to move in cycles, don't you think?" (93)

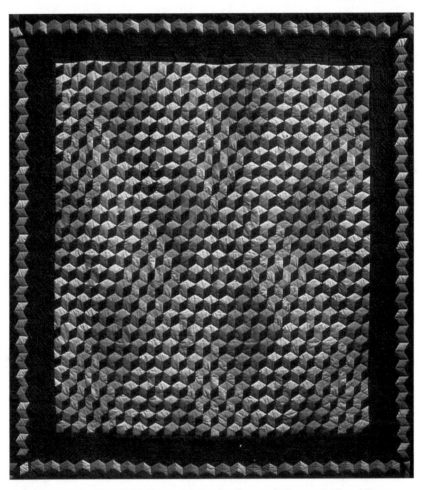

Figure 1. Mary Beth Bellah's "Can You See the Diamonds" uses the "tumbling blocks" quilt pattern and is a good example of adherence to linear, geometric form.

Figure 2. If even one piece of a patchwork quilt is improperly measured, cut, or sewn, the whole quilt can be flawed. In this example from the author's own work, a math error "revises" the traditional "trip around the world" pattern.

By linking Sarah with piecing and Lizzie with appliqué, Perry reveals the implications of the two quilt genres. Sarah's preference for the patchwork quilt emphasizes a reliance on the discernible geometric structure implicit in nearly all forms of pieced quilts. The difference between the two forms is aesthetic and philosophical. The patchwork is a geometric, grid-based quilt (that may or may not fracture the grid), whereas appliqué rejects the deep structure of the grid altogether. Because appliqué quilts are usually intended more for "show" than for "everyday use," they are better positioned to being read.[7] Hence, their iconography is an important element of their construction and interpretation. The pieced quilt, though an important assemblage of fragments, also risks fetishizing fragmentation and denying the literal events that produced the fragments in the first place. As therapist Lynne Layton writes of postmodern criticism's fascination with fragmentation, "The tendency in certain uses of postmodern theory to split off pain from pleasure is what enables a theorist to celebrate a fragmented subject or claim the fragmented subject as the authentic subject. But fragmentation arises historically, from private and public developmental traumas" ("Trauma" 121). Appliqué quilts are privileged in Perry's novel because they do not revere fragments in isolation; instead, fragments are contextualized within their traumatic origins.

The appliqué quilts crafted by Grace and Lizzie translate the wounds of Ayo's traumatic past into a narrative form. Lizzie's appliqué quilt places Grace's trauma in a narrative context, just as Grace's appliqué quilt tells Ayo's story. Appliqué's layering construction technique, which requires applying one piece of fabric on top of another, creates an entirely new product, one that is rooted in, yet different from, patchwork. Though they summon the fragmentary elements of patchwork, appliqué quilts signify on the traditional method by replacing the visual expectation of patchwork's linear, geometric grid with an examination of the interface between surface and applied figure. This textile interface is relevant also to scars on the body's textural surface. In the best of appliqué, the figures and images applied to the whole-cloth foundation appear to both blend into and pop out of their background. Quality is ranked, in part, by an appliqué quilt's seamless invisible stitching, which gives the appearance of "natural" (rather than constructed) inevitability. In this way, the best appliqué figures are like raised scars, riding the smooth flesh beneath. That Ayo's wounds are expressed, narrated in an appliqué quilt, is consonant with Dennis Patrick Slattery's interpretation of wounding: "To be wounded is to be opened to the world; it is to be pushed off the straight, fixed, and predictable path of certainty and thrown into ambiguity, or onto the circuitous path, and into the unseen and unforeseen" (*The Wounded Body* 13). The spatial configuration of appliqué, unlimited by the patchwork quilt's "straight, fixed" foundation, is better suited to tell Ayo's life story, which does not follow a linear trajectory.

When she is fourteen years old, Ayo accompanies her mother to the market to sell her hand-dyed fabrics. Ayo, who takes great pride in her mother's work and status, often reminds Grace and Lizzie that her mother is a "master dyer." Unfortunately, Ayo wanders too far away from her watchful mother and is abducted by slavers. After she is dragged aboard the ship, Ayo struggles with a slaver to keep her garment, which is made from her mother's hand-dyed indigo fabric. Her clothes are eventually torn from her body, but Ayo retains a small remnant of the cloth in her hand. As she tells her own daughter many years later, "I remember my fist being closed tight for what seem like years. . . . I had a piece of blue cloth balled up in there. Beautiful blue cloth" (*Stigmata* 132). When Lizzie inherits Grace's trunk, she finds the same piece of fabric: "The scrap of indigo-dyed cotton feels like a cloud in my palm, insubstantial and hardly graspable. That bit of nothingness is the only thing I have left of the master dyer. She had colored that cloth for me. A bigger piece makes up the dress of the girl child appliquéd onto the quilt, on her way to market, basket on her head. They tore that cloth from my body that day by the sea facing west, but I held on to something, balled it in my fist forever. Now, I look at what's left, wishing that I remembered the name of the full-brown woman" (47).

This indigo fabric remnant marks Ayo's traumatic break with her mother, her past, and her identity. The fabric that Ayo held in her fist during the months of the Middle Passage symbolizes her rage, grief, and loss. The presence of that fabric also signifies absence, a rending that suggests the impossibility of wholeness. Though tearing is fundamental to quilt construction and quilt metaphor (since fabric must be cut before it can be sewn together in a quilt), Ayo's torn life, like her torn garment, cannot be easily assimilated into a larger patchwork quilt of experience. Instead, when Ayo's garment is ripped, her sense of self is also torn, severing what Robert Jay Lifton calls a "lifeline," which if broken "can leave one permanently engaged in either repair or the acquisition of new twine. And here we come to the survivor's overall task, that of formulation, evolving new inner forms that include the traumatic events" (*Broken Connection* 176). Ayo cannot repair her lifeline by returning her fabric remnant to her torn garment. Instead, she tries to both repair her torn garment and acquire a new meaning for her life using her West African cosmology. As she tells her daughter, "We are forever. . . . We back and gone and back again" (17). Her lifeline is extended because of the need to be remembered and transmit her cry of rage far into the future. As Ayo's chosen female descendants, Grace and Lizzie, then, bear the burden of expressing and expunging Ayo's trauma. The description of Ayo's mother as a "master dyer" suggests a permanent imprint applicable to both the use of appliqué quilting and bodily epistemology as a means to know the traumatic past. Just as Ayo's indigo fabric is thoroughly saturated and fixed with color by the master dyer, so too is the iconographic imagery stitched onto the quilt (the indigo dress remnant is reconstituted *as* the dress in the appliqué quilt) and the wounds etched on Ayo's, Grace's, and Lizzie's flesh. As Ayo's daughter notices, "The marks are there, old but true" (109).

Grace's and Lizzie's belief in the veracity of their marks provides a context in which to speculate that the body is capable of registering history on its surface. Perry's deployment of the body brings to mind how slave narrators used the body in their work. Lindon Barrett has identified four patterns of representation in the slave narrator's treatment of the body: the body as intensive and extensive, the body in its relation to self-authorization, the body as a form of knowledge, and figurations of the master's body. By positioning the body centrally in the narrative, Perry's novel extends Barrett's analysis to contemporary novels of enslavement. Barrett's analysis of the body as a form of knowledge parallels my concept of bodily epistemology when he claims, "Simply put, more than it is brutalized, the body is meaningful in this mode of representation; there are attempts, whether positive or negative, undertaken by many to make *sense* of the African-American body rather than to apparently remove it from *sense* (as in scenes of brutalization)" ("African American Slave Narratives" 435; emphasis in the original).

Perry attempts to accomplish what Barrett identifies as a key mission of some slave narrators: to render the black body in a way that registers emotional, social, and historical significance. In *Stigmata*, Perry depicts Ayo's body as neither immutable nor immortal; however, her body's marks of trauma are permanent, tangible, and transferable to subsequent generations of her family. Perry's representation of the cross-generational persistence of black scars suggests a new development in the representation of slavery in historical fiction, one that proposes an alternative to the antirepresentational impulse of literary trauma theory. Though the novel's use of bodily epistemology may be seen as an unsophisticated treatment of the resurrected slave past, Perry's work also opens up new forms of inquiry into slavery's insolubility. Based on her work, it becomes more difficult to read the skin as a surface, and the surface as superficial. The body and the quilt, two popular objects of literary inquiry, are infused with new meanings when read together as a way to think about the traumatic past.

In *Stigmata*, the body is posited as a central mode of understanding the past, as first Grace and then Lizzie are made to bear Ayo's physical wounds and recall her life story. Perry deploys scars and wounding to emphasize the physical elements of Ayo's trauma and reinforce its ability to persist. The body, however, shares narrative space with the quilt as a way to remember and transmit the traumatic past. In this way, the novel uses bodies and quilts for the same therapeutic task. The quilt syncretizes the multiple meanings and implications of the body and language. By creating an iconographic narrative—that is, as physical as it is textual—Perry's novel presents quilts as a new mode of reading the traumatic past and recognizing its persistence.

Quilts are represented in *Stigmata* as transmitting and transgressing the bounds of dominant history. They also have a narrative and metanarrative function: within the story they have deep symbolic resonance, and just above the narrative the quilt orders the novel's representational form. Structurally, the novel is held together by a patchwork ethos. Perry brings together disparate fragments of interrupted lives and arranges them into a cohesive, nonlinear, grouping. The novel is ordered, but the pattern is not readily discernable. However, close inspection reveals that Ayo is the center of a nexus of historical and personal developments. Given Ayo's centrality, the traditional American log cabin quilt pattern provides a structural metaphor for the novel. With a fabric square in the center to which rectangular fabric pieces (logs) of different colors are added on either side, the log cabin is for feminist quilt maker Radka Donnell-Vogt "a universal convertible bisexual pattern protecting the union of opposites in human beings, and securing safe passage from one world into the other, from day to night, from life to death. Swaddling, doors, quilts, thus mediate in the dichotomy of inside and outside, that is, in the problems of physical, psychological, and social boundaries" (quoted in Showalter, "Piecing and Writing" 235). Perry also emphasizes the liminality of quilts: she uses them both as swaddling (Lizzie wraps up in the quilt when she opens the trunk) and as a door (Ayo reports that the door frames of slave cabins were hung with quilts). Though Donnell-Vogt's analysis successfully links two dichotomous categories, Perry's use of the quilt does not ensure "safe passage from one world into the other." In fact, one could argue that neither Grace nor Lizzie passes as safely from her own time period into that of their inaugural ancestor. Rather, Lizzie and Grace struggle to manage their multilayered consciousness. Grace's failure to understand Ayo's presence precipitated her traumatic departure from Johnson Creek. Though Lizzie is institutionalized for her own protection, it is there that she discovers the concept of stigmata. Perry invokes the phenomenon to explain what might well be considered a racially and culturally specific stigmata for African Americans.

There is a fundamental difference between *stigma* and *stigmata,* despite the latter being a variant of the former. *Stigma* suggests taint or stain, which bears racial meaning and has long been used to justify claims of black inferiority. As Charles Johnson notes in his essay "A Phenomenology of the Black Body," black corporeality "suggests 'stain' primordially. . . . [T]his stain of my skin gives in a sudden stroke of intentionality 'darkness,' 'guilt,' 'evil,' an entire galaxy of meanings" (126). From this brief glimpse and countless other narratives extending from slavery to police racial profiling, one could conclude that the black body itself is often considered a "stigma." Perry's novel, however, takes the important step of transforming the stigma of the black body into stigmata.

In the Catholic sense, stigmata is a physiological manifestation of history, a way for the past to make itself known and felt in the present. Within certain Catholic belief systems, stigmata is a sign of religious devotion. It is also a sign of what Ariel Glucklich describes as a form of "vicarious pain" that is evidenced in the "co-suffering on one's own body of Christ's wounds from the crucifixion" (*Sacred Pain* 29). Ron Hansen, author of the novel *Mariette in Ecstasy*, which features a stigmatic nun who is expelled from a convent, believes the function of stigmata is to provoke memory: "We are so far away from the Jesus of history that he can seem a fiction, a myth—the greatest story even told, but no more. We have a hint of his reality, and the shame and agony of his Crucifixion, in those whom God has graced with stigmata" ("Stigmata" 66). Perry radically revises stigmata by unmooring it from its Christian origins and meanings. The Catholic concept becomes a device to bridge two distinct but interrelated forms of knowledge: Ayo's abduction, enslavement, and the generation of Lizzie's family line becomes just as significant as Christ's martyrdom and the rise of Christianity.

Perry is not the first person to use the theme of Christian redemption to promote a proximate connection to black traumatic history. For more than a decade, St. Paul Community Baptist Church, a black church in Brooklyn, New York, has commemorated the Middle Passage and slavery with a series of annual programs, including ritual reenactments, dramatic performances, and liturgical dances. In one ceremony, the West African tradition of pouring libation to departed ancestors is coupled with the sacrament of Holy Communion. As the presiding minister proclaimed, "We are, because He is. We are, because They were" (Youngblood, *St. Paul*). Velma Maia Thomas, curator of the Black Holocaust Exhibit, titled her three-dimensional interactive book of slavery artifacts and memorabilia *Lest We Forget*, a clear reference to the popular Christian hymn "Lead Me to Calvary," which features the following refrain:

> Lest I forget Gesthsemane
> Lest I forget Thine agony
> Lest I forget Thy love for me
> Lead me to Calvary.

Trading on the assumption that most African Americans are historically and traditionally Christian, these two instances reveal an impulse to sanctify black captives as progenitors of African America. They suggest that blacks should approach the slave past with the same reverence usually reserved for religious worship. More radically, they seek to incorporate the black captive body into, and by subtle implication *for*, the body of Christ. Consider, for instance, the recent renovation of a black Baptist church on Chicago's South Side. When the New Mt. Pilgrim Missionary Baptist Church acquired a building that was previously a Catholic church, the new owners made an improvement on the facility. Rev. Marshall Hatch and church leaders raised thirty thousand dollars to install a stained-glass mural titled *Maafa Remembrance* behind the pulpit. The mural, adapted from Tom Feelings's dramatic illustrated book *The Middle Passage: White Ships/Black Cargo* (1995), is an image of a slave ship "personified in the Christlike figure of an African man. His muscular, chain-draped arms are outstretched. His body, from his torso to his calves, is the pit of a ship, drifting across the Atlantic Ocean with a cargo of men and women, sardine-packed and bound for slavery" (Fountain, "Church's Window" A14). This installation, which positions black captives as deities, is part of a long-standing movement to create more black Christian icons. It is most likely not intended to deify blacks, though this is a subtle consequence. These images portray black captives as martyrs with whom black congregants are encouraged to connect, identify, and revere. The Reverend Hatch suggests that the mural is a way to link blacks to God, yet when he gazes at the mural, another more unusual bond is revealed. As he told a *New York Times* reporter, "I was there at some point. . . . I was in somebody else, but I was present. That's my theology. It makes me whole to remember that this is what I've come through to get where I am" (ibid.).

Just as Mt. Pilgrim Baptist Church's stained-glass slave ship is moored in a building that used to be a Catholic church, so too does Perry renovate the stigmata for African American cultural ends. Perry's theology is founded, like Christianity, on a physical trauma that reverberates spiritually and emotionally throughout the ages. Ayo's wounds return because she is the initial inscriptee, the blank slate on which Lizzie's family history in the New World is written. She is permitted a powerful degree of longevity in a spiritual extension to her grand- and great-great-granddaughters. Scars and wounds are significant markers or evidence of physical trauma, testifying to both bodily integrity and its loss. Scars are signs of healing and constant reminders of trauma. However, the body is not uncontested terrain: the meaning and cultural work of scars are varied and unpredictable, often hinging on the status of the subject and the interpretation of the viewer.

Stigmata is introduced as a structuring concept for the novel and an explanation for Lizzie's condition by a priest. After she tells him the story of Grace's and Ayo's presence in her mind and body, Lizzie expects him to respond with the same skepticism as others. The priest, however, surprises her by diagnosing her experience: "Yes. Stigmata. I believe that's what you have. You hear about it happening in the Catholic Church. And often enough so that it's accepted as an authentic experience" (213). Perry effectively stages a dialogue between Catholic stigmata and Lizzie's racially specific version in order to allow the former to explain the latter. In this way, Perry canonizes Ayo. Just as Christ's wounds speak to Christians today, Perry suggests that Ayo's wounds can do the same for her descendants. Part of Perry's task, then, is to generate a story or mythos that will preserve the tales of anonymous, traumatized black girls and women and install them into a pantheon. In addition to naming Lizzie's condition, the priest also helps her on the path to recovery. After explaining that another stigmatic was a healer, the priest remarks on the reasons for Lizzie's wounds: "Maybe you're marked so you won't forget this time, so you will remember and move on. And Lizzie, I don't think you're meant to rot in a mental hospital" (213). His advice inspires Lizzie to take a more aggressive role in her care. Specifically, Lizzie learns to conform to the doctor's expectations so that she can be released and work on healing the rift in her family. Diagnosing her condition as stigmata, the priest helps to clear Lizzie's confusion about her mental health, essentially destigmatizing her.

However, it is important to note that the stigmata explanation does not persuade any of the novel's other authority figures. Lizzie's father flatly rejects her theory as a reason for what he perceives to be his daughter's mental illness. "That priest was giving you a story, Elizabeth, an interesting legend or something. It doesn't have a thing to do with you. You marching with the saints now, girl?" (217–18). His final question seems intended to shame Lizzie into concession, to urge her not to overinflate her importance. Another significant figure of power, her doctor, is equally reluctant to consider stigmata as a suitable explanation for Lizzie's wounds. When Lizzie proposes the stigmata hypothesis to her doctor, the doctor replies:

"I thought you told me your scars were from whips and chains," she says raising an eyebrow.

"But it's the same MO as stigmata, you see. A mysterious physical trauma. I wasn't praying when it happened, though. I was remembering. Remembering something unbelievably traumatic."

"I'm not dismissing your theory Elizabeth. I just . . ." She leans back and taps her desk with a pen. "There are rare cases, but I don't think you fit the criteria."

"It really hurts me, Doctor, that you won't at least entertain the thought as an explanation of my condition," I say somewhat sarcastically.

"I'm sorry you feel that way, but I'm here to help you, not argue about nebulous theories." (214–15)

The doctor's resistance highlights the difficulty of positing the body as a referent for the variant complexities of history and its persistence. Stigmatic experience, though accepted by some, is largely and suspiciously regarded as a supernatural phenomenon. Though believers in the paranormal may accept Lizzie's definition of her condition, Lizzie's father and doctor cannot afford to believe her. Though they humor her by admitting the existence of stigmata in its Catholic sense, their response implies that Ayo's story is unworthy of such an aggressive permanence. Perhaps to them, the black female body can bear stigma but not stigmata.

In her essay "Recovery Missions: Imagining the Body Ideals," Deborah E. McDowell cautions against restricting the study of black women's corpo-reality to fleshly exteriors: "But while the skin encases the body, it does not constitute the entirety of the body's compass, is not its beginning and its end" (208). Instead, she recognizes the need for a balance between the visible and invisible parts of the body. For instance, in an analysis of Sojourner Truth's grief over her stolen children, McDowell writes, "That those cries originate in the body's 'inside' parts, even if they are registered on the outside surface, suggests the importance of a view of the body that perceives the reciprocal relation between exterior and interior, between visible and invisible 'matter,' between the outside and the inside body" (209). Perry's refashioning of stigmata is an effort to balance the interiority of trauma and its physical manifestations. Rendering the marks on the flesh is but the beginning of a form of transformative knowledge and reclamation. Lizzie's scars are references, signs that begin to narrate the traumatic past of slavery. However, as the following display of her scarred back to her doctor suggests, her body is not self-explanatory:

> Then, silently, I turn my back to her, satisfied with her short gasp.
> Her gaze is hot, I can feel it as it steps tentatively through the maze of scars, from neck to waist and beyond, permanent remembrance of the power of time folded back upon itself. Proof of lives intersecting from past to present.
> "Sad thing is," I say, picking up the shirt to slip it back on, "what you're look-ing at was rather commonplace back then. Scars like these. That's the thing, Doctor, I'm just a typical nineteenth-century nigger with an extraordinary gift. The gift of memory." (204)

Lizzie's description of herself as "typical" resonates with a popular nine-teenth-century photograph of Gordon, a former slave. Naked from the waist up, Gordon is seated with his back facing the camera, which focuses on a maze of raised whip scars traversing his back. The scars, which vary in shape and length, cover nearly his entire back. Widely circulated in the nineteenth century for abolitionist and Union causes, the photograph was reprinted in *Harper's Weekly* (July 4, 1863) as the center of a triptych titled "A Typical Negro." The three panels show Gordon's transformation from a ragged fugitive slave enlisting in the Union army to an armed soldier ready to defend his country. Marcus Wood, in his study of the visual representation of slavery, suggests that Gordon's image was so interchangeable that it could be used to promote a variety of concerns, including "what the slave was prepared to do for the North" (*Blind Memory* 268).

Similarly, the unveiling of Lizzie's battered back reveals that wounds lack a stable meaning. Consonant with the paradox of the body, Lizzie's display to her psychiatrist both succeeds and fails. Lizzie's battered flesh successfully provokes an automatic response, the doctor's "short gasp." But the doctor's response is limited to shock, horror, or revulsion, rather than conversion to a belief in paranormal phenomena. Lizzie deploys her scars as evidence of the fluidity of time and as proof of the brutality that the black body was forced to endure in the nineteenth century. Her outside body, however, remains subject to interpretation. The doctor, though moved by the presence of the scars and hard-pressed to explain how these wounds could be self-inflicted, is bound by a professional ethos that will not allow Lizzie to go free until she is cured of her delusions. In this way, the novel critiques an overreliance on the body's flawed explanatory power.

Is it possible that by touching a scar, one can reference the precise moment of its creation? Can fingering a jagged grain of evenly formed stitches in the flesh resurrect the piercing of the needle, the pull of the thread? These questions suggest the dual meaning of part of this chapter's title, "Touching Scars," a phrase that relates to the interior perspective of the wounded and the exterior gaze of the viewer. From an external interpretive locus, scars (on another's body) may be emotionally "touching" in the sense of provoking a feeling of sympathy, pity, or repulsion in the viewer. Even if one touches another person's scars, the gesture does not fully render the wound's story, which must be supplemented by further explication. This is the lesson Lizzie must learn, and it indicates the conceptual strengths and limitation of bodily epistemology. From an interior perspective, touching one's own scars is a highly self-referential process, for only the scarred person knows precisely what her scars mean, what presence or absence they signify. An abdominal scar can reference a cesarean delivery or uterine fibroidectomy, both surgeries marked by the same dotted line. If it is true, as Dennis Patrick Slattery suggests, that "wounds, misshapen bodies, scarred or marked flesh always tell a story through their opening onto the world," then it is also true that scars can start a story, but not fully narrate it (*The Wounded Body* 14).

Thus far, my exploration of bodily epistemology has been based on female protagonists. Butler, Gerima, and Perry offer women characters as the best choice for time travelers, as prisms through which to understand slavery in a more physical way than standard modes of knowledge permit. Since I am working with speculative fiction, allow me to speculate a bit: what if Dana was Dan or if Mona and Lizzie were men? In two interviews, Octavia Butler explains that she initially developed a male character for the starring time-traveler role but found that she could not keep a twentieth-century black man alive long enough in the antebellum South to "sustain the character. Everything about him was wrong: his body language, the way he looked at white people, even the fact that he looked at white people at all" (McCaffery, *Across the Wounded Galaxies* 65). As she told Charles Rowell, "So many things that he did would have been likely to get him killed. He wouldn't even have time to learn the rules—the rules of submission, I guess you could call them—before he was killed for not knowing them because he would be perceived as dangerous. The female main character, who might be equally dangerous, would not be perceived so" (interview with Rowell 51). In Butler's imaginings, a black man's twentieth-century identity, specifically his masculinity, was incompatible with the demands of a cosmic return to the slave past.

In the next chapter, I consider two films produced in the early 1990s for young audiences that take up this concern. In their representation of sending a young black male to the slave past, these films reflect a larger cultural anxiety about black masculinity as it appears in hip-hop (which the films depict in their protagonists' preoccupation with money, music, and stylish dress coupled with a lack of interest in formal education and legitimate work). Though it is not my intention to dismissively label these films as *Kindred* in drag (without engaging the complexities of the gendered performative), the phrase is a useful means to access the gender and generational implications of the films. If part of Butler's motivations in *Kindred* was to "school" a Black Power brother in the hard lessons of his ancestors, *Brother Future* (1991) and *The Quest for Freedom: The Harriet Tubman Story* (1992) seek to impart the same knowledge to the hip-hop generation. I will consider the ways in which the films critique hip-hop through their rather standard sociological treatment of cool and reeducate (even rehabilitate) the black male teen protagonist by forcing him to reassess his twentieth-century present in terms of a brutal, if fantastic, experience with the slave past.

3. Teach You a Lesson, Boy

*Endangered Black Male Teens
Meet the Slave Past*

In July 2005, American parents learned of two unusual programs designed to teach teenagers valuable, yet difficult, lessons in gratitude and resourcefulness. Heifer International—an antipoverty and anti–world hunger organization operating in fifty countries—offers an immersion experience at its Heifer Ranch in Arkansas. The ranch's Global Village, a re-creation of living conditions in developing nations, is the site of a learning experiment that ranges in duration from one night to two weeks. Students (middle school through college age) are randomly divided into "family" units, given "resources such as food, firewood, water, or shelter. . . . Since the resources aren't equally divided, families must trade with each other to meet their basic needs, prepare their evening meals and settle in for the night" ("Heifer Ranch" n.p.). It is this uneven distribution of resources that makes the experiment vivid for many of its participants; some groups "receive more than others, while a group of refugees receives nothing. The exercise creates a microcosm of the real world where people have to trade firewood, cornmeal, water, or vegetables to survive, or depend on strangers." Though the scarcity element might invite comparisons with a televised *Survivor* episode, a camp leader warns in advance, "It's not about competition. It's for you to experience what it means to live like this." One church-group adviser brought sixteen teenagers from Boulder, Colorado, for this precise reason: "Here's a bunch of affluent, Caucasian kids. . . . They talk the talk, but I wanted to see if they could walk the walk" ("Teens" B1). Thousands of students each year go through the real experiences of trading, bartering, or begging for sustenance in this simulated environment. For many, this prompts insights into global hunger that are more immediate than those they might have studied formally.

In the main, the young people at a Global Village program are more or less "good" kids, interested in solving world problems. But what about another type of teen, one less concerned about global issues and more interested in himself? The ABC television network put the question this way: "What do you do with a teen who curses at you, breaks the law in your house and doesn't listen to anything you say?" ("Brat Camp" n.p.). For nine families, the solution resulted in the July 2005 premiere of another program created to teach teens a lesson: the reality TV series *Brat Camp.* Produced by Arnold Shapiro of the award-winning documentary *Scared Straight!, Brat Camp* removed nine unsuspecting, antisocial (and apparently white) teenagers from their daily environment and took them to SageWalk, an Oregon wilderness-based rehabilitation program for troubled kids. The sight of teens (who appear on-screen framed by captions such as "Compulsive Liar," "Steals from Mom," and "Violent Temper") learning survival skills as a form of therapy and behavioral modification is a huge audience draw. *Brat Camp* ranked among the top-ten televised shows for every week it aired, pulling in 8.5 to 10.5 million viewers per episode. The SageWalk wilderness program also garnered increased attention, as visits to its Web site rose from two hundred daily hits to more than nine thousand visits per day after the show's premiere.

Although Heifer International may have a more virtuous ambition (to create more globally minded teens) than ABC television (to generate viewers and advertising revenue), both programs tap into parental anxiety about the proper behavior, morality, and life path of their children. Though they predate the two programs mentioned above, two films in the early 1990s featuring antisocial black male teen protagonists share a remarkably similar motivation. Like the Global Village and *Brat Camp, Brother Future* (1991) and *The Quest for Freedom* (1992) are premised on the theory that physical labor, privation, and isolation from one's regular setting or comfort zone can influence a self-absorbed teenager's behavior. But rather than sending these disruptive teens to a third world camp or wilderness rehab program, these films offer the ultimate no-nonsense boot-camp location: the slave past.

In this chapter, I consider the ways in which bodily epistemology works as a reformatory strategy designed to rehabilitate wayward black youth and address anxiety about black males in the hip-hop generation. I read the films as both an exercise and a solution. They are an exercise in compliance, one that deploys the slave past as a disciplinary tool to manage the cultural anxiety created by black male teens. They also present themselves as a solution, a packaged panacea offered to teachers and administrators of school-age children and young adults who may not take school or other authority figures seriously. The films seek compliance of black male teens in a cultural context rife with black masculine expressions of rage (Public Enemy's "Fight the Power"), anarchy (NWA's "Fuck the Police"), insolence ("Parents Just Don't Understand"), and sexual prowess (Tone Loc's "Wild Thing" or any song by the 2 Live Crew). The films are a cinematic version of Scared Straight, a panacea program that overlooks the intricacies of the conditions of these troubled teens. Rather than explore the complex reasons for T. J.'s and Ben's current state, the films circumvent the considerable issues of public policy, racism, inner-city underdevelopment, and struggling public schools, and place the responsibility for their condition outside of America's mainstream squarely and solely on them. In the films, T. J. and Ben both *choose* their antisocial behavior. There are no larger social, political, or economic factors arrayed against them. T. J. is a smart aleck who mouths off to his teachers and rejects formal education in favor of the more lucrative underground economy. Ben is an idle and belligerent teen who aggressively talks back to his mother. The adverse effects of Reaganomics do not emerge as a plausible explanation for these young men's disillusionment. They choose to be outside of America's mainstream; they are not excluded from it.

In *Brother Future,* T. J. (Phill Lewis) steals electronics and sells them, whereas *The Quest for Freedom*'s Ben (David King) is indolent and insolent. Both boys[1] avoid school and care only about themselves. In the midst of running away— T. J. from the police, Ben from his nagging mother—the boys find themselves transported to a moment in the slave past: T. J. to 1822 South Carolina and Ben to 1849 Maryland, where they are forced to live and work as slaves. Their return to their own present can be achieved only by "doing for others."

Brother Future and *The Quest for Freedom* aim to address character deficits in urban black male teenagers. Both films depict the slave past as a rehabilitative location, and their narratives expose the protagonists to a combination of Joe Clark zero-tolerance discipline (as praised in the 1989 film *Lean on Me*) and prison-aversion and delinquency-prevention tactics popularized in the *Scared Straight!* reform movement. In both cases, the cosmic strategy of time-travel immersion effectively, thoroughly, and, best of all, inexpensively reforms the boys. Such a strategy is consonant with the Reaganomics ideology that promoted a shift from government intervention to "character development" as a solution to social troubles. The complex problems of T. J.'s selfish consumerism or Ben's nihilistic rage are easily solved by "doing time" in the slave past, which leaves the boys grateful for their position in the "free" present. The films imagine a universe in which moments of the slave past are resurrected to function as a jail or prison would in a crime-deterrence program.

I use the term *coercive memory* to describe the mastery with which the films urge a particular form of interaction with the slave past. Coercive memory narrowly selects the moments that should be remembered, shapes the image of that memory, and allows for only one response to that past. Like the concept of rememory in *Beloved,* where a past—but not finished—experience still awaits, moments of the slave past await these black male teens. The coercive element resides in the strenuous lessons (in twentieth-century obedience, gratitude, and self-sacrifice) that accompany the film's resurrection of the slave past. These films force the boys to interact with the slave past in a singular way, one that advances a reformatory agenda in their present: the boys' efforts to resist, talk back, or escape are thwarted. The protagonists perceive the slave past in such a way that serves the needs of the dominant culture. They are permitted to see the slave past only in the spirit of healing and reconciliation, not rage. These films exercise authority over the slave past as a way of exerting authority over unruly black teens in the present.

Unlike many prison-aversion programs that frequently backfire, these two educational films demonstrate successful resolutions. Once returned to the twentieth century, Ben grabs his books and prepares to apologize to his mother; T. J. gives up his "business" and seems on the path of racial uplift. The combination of coercive memory and bodily epistemology is part of a larger cultural desire to manage and control young black male behavior. The fantasy is motivated by a need to quell anxiety about the things that the emerging hip-hop generation had come to represent by the early 1990s. Though its popularity had increased to the point of mainstream co-optation and imitation, rap music of the early 1990s (and the hip-hop generation that produced it) both portrayed and engendered concerns about black criminality, black male reclamations of public space, and aggressive youth behavior. As the generation raised on civil rights and, in many cases, by those who were denied their civil rights, the hip-hop generation had become disillusioned, as the dream of equality continued to be deferred through the Reagan and Bush administrations. Although some black youth remained optimistic, others succumbed to despair, rage, or the lure and lucre of the underground economy. As Jewelle Taylor Gibbs explains in her book *Young, Black, and Male in America: An Endangered Species,* "The delinquency-prone adaptation styles are cultural 'options' which seem attractive to young, black males who feel alienated from white society and perceive few achievable routes to conventional success being available to them" (143). Each of these films presents a young black male who needs to rejoin the mainstream, to accept his role in the dominant culture even if it is in a subordinate position. Under the guise of character building, these films tell a story of reform and rehabilitation through the labor practices and physical discipline of American slavery. Ironically, and without self-reflection, these films use the slave past to coerce deviant black males to joyfully accept their subaltern position in American culture.

Using the slave past as part of a reformatory technique is consonant with the "get tough" disciplinary approach popular in the late 1980s and early 1990s. American culture, as reflected on a cinematic level, was deeply troubled by the problem of young black males and what was presented as their disorderly conduct. In the late 1980s and early 1990s, ghetto films, featuring black teens struggling to survive urban chaos, were a significant trend and audience draw. Some viewers were attracted to these films' use of rising hip-hop stars (like Tupac Shakur and Ice Cube), others enjoyed the heady soundtrack (featuring songs by Ice-T and NWA), and still others probably experienced a vicarious pleasure of reading the films as exposure to the front lines of the inner-city war zones. Films such as *Colors* (1988), *New Jack City* (1991), *Boyz N the Hood* (1991), *Juice* (1992), *South Central* (1992), *Menace II Society* (1993), and *Fresh* (1994) shared screen space with educational reform films—such as *The Principal* (1987), *Lean on Me* (1989), and later on *Dangerous Minds* (1995) and *The Substitute* (1996)—about troubled inner-city schools that miraculously improve with tough discipline from a charismatic authority figure. These films provide an interpretive context in which to consider *Brother Future* and *The Quest for Freedom* because, in effect, they share the same preoccupations: How can black teens be managed in this time of their increased mobility and visibility, when their cultural property—rap music (once marginal)—has become mainstream and is on its way to global prominence? How do we encourage black teens to believe in the American dream when it continues to elude them? How do we make our institutions and behavioral systems seem fair when they are actually discriminatory? In essence, how do we make a grim present appear to be more attractive? The solution is to relocate the mal-contents in an environment that is overtly more grim, where blacks are denied basic human rights, where freedom is an idea rather than an entitlement, and where the boys' complaints (though justifiable in the twentieth century) will become moot, nonsensical, and anachronistic. In this way, the films replicate what sociologist James O. Finckenauer calls the "panacea effect": the slave past is presented as a panacea for the twentieth-century ills that black youth have acquired during the Reagan-Bush era (see *Scared Straight!*).

These teen protagonists are drawn to represent the hip-hop generation, embodying the ideals of cool, selfishness, materialism, and ahistoricity. The disciplinary impulse of these films can be usefully explained by a reference to another slavery immersion film, *Sankofa*. In her critique of that film's representation of the slave past, Sylvie Kande bemoans what she regards as an oversimplified disciplinary vision: "The therapy he envisions for all the

Monas of the world is a kind of re-education through work on the plantation—a tropical gulag, so to speak" ("Look Homeward, Angel" 132). The
gulag concept, though not appropriate, I think, for *Sankofa*'s protagonist,
goes a long way toward explaining T. J.'s and Ben's return to the slave past.
These films are part of an intraracial struggle between the hip-hop generation
and the civil rights era that preceded and created it. The film thus depends
on a depiction of the slave past as not only historically "authentic" but also
capable of producing an emotionally genuine response. It is this affective
transformation that will erode the teens' facade of cool and put them on the
proper path to racial uplift, promising to (perhaps) provide a place for them
in the mainstream American economy and society.

Presenting slavery as a disciplinary tool reflects the ways in which the
slave past can be used as a malleable literary and cinematic trope. As Fred
D'Aguiar writes, "Each generation inherits an anxiety about slavery, but the
more problematic the present, the higher the anxiety and the more urgent
their need to attend to the past. What the anxiety says is quite simply that
the past is our only hope for getting through this present" ("The Last Essay"
132). If these films are any indication, it would appear that, according to the
older generations who make the films, the hip-hop generation has not yet
found an empowering or useful method to regard the slave past. Instead,
Brother Future and *The Quest for Freedom* both offer the anxious "parents"
of these troubled black teens the slave past as a way to help their offspring
straighten up and fly right. These films use the slave past to teach the boys
a lesson, to reveal the privileges they take for granted, to get them to value
their freedom by depriving them of it.

The scared straight approach, first started in the late 1970s, was a popular
program and one that generated positive responses, despite its lack of testing
or proven results. Initiated in the 1970s by the New Jersey prison system, the
prison-aversion program Scared Straight is now a generic descriptor of any
session designed to forcibly educate at-risk youth about the consequences
of crime and the perils of prison life. The lure of these programs can be
attributed partly to their low cost, but also to the ways in which they punish rather than treat potential offenders. The "get tough" approach did not
mollycoddle or encourage; rather, deviant behavior was modified by giving
young kids a taste of the negative consequences of their behavior. *Brother
Future* and *The Quest for Freedom* use this strategy in reverse. Rather than
showing the teenage boys a glimpse of their grim future should they continue
on the path of delinquency and nihilism, the films show the boys the depth
(or at least one level) of their grim, enslaved past. The films locate the boys
in an enslaved role where their reeducation will take the form of manual

labor and physical violence with its concomitant emotional containment. This situation will clash with the boys' conspicuous hip-hop attitude, which will be either eliminated or modified to better serve them in the past and eventually in their present. Their key to freedom lies in their ability to help others, even at the expense of themselves. Thus, the slave past is crafted here as a location to transform young black men from being loud, brash, and self-involved into what the films imagine as an improvement: moral characters who are selfless, compassionate, responsible, and perhaps even willing to work for minimum wage.

Crime and delinquency scholar Anthony Petrosino summarizes *Scared Straight!* in this way: "Deterrence is the theory behind the program; troubled youths would refrain from lawbreaking because they would not want to follow the same path as the inmates and end up in adult prison" (Petrosino, Turpin-Petrosino, and Finckenauer, "Well-Meaning Programs" 356). The program's popularity—fueled by a conservative ideological climate and its low cost—represents what researchers call a panacea phenomenon in government policy, "the search for simple cures for difficult social problems" (357). And despite actual data showing "no crime reduction effect for *Scared Straight!* and other deterrence-oriented programs," *Scared Straight!* was again validated in a 1999 follow-up documentary hosted by African American actor Danny Glover. The MTV special *Scared Straight: Twenty Years Later* claimed a high rate of success in reforming potential criminals. As the show's producer says, "You don't know how many people have come up to me and said, 'I was a juvenile delinquent and when I saw this, I stopped, I changed'" (357–58). Despite this purported enthusiasm, such delinquency-prevention programs, when reviewed by scholars analyzing exit surveys and control-group studies, have been shown to be ineffective.[2]

Though research consistently shows that such deterrence programs do not work, these projects continue to be praised and funded. Anxiety about increasing crime results in a "perception that any alternatives to getting tough, such as treating offenders, do not work" (368). The predominant cultural attraction to the "get tough" method of crime prevention produced and reflected the overwhelmingly positive response to the program. Exit surveys and interviews with "inmates, juvenile participants, parents, corrections personnel, teachers, or the general public" yield claims that "almost everyone believed the program was doing good" (369). Despite the rigorous studies that prove the program to be ineffective, the lure of the *Scared Straight!* program remains strong. I suggest that the documented positive response is an indicator of increased cultural unease about criminality and deviance. People believe that *Scared Straight!* is effective because of a fundamental need for it to be so. After all, if prison does not deter crime, then what does? Rather than focus on more creative and complex strategies of intervention, these programs rely on the simple solution—using a flawed system already in place—to cure the problem.

My interest in these films concerns the disciplinary fantasy embedded in the representation of a "return" to the slave past. Though the films have different funding sources and distribution outlets—*Brother Future* was funded by and aired on PBS, whereas *The Quest for Freedom* was directly marketed (by phone, newsletter, and word-of-mouth) to schools and libraries[3]—both share the fantasy of reforming black male teens who, through their hip-hop attitude, represent an increasing threat to American civil society. In what follows, I consider how these films use the historical event of American slavery—focusing on a discrete moment in that past—to cultivate an attitude of gratitude in black male teens living in the twentieth-century Reagan-Bush era. In so doing, these films promote the idea of compassion, humility, and sacrifice as the cure for (f)ailing black communities in the 1990s. These films offer two black teens a homeopathic dose of the slave past as a simple cure for the symptoms of a disturbed present.

Their representation of slavery, which the films decry as an institution, is one that subtly grants slavery legitimate status as a foundation or source for black identity formation. The films take pains to depict the past as more rich and authentic than their present-day settings. The attempts to create a slave past shot "on location" imply that the slave past can be reconstructed if one returns to its "original" sites and that this revisiting requires more attention to detail to be successful. Filming on location at heritage sites such as Magnolia Plantation in Louisiana or Boone Hall plantation in South Carolina provides the film with a rich visual archive of the past that is conspicuously absent in the film's generic twentieth-century urban setting. From Dumpster to palm trees, the representation of public space in the twentieth century differs greatly from that of the nineteenth century, where the emphasis on visible reenactment, in terms of costuming, scene construction, and transportation, shows signs of an effort to create a nineteenth-century past that concretely, visually corresponds with the lived experience of that era. The films imply that the present is anonymous, the past specific. In this way, the films offer an unwitting critique of the importance of "the street" in a hip-hop context. The dismally generic quality of the street in *Brother Future* or the hood in *The Quest for Freedom* contrasts significantly with the value and high emphasis placed on these locations in rap music and videos. In both cases, the street reflects its use as a convenient referent for the hip-hop context that informs each boy's identity.

Rap music, especially in the late 1980s, cultivated the street as an authentic location and source for black youth identity. Tricia Rose's observations about rap video production are relevant to the depiction of the teens' twentieth-century context, since the urban locations "usually affirm rap's primary thematic concerns: identity and location." As Rose notes, "Rap music videos are set on buses, subways, in abandoned buildings, and almost always in black urban inner-city locations. This usually involves ample shots of favorite street corners, intersections, playgrounds, parking lots, school yards, roofs, and childhood friends" (*Black Noise* 10). Contrary to the appreciation, even fetishization, of the street in hip-hop, the urban locations of *Brother Future* and *The Quest for Freedom* are generic and grim. Though T. J. boasts to those he meets in the past that he is from Detroit and Ben confides to Harriet Tubman that he is "from L.A.," there is nothing in the depiction of these present-day locales to suggest the specificity of these cities. This is curious, considering the racial markings of each place. Both cities produced what is known as a distinctly black musical style: Detroit as the home of Motown and Compton as the beginnings of NWA (Niggaz with Attitude). These cities are also known for expressions of black rage and social protest in the form of riots. Still, in these films, the decision is made to have the present pale in comparison to the past.

The reeducation of black male teens takes the form of a violent immersion in moments of the American slave past. In this imaginary scheme, visiting Harriet Tubman or Denmark Vesey forces each young man to compare his present-day existence with the slave past. But since coercive memory is at work here, the protagonists are allowed to cultivate only certain responses to that past. In this way, these teens are not allowed to see themselves as victims in the 1990s. Any complaints about their present-day predicaments pale in comparison to the conditions of the slave past. The films deflect criticism of the present by offering a past that is more overtly oppressive. The films critique the protagonists' hip-hop attitudes toward education (preference of street credibility over formal school), work (rejection of the service industry), and entitlement (their selfishness). While in the past, the boys must learn the value of formal education and physical labor, which the films link to freedom.

As educational films geared toward middle and high school students, *The Quest for Freedom* and *Brother Future* offer increased understanding of black history and the subjection of blacks in the antebellum South as a method of reforming troubled teens in the 1990s. The films aim to erode student and viewer apathy about the past and critique what they depict as the self-absorption, image preoccupation, and other troubling behavior of contemporary teens. Unlike their black female counterparts, however, these young male characters present a challenge to the mode of time travel and bodily epistemology as a strategy to understand the slave past. Their youth and masculinity make them targets for the application of a critical, if imaginary, reform effort. If the female protagonists of the previous works reflect a meditation on the status of black female sexuality and power within a white patriarchy, the place of black masculinity within the same patriarchy is also hypervisible. There are crucial differences between placing a contemporary black woman in the slave past and "returning" a black male to that same time and place. The imaginative ventures I have discussed earlier—*Kindred, Sankofa, Stigmata*—feature a woman whose time travel is motivated by a judgment error in the present, or by a need to complete or complement the story of an ancestress. In each case, their gender makes them automatically subject to male power, just as their race marks them as social inferiors. Black women, these texts imply, are more malleable to the conditioning processes of subordination. These black women characters can be sketched more believably as compliant subjects largely because women are expected to occupy this role in patriarchal culture.

Because of this assumption of female malleability, imagining a present-day male returned to the slave past is a more tricky prospect. I claim that there is a tacit assumption—borne out by examples as diverse as Frederick Douglass's two-hour fight with Covey or Linda Brent's "choice" of a white "lover"—that men can physically free themselves from the bonds, whereas women's responses to enslavement are less likely to involve physical battle. Slavery, many slave narratives suggest, deprives men of manhood in a way that is ostensibly less detrimental than the way a woman is deprived of her womanhood.

Brother Future and *The Quest for Freedom* take up a scenario that is rife with this concern of black masculinity but avoids its deeper complexities by making its protagonists teenagers (not quite adult). Though the films proclaim themselves to be family entertainment—and have been commended as such—beneath the facade of wholesome viewing and moral uplift lurks a less kind and gentle strategy of reform. It is important to consider the films not only as an intervention in the teaching of history in secondary schools but also as part of the larger debates about the "endangered black male." Fitting within the era in which they were produced and released—the turn of the 1990s—the films' solution to black male delinquency reflects a distinctly Reagan-Bush quality of conservatism that deflects attention from social, economic, or other structural elements that adversely affect black life while seeking to reinvigorate a work ethic and emphasize the importance of an attitude of gratitude from antisocial or delinquent black male teenagers.

Rather than rely solely on representations (such as slave narratives or documentary and archival records) to access the past in the present, these films depict a scenario in which the past can be revisited and relived, in real time. Additionally, the films suggest that a more proximate connection with the slave past can change delinquent behavior in the present. The return to the past—or, rather, the *turn* to the past—is part of a larger effort to better understand the difficulties of the ancestors to whom present-day blacks are obliged. Consonant with this view, the past is depicted as a more brutal and more vivid environment than the present. In the case of *Scared Straight!*, authority figures who send their students to such programs seek to counterbalance the street mythology of prison, which is at times glamorized in some sectors of hip-hop, with the lived experience of incarceration. This urgent need to impart "the truth" motivates many *Scared Straight!* supporters. For example, the director of an in-school suspension program who took her at-risk middle school students to a Washington, D.C. jail in the spring of 2001 said, "I wanted some of these kids to experience the jail—you know, the clink-clink, the bars." As part of their deterrent visit, the kids were "intimidated by guards, strip searched, forced to undergo a body-cavity search, and left in the presence of a masturbating inmate" (Bellinger, "Scared Crooked" n.p.). The "reality" of jail, as stressed in the phrase "you know, the clink-clink, the bars," is presented as an opportunity to change juvenile behavior. These films and *Scared Straight!* share the same reform approach by emphasizing the distinction between the past and present, jail and freedom. The programs and the films show that through fear, intimidation, abuse, and sexually coded violence, the troubled boys will choose to change their ways, learning to fear and loathe incarceration and appreciate freedom.[4]

The experience of the children at the D.C. jail might support a conclusion that prison is a modern-day analogue to American slavery; one could argue that increasing prison populations, with huge numbers of black and minority males imprisoned, reflect both an uneven application of the law and a need for a captive workforce as more prisons become privatized producers of goods and services. *The Quest for Freedom* and *Brother Future* foreclose this avenue of explication, however. In these films, the past is past, finished, whole, complete, and contained, whereas the present is evolving, open, fecund, and possible. The past does not impinge upon the present, and present-day values are inoperable in the past. These films claim an authority over history that allows the past to serve a conservative agenda in the present. Although many blacks complained about the Reagan-Bush administrations, the films' version of the past and (a newly improved) present renders such claims moot or petty. According to the films' logic, blacks are free in the present and should pursue the many opportunities available to them in the early 1990s. There is no ironic reflection on the fact that it takes a grim reproduction of slavery to make young blacks aware of the advantages afforded them in the Reagan-Bush years.

The eight years of Ronald Reagan's presidency (1981–1989) were difficult for many American blacks. A report on the economic status of blacks in 1987 claimed that "since the advent of the Reagan administration, black family income has declined, poverty rates have increased, and the labor market difficulties of blacks have intensified. Moreover, racial inequality in income, employment, and wages has also increased." In this report David Swinton poses the following questions to understand the impeded economic growth of blacks under six years of Reagan's presidency: "Is the lack of economic progress for blacks a result of black failures in motivation, behavior, morals, or preparedness; or does the lack of progress result from failures in the economy or Reagan administration policies? The evidence suggests the blame should be placed squarely on Reagan administration policies" (Swinton, "Economic Status" 49). Reagan's proclamation of "a new day" in America heralded an era of increased spending on national defense and decreased spending on national social services. In 1988, National Urban League president and chief executive officer John E. Jacob remarked that "the past eight years has seen the rich get richer and the poor get poorer. In effect, there has been a huge transfer of resources from the poor to the affluent. Inequality has always been a serious national problem, but in the past eight years we have become a far more unequal society" ("Black America, 1988" 2). The end of "big government" left many social programs insufficiently funded or totally eviscerated. Essentially, under Reagan, the previous decades' War on Poverty was transformed into a war on the poor.

An ideological meanness accompanied the government's new tightfistedness. Using a welfare-causes-poverty argument, the conservative government blamed the poor for being poor. As an additional sign of the government's disregard for blacks, Reagan's administration refused to meet with the Congressional Black Caucus, and black requests for implementation of hard-won civil rights were ignored or dismissed. It is this context of the Reagan years—a "regressive period in our national life: a time when some Americans got richer, but our society as a whole got poorer, and blacks were driven further from the goal of equality"—that provides the ideological grounding for *Brother Future* and *The Quest for Freedom*. The idea of getting tough—on crime, drugs, drinking, promiscuity—prevailed, and the major target for these efforts were black youth, especially males.

The disciplinary fantasy of easily reforming troubled black teens is most clearly and urgently presented in the shorter of the two films, *The Quest for Freedom*. Here, the protagonist is immediately depicted as in need of an attitude adjustment. The forty-minute film opens with a shot of a library, followed by a montage of clips from other videos. The narrator describes the library as "a place of books, a place of imagination. Walk through this door into adventure." The narrator introduces the protagonist as a "young man from our own time" who is "in search of something he doesn't even know he's lost." The video packaging states that Ben has "lost the courage to dream." His present-day context is meant to suggest an urban apartment dwelling, possibly a housing project: concrete buildings and black iron fencing. His bedroom, with posters of sports figures, trophies, and video games, aims to represent a typical teenager. We first learn the protagonist's name when his mother shouts for him to wake up and get ready for school. Benjamin, still in bed, is groggy, reluctant, and then angry. When she pulls the blankets from his bed, he jumps up and yells, "Woman, what are you doing? I'll do as I please." She retorts, "Well, you can just get out then. This is my house, and you'll do as you're told. I'll have no son of mine growing up dumb on street corners." Ben agrees: "Fine. I don't need this sorry place, and I definitely don't need you." Grumbling to himself, he grabs a bag and walks into his closet to pack his things: "Can't tell me what to do. Telling me to go to school? What's school going to do for me?" Once in the closet, the door closes behind him, and he finds himself trapped. Turning to what was once the closet's back wall, he sees the librarian and his collection of books. Wandering in confusion toward the seated librarian, Ben demands to know, "What happened to my room?" When the librarian does not give him a satisfactory reply, Ben grabs him by the collar and threatens violence if his bedroom is not restored. The librarian offers him a biography of Harriet Tubman. Pushing the proffered book aside and grabbing the librarian by the lapels, he threatens, "You ain't gon' get any older unless you tell me where my room is." The librarian replies, "Oh, when you put it that way, you might try going back the way you came," and indicates the closet door adorned with Michael Jordan's picture (Jordan is midflight, basketball in hand, poised to slam-dunk). The librarian makes a last-ditch effort to interest Ben in Tubman's story by saying, "You sure you don't want to read about Harriet? I think you'd like her. She's a lot like you: strong, independent." Ben, framed now by the words *Michael* and *Jordan,* rejects the offer with the reply, "Step off me, you fossil." Opening the closet door, he walks onto a wooden porch and into the hands of several slave overseers, one of whom, after a spirited, if brief, struggle, renders him unconscious. Here, Ben's head trauma is also his inauguration into the larger traumatic location of the slave past.

This method of locating Ben in the past is significant in its critique of black masculinity, the place of black men in public space, and their location in the domestic sphere. The image of Michael Jordan—a global phenomenon whose basketball talents made him a transnational icon of black athleticism and masculinity for considerable fame and profit—is offered as a role model that Ben has claimed for himself. At this point in the film, Jordan is Ben's hero (as per the instructions of Gatorade's catchy "Be Like Mike" ad campaign of the early 1990s). This attraction could also be a sign of the importance of a black man claiming public space, asserting a fundamental right to be "free" and advancing that right into global recognition. There is little need to rehearse why Michael Jordan was such a powerful symbol in the early 1990s, but it is interesting to consider why the film offers him as an example of a modern-day hero who has failed to put Ben on a good moral path. Ben's attraction to Jordan's image reflects in part an obsession with wealth and the "easy" road to success that characterizes, according to its chroniclers, the hip-hop generation. Ben's domestic situation—living in a "gritty" urban environment with a mother who rushes him off to school because she has to "go to work" and his desire to remain at home, snuggled in bed—is intended to be seen as more than the usual teen apathy. Ben's reluctance to go to school is cast as antisocial behavior resulting from his preference to hang out with his friends in the street. Contrary to his mother's exhortation that "no son of [hers will be] growing up dumb on street corners," Ben is depicted as alternately un-motivated and angry. Although *The Quest for Freedom* does not provide a clear source for Ben's feelings, his rage reflects what Cornel West describes as black nihilism, a sense of "psychological depression, personal worthless-ness, and social despair so widespread in black America" (*Race Matters* 13). Ben's anger, represented by the way he figuratively strikes out at his mother while actually leaning his body toward her, produces a charged atmosphere that suggests a pronounced nihilism. West's comments are useful ways to approach Ben's character: "The frightening result is a numbing detachment from others and a self-destructive disposition toward the world. Life without meaning, hope, and love breeds a coldhearted, mean-spirited outlook that destroys both the individual and others" (14–15).

Ben's domestic scene and his retreat to his closet are significant insofar as "his room" is both a haven (a private space as shown by his video games, comic books, and posters) and a site of conflict. That Ben's time travel begins "at home" (rather than in school, as it does in other "In Search of the Heroes" videos or in the street as it does for T. J. in *Brother Future*) is a component of the film's critique of black male teen behavior. The house, as Maurice O. Wallace writes, "is the very image of the structure of black masculinist consciousness as well as a principal object, materially and metaphorically speaking, of African American men's literary and cultural figuration" (*Con-

structing the Black Masculine 120). Ben's status as a juvenile means that his domestic space, his room, is always subject to another's authority, yet unlike school it is more private and reflects his preferences. Wallace's work on the black masculine desire for home illuminates Ben's situation. Wallace writes that black men's need for "the comfort and concealment of the home, is never merely an external affair. It is always, if in varying degrees, a liberating interiorization (closeting) as well" (123). Given the freedom implied in the home space—Wallace claims that home permits a retreat from, among other things, the hypervisiblity of black men in public spaces—Ben's abduction from this site and the film's use of his closet as a liminal space between the past and the present are suggestive. It is from this vantage point that the film launches its fantasy of containment and reform, one that aims to remedy the complex problem of Ben's nihilism, rage, and despair by placing him in a worse predicament.

Ben's first experience in the slave past initiates the film's disciplinary fantasy by critiquing and containing black male resistance. Comedian Eddie Murphy, in his 1987 stand-up comedy film *Eddie Murphy: Raw,* offered a similar critique of black violence in the face of enslavement. In one routine, Murphy responds to a contemporary black man's claim that he would never have been a slave. The man says that he would have vigorously, yet in cool-pose mode, resisted by telling his white captors to "suck my dick." Murphy mocks this man's bravado by explaining to the audience that "the first motherfucker off the boat probably said, 'Suck my dick.' Then twenty motherfuckers with whips said [sound of whips lashing]." As Murphy suggests, black male resistance would have been difficult, if not impossible, in the face of the overwhelming numbers. The hypermasculine quality of this resistance—telling the captors to "suck his dick"—is significant in the ways that slavery is imagined as depriving men of manhood. In this scenario, one man forcing another to perform fellatio is a sign of dominance, and the only alternative is the subordinate position, of being forced to give fellatio. I would like to consider the Murphy scenario of resistance as a model for Ben's initial encounter with the slave past. As mentioned above, Ben fights the men who seek to capture him. When Ben walks through the door that he thinks is his bedroom closet, he is punched in the face, spun around, and pushed into a wall. In this position, Ben's shirt is partially torn from his body, and his exposed back is lashed with a whip, which leaves a bloody mark. Ben then elbows his assailant in the face, knocking the man to the ground, at which point more men join in to subdue him. He is pushed down, is repeatedly kicked, and has a rifle barrel pointed at his head. The man seems ready to fire when a woman's voice intervenes, saying, "Don't do it, massa. He's just a dumb African boy. He don't know no better." A white man grabs Ben by the throat and growls, "You're gonna learn. You're gonna die," just before he hits Ben in the face with a rifle butt, rendering him unconscious. Thus begins Ben's lesson. During his incarceration in the slave past, he must learn to help others and value his twentieth-century freedom. The film proposes to teach him this lesson by providing firsthand experience with a brutal past.

In their study *The Presence of the Past: Popular Uses of History in American Life,* Roy Rosenzweig and David Thelen examine the ways in which Americans use the past to evaluate their present. Exploding the standard view that Americans care little for the past, Rosenzweig and Thelen, through surveys, interviews, and focus groups, discovered that "the pursuit of the past is a national preoccupation, it seems, but one with many variations" (22). A twenty-four-year-old African American woman from Detroit, expanding on the clichéd sentiment that "experience is the best teacher," told the scholars, "It's important because you're there. You can hear what people say and see it yourself and experience it. You know for yourself." Analyzing this claim, Rosenzweig and Thelen write that for many respondents, "the real advantage to experiencing something at first hand was not so much knowing its details—who said or did what—but sensing the multiple meanings and possibilities evident only to participants" (92). According to their findings, history classes were the least-effective method for discovering meaningful lessons from the past. Though one doesn't necessarily need such evidence to explain why the films depict T. J. as falling asleep in black history class or Ben's general distaste for school, the ineffectual interpretation of formal schooling is a useful element in the staging of the boys' return to the past. Like Octavia Butler's Dana, who agrees with her white fiancé's invitation to marry in "Vegas and forget [they] have relatives," and Haile Gerima's Mona, who flagrantly disregards the sacred space of the slave dungeons, T. J.'s transgression is his lack of interest in American history and, more important, the black past. He is depicted as choosing to fail in school, answering his black-history teacher's inquiry, "You have a brain—when will you use it?" with the quip, "I'm saving it for a special occasion."

Brother Future attempts to reach young audiences by emphasizing hip-hop as its formative context. The film opens with the sounds of syncopated beats and an image of a brick wall. Against this sound track, the words *Brother Future* are written on the wall in spray paint with the accompanying hissing sound. These are the first indications that we're in for a hip-hop film. As Katrina Hazzard-Donald suggests, reflecting the prevailing conception of hip-hop, "The genre includes rapping and rap music, graffiti writing, particular dance styles (including breakdancing), specific attire, and a specialized language and vocabulary. Hip hop appears at the crucial juncture of postindustrial stagnation, increased family dissolution, and a weakened struggle for black economic and political rights" ("Dance in Hip Hop Culture" 244–45). The film so completely follows this description of hip-hop culture that the parallels cannot be coincidental. T. J. is preoccupied with his clothing and accessories (he retains his Nikes, dark sunglasses, and hat throughout the film), and his language and banter are conspicuously hip. The Detroit of this film looks stagnated, and the "family dissolution" element is revealed when T. J. is shown to live with his grandmother, rather than two parents. The film oscillates between an unsympathetic vision of the hip-hop generation and a fleeting hope in its redemption. By the film's end, however, it is clear that the only hope for the young black delinquent's reform is through bodily epistemology (being forced to "go there to know there"), a cosmic immersion in the slave past.

Characterized by beauty supply shops, bodegas, and other nondescript storefronts, the film's urban landscape is marked by milling, multiracial bodies, which coupled with the percussive syncopated beats of hip-hop suggest "the street" as its dominant and most meaningful setting. To further establish the street as a primary location, the film first shows T. J. when he partially emerges from a Dumpster in which he hides to watch two men loading a van with boxes visibly labeled as containing electronic goods. T. J.'s Dumpster hiding place is a sign, I believe, of the generation gap at work in the film's production. The film's producers may stash T. J. in a Dumpster as a sign of urban decay or even as a symbol of his "trashed" life, but it does not fit with T. J.'s cool, image-preoccupied, hip-hop attitude. His character might hide *behind* a smelly Dumpster, but not in it. When the van that T. J. monitors is unattended, he springs from the Dumpster, grabs a videocassette recorder, a Nintendo video game system, and a portable compact disc player from the back of the van and sprints away. Later, we see T. J. and his friend Crunch selling the goodies to other black kids from the trunk of a car. Crunch is not fully invested in T. J.'s scheming, even though he is impressed with the loot.

> Crunch: Yo, T. J., man. This is fresh. Where'd you get all this stuff?
> T. J.: Don't worry about it.
> Crunch: You stole it.
> T. J.: Hey, brother. You can't steal something that's already been stolen.
> Crunch: Word.
> T. J.: That's right. I'm an entrepreneur.

T. J. is doing a swift business of selling the now twice-stolen electronics from his car trunk. It is here that rap music is specifically invoked as part of

T. J.'s sales pitch. As a way to sell more goods, T. J. performs for his buying public. With Crunch providing the background sound of the "human beat box," T. J. raps:

> Your money is paper and paper is wood
> but in your pocket it's doing no good.
> But in my hands it will feel so right, and these jamming sounds
>   will rock all night.
> See they call me the peddler for reasons different and same.
> I'll always be the winner of this here game.
> You ain't got a lot of time, so waste it not.
> You'll get the get, and I'll get the got.
> Word.

This impromptu performance is significant on several levels. First, this sales pitch articulates the ways that rappers invert "status hierarchies, tell alternative stories of contact with the police and the education process, and draw portraits of contact with dominant groups in which the hidden transcript inverts/subverts the public, dominant transcript" (Rose, *Black Noise* 101). As a rapper, T. J. justifies his criminal acts as part of the natural law of supply and demand. He is not a thief but a "peddler" who appropriates already stolen goods for his personal gain. The performance also presents a popular vision of rap music in the late 1980s. The "human beat box"—made by cupping both hands over one's mouth to create a hollow chamber that emits bass sounds—was an early example of the inventiveness and spontaneity of hip-hop. Similar to scratching on records to find new uses for old materials, the human beat box created a rich audio foundation for rappers without the technology of the synthesized beat box. In some ways, the body supplemented or even replaced the technology, as rappers talked over and through the percussive sounds. Though rap artists like Doug E. Fresh and the Get Fresh Crew and Biz Markie creatively refined the craft of the human beat box, by the time the human beat box hit the mainstream (most notably in the music of the Fat Boys), many adults (especially parents of the teens who could not get enough of the music) were incredulous about the popularity of what appeared to be young black people bopping their heads and spitting into their cupped hands. T. J.'s rap—in addition to his dress, ambivalence toward school, and a preference for hustling—marks him as a member of the hip-hop generation. Obviously, he is devoted to that generation's concept of cool.

In its critique of young black men of the early 1990s, the film explores the meaning of cool and diffuses it in an attempt to counter the ambivalence of young black men. As suggested by the inclusion of rap music in T. J.'s sales pitch, the film depicts hip-hop as a significant part of black teen identity. The film is troubled by T. J.'s preoccupation, which has been explained thus: "Even more important than fashion, style, and language, the new Black culture is encoded within the images and lyrics of rap and thus help define what it means to be young and Black at the dawn of the millennium. In the process, rap music has become the primary vehicle for transmitting culture and values to this generation, relegating Black families, community centers, churches, and schools to the back burner" (Kitwana, *The Hip Hop Generation* 202). Though this statement may overstate the case a bit (surely not all black youth are avoiding other meaningful activities by watching rap music videos all day), it perfectly describes T. J.'s interests and worldview. He is not interested in school or his grandmother's opinion ("You think I go home and tell my grandma everything I do? It's bad enough when she finds out I'm not in school. Then she starts preaching"). T. J. is depicted as someone who looks out only for himself:

> T. J.: You got to live your own life, brother.
> Crunch: Man, I got a life, and I want to keep it.
> T. J.: You call this a *life*? Man, come on. I'm gon' make myself some real dough. I'm gon' be living on the hype tip.
> Crunch: Sounds like five to ten in the pen.
> T. J.: Man, you got to get it while it's kickin', brother. Tomorrow ain't gon' last forever.

It is not conducive to the film's goals to consider the legitimacy of T. J.'s pointed (and apparently rhetorical question): "You call this a *life*?" Gesturing at the street scene around him, T. J. might well be referring to the urban decay and embattled conditions of black life where blacks remained "'separate but not equal,' still-dependent on the paternalism of the white power elite, still disenfranchised and powerless, still treated as second class citizens in the land of their birth, and still dehumanized and depersonalized, exploited and extorted, neglected and narcotized" (Gibbs, *Young* xxii). The film does not pause to consider the reasons T. J. seeks profit from the underground economy or why these transactions are so lucrative. Instead, the film emphasizes T. J.'s selfishness and his desire to "live his own life." This carpe diem attitude, coupled with his dismissal of the lessons from the past, does not earn him "five to ten in the pen," as Crunch fears, but rather a trip to the slave past. The disciplinary urge of the film is simple and clear: T. J.'s criminally minded solipsism is not only a character flaw but also a detriment to the black community. Though he frequently uses the word *brother*, he lacks a communal ethos and is uninterested in racial or brotherly uplift. The film plans to reform T. J. by making him "do for others" and in turn appreciate the twentieth-century opportunities that appear to him only after spending time in the slave past. His cool pose is the thrust of the film's rehabilitation efforts. Like most "After-School Special"–type films, this one seeks to impart a moral lesson, to solve a problem, or to address an issue. These films try to speak to its audience of school-age young people on their own level and with things they value or understand.[5] Difficulty arises, however, because of the generation gap between students and teachers, between the audience and the producers of the films.

The hip-hop generation has been defined as that group of black Americans born between 1965 and 1984. As such, "our generation is the first generation of African Americans to come of age outside the confines of legal segregation" (Kitwana, *The Hip Hop Generation* 13). Some claim that the central element of this group's identity is living in an integrated America, where the legal and social gains achieved through the civil rights movement are a matter of simple entitlement. Whereas their predecessors experienced "segregation and second-class citizenship firsthand," the hip-hop generation "was socialized on a steady diet of the American dream. We grew up with television sitcoms, film, and advertisements that portrayed [the American dream] as a reality. Lip service to equality, civil rights, freedom of movement, and integrated schools and neighborhoods created high expectations for our generations—even if we didn't experience it firsthand" (41). Hip-hop chroniclers like Bakari Kitwana and Todd Boyd illustrate a generational division between the hip-hop generation and the civil rights and Black Power generation. This division between new school and old school is a commonly repeated phenomenon, since many individuals define themselves in relation to and against those who preceded them. In hip-hop, the conflict was most popularly and comically borne in DJ Jazzy Jeff and the Fresh Prince's hit single "Parents Just Don't Understand," an anthem for misunderstood teens in the late 1980s. Less humorous are new-school claims that the old school is self-absorbed and unwilling to accept the prominent position of hip-hop. As Boyd writes, "America has now turned Martin Luther King's dream into a long weekend. In other words, civil rights has passed; get over it!" (*The New H.N.I.C.* 153). In *Brother Future* and *The Quest for Freedom*, this intergenerational conflict motivates both the plots and the black teenagers' return to the past.

T. J.'s preoccupation with his image and his business (fencing stolen goods) reflects what some hip-hop chroniclers have characterized as an important value for the hip-hop generation. As Bakari Kitwana writes, "Everyone wants to make it big. For many, the American Dream means not just living comfortably, but becoming an overnight millionaire while still young. . . . Although such attitudes existed in previous generations, with the hip-hop generation, it is a near obsession. And this desire to achieve not simply financial security but millionaire status is the driving force of our generation's work ethic" (*The Hip Hop Generation* 46). Kitwana and others cite the meteoric rise of black sports figures such as LeBron James or rappers such as Sean "Puffy"/"Puff Daddy" Combs or Nelly as hip-hop models for apparently easy black male financial success. Though these men *do* work for their money, as athletes and entertainers they are outside the traditional labor markets. For young men like T. J., who want to make it big quickly, the underground economy is the best chance at speedy success. It is important to note that T. J. is not a drug dealer, nor is he involved in a gang. By stealing stolen merchandise and selling it, T. J. participates in the underground economy, retains the "respect" of his peers, yet does not alienate the sympathies of adults or others who would be offended at T. J.'s role in the destruction of his own community. Stealing and reselling already stolen electronics (stolen from the back of a van, not from someone's home), when compared to furthering the cycle of violence or drug addiction among his peers, are pretty petty offenses. In this way, T. J. is still redeemable in a way that many other underground young black men are not.

T. J.'s attitude toward work is heavily filtered through his definition of cool. Given the type of legitimate work opportunities and the "subordination" required to keep such a job, T. J.'s dismissive attitude toward work follows the black masculine cool pose of both the 1970s and the late 1980s. Julius Lester, writing in the 1970s, claimed, "To a black man, work means putting yourself directly under a white man on a job and having to do what he says. Refusal to do so means being fired. Thus, work becomes synonymous with loss of respect" (quoted in hooks, *We Real Cool* 23). Nearly a decade later, Nathan McCall describes a similar view toward work: "I took on the attitude about work that a lot of the brothers I knew had: 'If getting a job means I gotta work for the white man, then I don't want a motherfuckin' job'" (25). These explanations of why one *won't* get a job is in part a cool-pose response to the limited types and number of jobs a young black man *can* get: "By the 1980s, young Blacks who lacked the education demanded by these new high-tech jobs, especially workers concentrated in urban centers, had few places to go within the mainstream economy aside from minimum-wage jobs being created by the service sector" (Kitwana, *The Hip Hop Generation* 29). As sociologist William Julius Wilson argues, "Where jobs are scarce . . . many people lose their feeling of connectedness to work in the formal economy; they no longer expect work to be a regular, and regulating, force in their lives." Young people reared in this context may "rely on illegitimate sources of income, thereby further weakening their attachment to the legitimate labor market" (quoted in ibid. 35). T. J. is happily one of these young men unattached to the labor market, financially thriving by selling stolen goods from the trunk of his car. His success reflects the results of a 1989 youth survey that claimed that "more than half of young Black men felt that they could do better financially in the underground economy than in the mainstream economy" (40). The film places the burden of this irresponsible view of work squarely on T. J., not considering the effects of globalization, NAFTA, or other government and business interventions that eliminated manufacturing and other jobs in cities like Detroit and Flint, Michigan. Although there may not be enough legitimate work for young black men in Detroit's inner city, the film depicts labor opportunities aplenty in the antebellum South.

After selling the last hot CD player, T. J. and Crunch are approached by a white police officer, who yells, "Hey, you! Freeze!" Crunch, protesting his innocence, assumes the position to be searched by an officer—hands up and braced against the wall, legs apart, dropping his American history book to the ground, where it lands faceup. T. J. makes a run for it, but gets hit by a car, and is rendered unconscious. This head trauma marks his introduction into a new world that is marred with trauma for blacks: the slave past. The last words we hear the officer say to Crunch—"Do you have any identification on you?"—will also apply to T. J.'s arrival in the nineteenth century. This encounter with the police is the gateway for T. J.'s return to the slave past; that the state is responsible (in a way) for this return is relevant, considering the hip-hop generation's attitude toward law enforcement. As Bakari Kitwana writes, "For hip-hop generationers ourselves often on the receiving end of such encounters [negative interaction with the police], police brutality serves as a constant reminder of the days of Black enslavement in America" (*The Hip Hop Generation* 39). This is a crucial point to help explain why, when fleeing the police, T. J. falls through the space-time continuum into the slave past, where he is immediately picked up by slave patrollers, the proto-policing force. Both his exit from the twentieth century and his entrance into the nineteenth century are marked by an encounter with the state and its mandated control of black criminality and black bodies.

T. J.'s first interaction with the past is with two white men on horseback. Still thinking he's running from the Detroit police (even though those streets have now been replaced by bright-green palmetto bushes, trees, vegetation, and sandy ground), T. J. maintains his cool pose after he is grabbed by the first patroller. T. J. seeks to set the tone for the encounter by interrogating his captors:

T. J.: You guys undercover? Look, I ain't got no stuff on me. You can frisk me.

Patroller no. 2: Shut up, nigger.

T. J.: Nigger? Look, don't make me bust a move on you. There's a law against police brutality.

Patroller no. 1: There's a law against runaways, boy.

T. J.: Runaways? I ain't a runaway. I got a home.

Patroller no. 2: How come you ain't in it?

T. J.: I don't know. The last thing I remember . . .

Patroller no. 1: We takin' you in.

T. J.: You got to read me my rights.

Both patrollers laugh.

Patroller no. 1: You ain't got no rights, boy.

T. J.: Man, I'm innocent until proven guilty. What is this?

Patroller no. 1 *(tying T. J. to the back of the horse)*: We goin' to market, boy.

Patroller no. 2: How far to Charleston?

Patroller no. 1: Four or five miles.

T. J.: Miles? You want me to walk? . . . Look, guys. This is cruel and unusual punishment, now. I'm a juvenile! I'll sue.

This conversation reflects a host of differences—in social status, race, and age—but it most clearly establishes the contrast between the past and the present. It is useful to consider T. J.'s misguided interpretation of the slave patrollers as police officers as well as the patrollers' perception of T. J. as a runaway. T. J. does not consider himself a runaway because he has a home. In the patrollers' minds, T. J. is a runaway because he is a black male without proper documentation. The film misses an opportunity to consider the similarities between T. J.'s flight from the Detroit police and his fall into the hands of a nineteenth-century slave patrol. (Is it so farfetched to imagine a twentieth-century police officer addressing T. J. as in the above dialogue?) Much could be made of the parallels between T. J.'s delinquency and his preference for the street over the home and the criminalized condition of a nineteenth-century black man escaping to freedom. Instead, the film presents the message that the street is unsafe, that criminal behavior will be punished. The film offers a *Scared Straight!* solution to reeducate T. J. about the privileges of this present-day life. He will undergo a training process that will figuratively unman him, eventually fostering an attitude of gratitude.

T. J.'s seasoning process begins with his incarceration. In the jail, he continues his cool pose and reinforces his own confidence by telling himself "this is a nightmare" and announcing to no one in particular that he is "about to bust a move on this place." When he sees another chained black man sitting next to him, he asks, "So what you in for? Yo, man. I'm talking to you. You speak English, man?" T. J.'s cool, a central component of his twentieth-century identity and an aspect that troubles the film, emerges here to protect him from the diminishing effects of being held captive with slaves awaiting their fate. His query to the other black man speaks of his bravado and a determination to not be affected by this change in context. Like Dana in *Kindred* who travels to the past with a duffel bag full of twentieth-century provisions, T. J. travels with his most prized twentieth-century possession: an unassailable sense of cool. As Bakari Kitwana declares, "The rebellious 'don't-give-a-fuck' self-portrait of many young Blacks in popular culture (primarily in rap music lyrics, videos, and film) has been consumed as definitive and authentic" (*The Hip Hop Generation* 42). T. J. is this type of consumer. His hairstyle (the then popular flattop fade), gold-rimmed sunglasses, Nike basketball shoes (which he calls "kicks"), and silk shirt all proclaim his preoccupation with a cool image. The auction block is the first location that marks his place in the slave past, beginning the erosion of his sense of cool. He is forced to disrobe and put on different clothing, thus removing most vestiges of his twentieth-century context, though he retains his gold-rimmed dark sunglasses and high-top Nikes. The sunglasses and sneakers, like his conspicuous hipness, will be constant markers of T. J.'s difference from his surroundings. These differences, however, will not be enough to spare him the profound social costs of having black skin in 1822 Charleston. Awaiting his turn to be sold, T. J. struggles to retain his twentieth-century cool pose, even though he is shaken at the sight of a black family being separated on the auction block. T. J.'s own sale emphasizes the brutality of the property relations of enslavement and additionally reads his body as interchangeable property (the auctioneer calls him a "stray") that can be sold and resold. For T. J., this process demonstrates both the subjection of enslavement (by objectifying black bodies) and the low value of his body in this market. The black man who was sold before T. J. was described as a strong man who has "fathered a healthy child. This man is prime stock. He'll bring in your cotton." T. J., on the other hand, is what Cooper is looking for, "the best quality for the dollar," a bargain. The auctioneer (presented here to T. J. as a grim reminder of what he used to be in the twentieth century, a peddler of stolen goods) tries to drum up interest in purchasing the "stray": "It looks like nobody worked this boy anyplace. His hands are soft. Must have kept him in the kitchen. He's young. He's alert. Could take a little discipline. This could turn out to be a good'un, folks. Now, who'll offer me a hundred dollars?" T. J. is, in the economy of slavery, not a man but a boy with less value than an adult. The auctioneer's emphasis on T. J.'s "soft" hands and his place in the kitchen feminizes T. J. by locating him in the domestic sphere. T. J., however, works hard to shrug off this designation and refuses to accept that he is a slave. When he meets Josiah, whose job it is to introduce T. J. to life in the field, T. J. is insistent about the impossibility of his time-travel experience. Convinced that he is having an extended nightmare, rather than the nightmare of history, T. J. tells Josiah:

> T. J.: Aw, man, I got to wake up.
> Josiah: You don't look sleep.
> T. J.: Hey, what if this isn't a dream? What if this is really happening to me? Just because some fool gives another fool 125 bucks doesn't make me a slave.
> Josiah: That there's Master Cooper. He owns me. Now he owns you.
> T. J.: Yo, nobody owns me.

T. J. not only protests the unreality of time travel but also rejects the economic rationale that makes such a transaction legal. One hundred and twenty-five dollars does not make T. J. property; Josiah, whom T. J. befriends and eventually sacrifices himself for, tries to school T. J. in the rudimentary facts of his new existence. T. J.'s declaration that "nobody owns me" remains with him throughout his journey into the past and marks his difference from (and acts as the audience's entrance point into) the era of slavery.

T. J.'s move from twentieth-century Detroit to nineteenth-century Charleston is made more difficult by his devotion to the principles of cool and the ethos of hip-hop. These are the elements of his character that the film seeks to reform through immersion in the slave past. Though sociologists studying the "cool pose" correctly assert that all black men do not fit their profile, T. J.'s character is fully informed by such a pose. As Richard Majors and Janet Mancini Billson claim, "[The] cool pose is a ritualized form of masculinity that entails behaviors, scripts, physical posturing, impression management, and carefully crafted performances that deliver a single, critical message: pride, strength, and control" (*Cool Pose* 4). T. J. is nothing if not cool. His age, approximately sixteen, and social position, a high school junior, demand it, for as James Stanlaw and Alan Peshkin assert, "Being cool is not a way of life for teenagers, it is life" (quoted in ibid. 1). T. J.'s mission at the start of the film is to convince his less cool friend and sidekick, Crunch, to become his partner in crime. Crunch is hesitant because he does not want to spend any time in juvenile hall and fears that his "mother would kill [him]" if she discovers what he is up to. Crunch tries to reinforce the traditional values of formal education by encouraging T. J. to avoid things that will force them to "repeat their junior year." But T. J., who is making good money in the underground economy, seeks to expand his financial opportunities and has no further need for high school since he earns "straight As in these streets." The street is the site for legitimacy and currency in T. J.'s hip-hop universe.

But privileging this location puts him in physical danger (which is cool) and makes him a likely candidate for reeducation through cosmic abduction (which is less cool). To become a better "brother" and less of a "bother" in contemporary America, T. J. must learn to disavow his cool pose. To this end, T. J. undergoes a series of humiliations designed to teach him the value of school, hard work, economy, and selflessness, all of which he has neglected or dismissed in the twentieth century. Thus, *Brother Future* deploys slavery as a disciplinary tool within the film and uses it as a cautionary tale for its young viewers.

To emphasize the film's goal as a teaching tool, I turn briefly to online reviews. I am not trying to pose these comments as expert testimony or brilliant critical analysis. Rather, I claim that these reviews reveal important information about the ways in which the film is received in classrooms, living rooms, and other viewing sites. The cultural functions and effects of the film are clarified in the user commentary, and I am appropriating these insights to advance the claim that the film has reformatory potential. One fan enthused: "This movie touches that heart of many teenagers that fail to ascertain the importance of an education. I highly suggest that this movie become a part of every home's video collection, and every elementary school's and high school's library." Another person writes, "As a family, we loved this movie. It helped my daughters appreciate more the blessings of being free, getting an education and the joy of reading." Another viewer offers this recommendation: "This movie should be a requirement for all teenagers to see before entering middle school" (Amazon.com, "Customer Review" n.p.).

These fan comments—though not representative of all viewers—suggest a desire to inspire apathetic teens to participate more actively in mainstream society. The idea of making *Brother Future* required viewing for middle school admittance speaks to a cultural anxiety about the target audience. These recommenders participate in and endorse the film's project, one that implies that troubled teens might alter their self-involved course, unlearn habits of selfishness, and relearn compassion, tolerance, and self-sacrifice. These endorsements suggest that the film might have a transformative effect on its teen viewers while betraying a cultural and generational anxiety about the state of young black America. Fears of black male youth, increasing steadily since the late 1980s, had reached such a high point that in 1994 the *New York Times Magazine* devoted an entire issue to the question, titled "The Black Man Is in Terrible Trouble. Whose Problem Is That?" The focus of this cultural anxiety was in large part rooted in young "inner-city" black men whose behavior was deemed responsible for increased crime rates (as seen in television and other media reports of gang violence, "wilding," and black kids killing each other for their expensive Nikes). This context helps to explain the disciplinary impulse in *Brother Future*: troubled young black males need help and behavioral modification. The best remedy for a troubled present, *Brother Future* suggests, is exposure to an even more troubled past.

Physical abuse is an important element of T. J.'s reformed character. Beatings, particularly the way they are posed, unman and infantilize T. J., targeting his mutually constitutive personality traits of cool and hip-hop. *Brother Future* features two scenes of whipping violence, both man-on-man: Zeke, the black overseer, whips T. J. in private, and later Josiah is publicly beaten by Master Cooper. The second beating scene is an unintended consequence of the first. After he is whipped by Zeke, T. J. plots revenge against him. He places a book in Zeke's quarters, knowing Cooper will discover it and punish Zeke for taking it. Unfortunately, a sheet of paper on which Josiah had been practicing writing his name was hidden in the book. Cooper publicly beats Josiah to make an example of him. I focus my attention on the encounter between T. J. and Zeke because this event is a crucial element in his experience in the slave past. Also, it most clearly makes the film's point about the twentieth-century freedoms that T. J. takes for granted by subjecting him to a sexually coded physical attack that aims to deprive him of his cool, hip-hop attitude. The private beating scene in the barn recalls Maurice O. Wallace's argument about the homosexual abuse that vulnerable slave men experienced under the lash.

Much important work has been done on the complex issue of sexualized violence in slavery, especially the telling scene of Frederick Douglass's witnessing his aunt Hester's abuse as an inauguration into slave life. I would like to briefly revisit some of those arguments to help frame my critique of T. J. and Zeke's scene. Particularly, I engage Wallace's reading of Douglass's resistance to Covey as a way of protecting Douglass's heterosexual masculine self to better understand the function of T. J.'s whipping at the hands of the black overseer. Building on the insights of Deborah McDowell and others who have persuasively argued that Douglass's closeted viewing of his aunt's whipping is an act of voyeurism that marks his difference from and possible superiority to her, Wallace concentrates on the similarity between Hester and young Fred when he claims that "both male and female bodies under slavery were vulnerable to the sexual impositions of the master" (*Constructing the Black Masculine* 90). Thus, Douglass's vigorous resistance to Covey's efforts to subdue him represents "a counterattack of psychosexual agency against the bodily trespasses of a lecherous overseer" (91). This physical struggle reveals how, in his own words, Douglass "was made a man" and, in Wallace's words, represents the acquisition of "manhood by a self-conflictive renunciation of the libidinal feminine" (94).

Brother Future repeats this scene but in reverse, almost as a photographic negative, by showing T. J.'s whipping as an act of unmanning him: a black teen beaten by Zeke, an older black male overseer. Zeke's brutality aims to discipline T. J. for running away and forces his submission to the slave hierarchy. In the process, the scene also critiques the staunchly heterosexual masculine identity of the hip-hop generation. The structure and postures of this scene offer a compelling site for examining the gender politics of hip-hop and the ways in which the film seeks to reform its protagonist.

Hip-hop has assumed an aggressively masculinist heterosexual posture as its definitive stance. To reform their hip-hop teen protagonists, both films challenge and seek to subdue the boys' heteromasculine identifications. An instance of hip-hop's aggressive heterosexuality can be seen in Todd Boyd's book *The New H.N.I.C. (Head Nigga in Charge): The Death of Civil Rights and the Reign of Hip-Hop,* which offers a highly charged vision of hip-hop's dominance over the previous generation. In his battle of the generations, "civil rights royalty" Rosa Parks—in filing a lawsuit against the hip-hop group OutKast's unauthorized use of her name as a song title with the line "everybody move to the back of the bus"—represents the "contempt that many older Black people feel toward their youthful descendants. In return, the hip hop generation says a collective 'fuck you,' asserting its independence and freedom of self determination" (3, 11). Boyd's study festively dances on the grave of the civil rights movement: "It is obvious that hip hop has not only overtaken civil rights as the dominant sentiment in modern Black life, it has consumed it" (10). His glee is especially evident in his favorable comparison of the new school with the old: "Hip-Hop is concerned, on the other hand, with being 'real,' honoring the truth of one's own convictions, while refusing to *bend over* to accommodate the *dictates* of the masses. Unlike the previous generation of people who often compromised or made do, in search of something bigger, hip-hop sees compromise as false, fake, and bogus" (151–52; emphasis added). Perhaps the italics are not necessary to get a visual of what Boyd uncritically describes as the accommodationist stance of the civil rights movement, but it is important to concentrate on his word choice. I emphasize these terms because there is a crucial difference, in predominant hip-hop parlance at least, between the words *bend* and *bend over,* especially given its proximity to the word *dictates* (which I read here with phonetic and thematic stress on the *dick*). Not to overemphasize this point, but I suggest that in Boyd's hyperheterosexual (and perhaps homophobic) imaginings, he casts the civil rights generation as one constantly submitting to the "sodomitic threat" that Douglass so vigorously resisted (88). Rather than embracing it as an understanding of the internal, "libidinal feminine," the hypermasculinity inherent in Boyd's definition of hip-hop—which reflects the prevailing view—must subdue the feminine (external and internal) through violence. From the ubiquitous pimp image to the seemingly endless debate over the offensiveness of the terms *bitch* and *ho* in the lingua franca of hip-hop (Dr. Dre's 1996 song "Bitches Ain't Shit" covers all bases with the line "Bitches ain't shit but hos and tricks"), there are many places to turn to demonstrate the insistence of male dominance in hip-hop. I choose the following quote from the sexually explicit, nationally popular South Florida group 2 Live Crew to explicate what I consider to be a highly influential aspect of hip-hop's masculine drive. Their 1990 album, *Banned in the USA* (a partial reference to the legal battle over their 1989 album, *As Nasty as They Wanna Be,* which Florida's state court deemed "legally obscene," blocking its sale, a ruling the Supreme Court would later overturn), featured the 3:02 song "Face Down, Ass Up" with the refrain, "Face down, ass up / That's the way we like to fuck," repeated in the song's chorus.

It is my claim here that this "face down, ass up" position (also known as "doggy style") is significant on several registers. Paul Gilroy has articulated a conception of "doggy-style *style* [a]s part of a public conversation about sex and intimacy, power, powerlessness, and bodily pleasure that can be reconstructed even from the fragments of antiphonal communication that have been captured in commodity form and circulated multi-nationally on that basis" ("'After the Love'" 74; emphasis in the original). Gilroy reads the preponderance of doggy style in hip-hop as a sign of "the positive value of intersubjectivity in black political cultures which are now subject-centered to the point of solipsism." I claim, however, that Gilroy is overly optimistic about the potential for doggy style to generate a new form of intimacy and political action. I am not fully convinced that doggy style evades "a naïve or pastoral mutuality" in favor of "dual solitude" that "proposes another mode of intimacy that might help to recreate a link between moral stances and vernacular metaphors of erotic, worldly love" (ibid.). In my estimation, doggy style (face down, ass up) reinforces (even as it makes more clear) the relations of power inherent in sexual cont(r)acts, wherein one partner's desire is enhanced by the submissive posture of the other. (This is not to say that pleasure is unavailable to the subordinate[d] partner. Rather, my stress here is that the dominant position is the privileged one, the one of mastery, the one who "fucks." In popular imaginings of doggy style, male rappers do not envision themselves "face down"; that is reserved for the "bitch.") 2 Live Crew's imagery is also usefully mutable in that "ass up" could refer to both rear-entry vaginal and anal sex heterosexually or the act of anal penetration between men. Most useful for the terms of my argument, this sexual position has become the libidinal and ideological grounding of mainstream hip-hop, a genre firmly rooted in patriarchy, masculine dominance, and feminine or feminized subordination. Tunes like "Pimpin Ain't Easy" and "No Vaseline," the once common shout-out "Gs up, hos down," the reverence for the "playa" or "pimp," and the immense popularity of Snoop Dogg's album *Doggystyle* are small but important indicators that this position offers images of young black men exercising mastery in a variety of contexts: the sexual arena, ho-mosocial venue of prison life, general intergender conflict, and interracial stress within American culture.

I divert attention to this matter to provide a richer understanding of T. J. and Zeke's whipping scene in *Brother Future*. T. J., using a forged pass, flees the plantation, only to be intercepted by patrollers. T. J.'s escape attempt might have proceeded if Zeke hadn't intervened and knocked him to the ground with one backhand blow to the head. (Significantly, this type of punch is known in hip-hop lingo as the "bitch" or "pimp" slap. This blow is one of the more colorful methods the pimp uses to keep his stable of women in line. Borrowing from blaxploitation films, hip-hop has resurrected the pimp as the apex of cool (Nelly's "Pimp Juice" or 50 Cent's "Magic Stick" are good, if comic, examples). In this context, the pimp slap is revered, I think, because it blends violence and cool. Using the back of his hand (a dismissive gesture like brushing away an insect), the pimp—given his advantage in strength—can usually knock a woman down or at least get her attention. This physical act is gendered on the axis of male-female, dominant-subordinate, pimp-pimped. When Zeke pimp-slaps T. J. to the ground (in front of the white patrollers), the boundaries of power are firmly established: T. J. is subordinated, "bitched out." The next scene is shot inside a darkened barn, made to seem even darker when contrasted with the natural daylight shining through the open door. The contrast between inside and out, light and dark, is rendered cinematically meaningful by shooting T. J.'s profile in silhouette. T. J.'s wrists are tied to a post, and he is talking fast to dissuade Zeke, who is standing behind him, from whipping him:

> T. J.: Zeke, how can you do this to me?
> Zeke: I'm gon' teach you a lesson, boy. You ain't gon' never run away from this plantation again.
> T. J.: But, Zeke, it's not your plantation, man. You a slave just like me.
> Zeke: Oh, yeah?

T. J.'s pleading with Zeke is domestically significant in at least two ways: a child begging not to be beaten by a parent or another adult and a woman begging her husband or boyfriend not to hit her again. In both cases, the powerless appeals to the mercy of the powerful. In his attempt to negotiate with Zeke, T. J. (mistakenly) seeks to draw on their similarities, their shared racial and servitude status. In this way, T. J. shares the perception of white-black dominance of an African American woman, in Rosenzweig and Thelen's study, who would prefer the slave past to the crime-ridden present because back then "it was the white man doing it to you."[6] T. J. cannot understand Zeke's investment in the plantation's hierarchy, the privilege he gains from being, as another slave character, Isaac, calls him, "the white folk's nigger." One way for Zeke to mark his superiority to and difference from T. J. is to beat him. Though this whipping can be seen as an example of black-on-black crime, the gender factor cannot be overlooked. As a whipping scene, this moment can be illuminated by considering the ways in which it enacts a form of sexual violence and pornography similar to that of the nineteenth-century slave narratives but also frequently invoked in hip-hop in overt and covert means. I suggest that homosexuality is transmuted in this scene. Just as heterosexual control underpins Aunt Hester's abuse and also as the "sodomitic threat" that Covey wields over Douglass, this intraracial beating bears sexual markings. But unlike Douglass in his battle with Covey, T. J. is unable to "rise." Zeke subdues T. J., thus challenging the teen's manhood and his cool.

We hear but do not see the event of T. J.'s whipping. Above T. J.'s cries, we hear Zeke taunting T. J. with the words "Just like you, huh?" The sound of the tortured interaction gets the attention of the two main female characters on the plantation. Mortilla, the cook, comes out of the big house and listens, while Caroline, hanging up laundry, looks at the open barn door. It is significant to note that both teens are beaten "off-screen." In Ben's case, the camera fades to black, and the scene cuts to Ben lying facedown on a mat while the Harriet Tubman character attends his wounds, telling him to "hold still—they done beat you real bad." The images of the wounds are greatly emphasized in both films. The films cinematically refer to the widely circulated nineteenth-century photograph of Gordon, the former slave whose back was covered in whip scars, mentioned in Chapter 2. The film uses this image to conjure the physical brutality of slavery; these teens are now marked by the past. In addition to physical scars, the emotional impact of the whippings reinforces their subjection, which is coded as feminine. In this way, the critique of hip-hop's hypermasculine ethos is made by the submissive homosexual coding of the beating and the vulnerability of being attacked from the back. Additionally, both boys have their wounds remedied by women, further emphasizing their dependence, which is part of the lesson they must learn. As Mortilla tells T. J., "You got to do for others and let others do for you."

Each protagonist, while stranded in the nineteenth century, must deduce how to free himself from his incarceration in the past. The films' logic would have it that the boys have earned their time-travel abduction through their deviant behavior. Once their antisocial traits are put to the service of others, the boys prove their worthiness to rejoin twentieth-century society. T. J., who in Detroit is known as "the peddler," is shown to sell skillfully the produce from Cooper's plantation in an open market. Later, he tells Josiah and Caroline that he sold not only Cooper's wares but also the goods of other merchants for a percentage of their profits. He then gives Josiah and Caroline a bag of money to help them escape. He also acts as a diversion when the fleeing couple is pursued by Zeke and Cooper. Ben, who during his time in the past demands to know "what this has to do with me," uses his fighting skills to defend Harriet from an overseer intent on thwarting her first escape. He then accompanies Harriet on the journey from Maryland to Pennsylvania, witnessing her celebration once she reaches the free state. For both teens, these selfless gestures, which are appropriations of the flaw that initially got them into trouble, trigger their return to their everyday lives. Once home, the boys show immediate signs of reform: T. J. tells Crunch that he is no longer interested in hustling, whereas Ben determinedly clutches his schoolbooks. Both teens have thoroughly learned their lesson.

What are the stakes involved in using the past to instruct or rehabilitate black male teens in the present? Is it appropriate to use the slave past as a form of motivation? To address these questions, consider the following anecdote from a recent visit to Thomas Jefferson's home, Monticello, during the museum's Plantation Community Weekend.

Three times a year at Monticello, "historic interpreters revive the sights and sounds of Mulberry Row's past as they demonstrate some of the trades and skills practiced when Monticello was a thriving plantation owned by Thomas Jefferson." Dylan Pritchett, an African American storyteller and former Colonial Williamsburg historical interpreter, works at the site, portraying Lewis, an enslaved worker documented in Jefferson's papers. I met a black family during one of these weekends. Dylan Pritchett's presentation was concluding with a musical activity. He distributed instruments (drum, bells, shakers) for the audience to play. He then asked for "a white man who could dance" to come forward, explaining that slaves could not gather for their weekly recreational period without a white man's presence. As children took up the instruments and listened to Lewis's instructions on the correct rhythm, a young black man in the audience tried to get another younger male to participate, saying slyly, "You could rap." Lewis's character continued to solicit volunteers, but the younger man remained where he was. Slumped forward on a bench near the periphery of the group, he wore the uniform of the hip-hop teenager: oversized basketball shirt, shorts that reached below the knees, and unlaced high-top Nikes. The other young man, his older brother, wore a sweatshirt emblazoned with the name of a midwestern university. His mother wore a similar shirt. When I commented on the mother and older son's matching sweatshirts, the mother replied that the shirt—which bears the logo of the older son's current university—was intended as a gift for her younger son, but "he won't wear it."

The mother explained that the three of them had driven from Illinois to Virginia on a kind of heritage tour. They had visited Pamplin to see slave quarters, Appomattox to see where the Civil War had concluded, and Virginia Beach ("just for fun"), and were planning a visit to Mount Vernon after Monticello. Pointing to her younger son seated on the bench, the mother said, "This trip is for him." She wanted him to "appreciate the privileges" that he has today, to encourage him to make better choices. Her oldest son, age twenty-three, is graduating from college and is moving on to law school. The youngest, age fifteen, has matriculated from a Catholic middle school to an urban public high school. His mother claims that in his new school, her youngest son has gravitated toward a bad element. She blames herself for his adoration of the hip-hop, ghetto-thug lifestyle: "I was in nursing school when he was coming up." Hoping to improve his education, "I spent a lot of money to put him in Catholic schools." Now, she fears that he is unlearning those values. As we talked and as they spoke with Pritchett, the youngest son remained removed from the conversation. Sitting on a bench or standing apart, he was frequently pointed out by his mother and brother as they talked about failing schools, crime, and deviant youth behavior.

Noticing the apparent split between the brothers or how the mother treated her older son differently than her younger, Pritchett told the pair a proverb he learned from his grandmother: "You can catch more flies with sugar than you can with shit." The adage implies that perhaps the mother was being too hard on her youngest son, who would come around in due course with good treatment. But I would like to consider the possibility this comment raises for the efficacy of living history as a method of correction. Living history, like all performance and history, is open to interpretation and cannot be forcibly internalized. Unlike the carefully scripted conversions in *Brother Future* and *The Quest for Freedom*, one cannot control how lessons from real-life visits to sites of the past are received.

A black family making a trek from Illinois to (and through) Virginia slave plantations for the benefit of an ambivalent black male teen suggests the ways in which domestic tourism of slavery might work as a way to confront traumatic history and use that encounter as a motivator in the present. Thus far, I have discussed bodily epistemology as a representational strategy that privileges realism and embodies meetings between the slave past and free present. For some tourists, however, the governing ethos of bodily epistemology—go there to know there—has a more literal relevance, as is indicated by a particular form of travel: heritage tourism devoted to slavery. An increasingly popular mode of travel among African Americans, slavery-heritage tourism includes travel to African slave castles and the dungeons where captive Africans were held before embarking on the Middle Passage. This geographic and physical movement not only represents a crossing of international boundaries but, for some blacks who consider themselves pilgrims rather than tourists, it is also a symbolic form of time travel. For those blacks who are unwilling or unable to travel internationally in search of remnants and records of the slave past, domestic tourism can meet a similar need on American soil. Sites such as Monticello, Mount Vernon, and Colonial Williamsburg, to name only a few museums in Virginia, offer representations and programs about slavery. In the next chapter, I consider slavery tourism and read several venues for the cultural and memorial impact those places have for African Americans making sense of the legacy of slavery.

4. Slave Tourism and Rememory

> If the past is a foreign country, nostalgia has made it "the foreign country with the healthiest tourist trade of all."
> —David Lowenthal, *The Past Is a Foreign Country*

> Each generation [of blacks] inherits an anxiety about slavery, but the more problematic the present, the higher the anxiety and the more urgent their need to attend to the past.
> —Fred D'Aguiar, "The Last Essay about Slavery"

Since the mid-1990s, tourism theorists have identified a new trend in recreational travel. Instead of engaging the "innocent" amusements of a Disney theme park or observing the natural splendor of a mountain range or reenacting frontier life by taking a cattle-drive trip, many travelers are opting for what some scholars have identified as the "dark" side. Visitors to Dallas can retrace John F. Kennedy's last journey, in a car identical to the one in which he was assassinated, complete with "a recorded soundtrack of clapping and cheering until, outside the school book depository, shots ring out and the car speeds to the hospital" (Barton, "Travel" 2). In Paris, tourists can take the "Princess Diana trip," which follows her final route "through the streets of the city in a black S class Mercedez [*sic*] Benz, identical to that in which she died" (Simpson, "Tourism Is Taking" 4). According to tourism theorists, these visits to "black spots" (Rojek, *Ways of Escape*) are a form of "dark tourism" (Lennon and Foley, *Dark Tourism*) that is steadily growing. The popularity of sites of mass destruction and atrocity (such as increased visits to concentration camps), battlefields (the Vietcong tunnel system has recently been widened to accommodate tourists), and markers of celebrity death, murder, or suicide (James Dean's grave, Anna Nicole Smith's residence, the club and sidewalk where River Phoenix died of a drug overdose) represents a fascination with death and destruction. The transformation of these "black spots" into "dark" tourist attractions is, for Chris Rojek, "a powerful example of the relabelling of signs to convey a more 'leisurely' significance and the redeployment of land use for the purposes of recreation" (*Ways of Escape* 170).

In this chapter, I consider slave tourism, an explicitly (for many blacks) nonleisurely form of travel and spectatorship that might well fit under the rubric of "dark tourism" to a "black spot." That the words *black* and *dark* are used in these theories to invoke the sinister meanings of death and disaster with little attention to the racial (and racist) implications of such language suggests potency of the black-white dialectic in both figurative and literal terms. My critique of the "black spot" or "dark tourism" concept directly relates to the general inattention to slavery; as historian Nell Irvin Painter notes, for many, slavery possesses "neither a literal meaning nor consequence; it serves only as a potent, negative metaphor" ("Soul Murder and Slavery" 130). To promote the literal or embodied element of slavery, slave tourism references slavery as a real and meaningful anchor for African American identity. Revisiting Haile Gerima's 1993 film *Sankofa* to more closely consider its tourist impulse, I also read several museum representations that use urgently referential strategies to present slavery as a literal, embodied event. I contemplate the risks and rewards of a realist approach to reveal the ways in which those different modes of representing and referencing slavery appeal to different segments of the black audience. In their representation of the slave past as insoluble, these venues provide an alternative to the predominant mode of trauma theory that defines trauma as elusive and unknowable. And, in some cases, through the cathexis of the image, these locations and Gerima's film engender a therapeutic process for some black spectators.

The slave castles at Elmina and Cape Coast in Ghana, Gerima's film *Sankofa*, Baltimore's National Great Blacks in Wax Museum, and Colonial Williamsburg's 1994 slave auction reenactment provide spaces in which to consider the ways tourism can be used to reference the traumatic past. These sites are also opportunities to explore the implications of different modes of representing slavery, especially as it relates to addressing slavery on a therapeutic level. These locations attempt to express traumatic knowledge through a mode of representation that relies on what Toni Morrison describes in *Beloved* as "rememory." As Sethe explains to her daughter, "If you go there—you who never was there—if you go there and stand in the place where it was, it will happen again; it will be there for you, waiting for you" (36). Whereas Sethe's remarks are intended to warn Denver about the dangers of an intractable past—"So, Denver, you can't never go there. Never. Because even though it's all over—over and done with—it's going to be always be there waiting for you"—sites like the National Great Blacks in Wax Museum and Colonial Williamsburg, the slave dungeons at Elmina and Cape Coast castles, and *Sankofa* are seriously invested in the idea that the traumatic past is waiting to be reexperienced. The film *Sankofa* is a historical venture set in a Ghanaian slave castle: Mona, a young black fashion model, is remanded to a violent slave past, and the viewer is compelled to watch. At the wax museum, a visitor's walk into the model slave ship is accompanied by the sound of a slave trader announcing new arrivals, while the One Africa tour group places black visitors to Ghana's slave castles in the slave dungeons to reflect on the captive moment. In 1994, Colonial Williamsburg's African American Interpretive Programs (AAIP) department attracted national attention and sparked a bitter controversy when it announced plans to reenact a slave auction—a composite of actual auctions at that location in the eighteenth century—on the steps of one of its historic buildings. This event drew an unprecedented number of spectators who gathered to both oppose and witness this reembodiment of American slavery.

I divide my discussion into three parts. Because *Sankofa*'s representation of tourism corresponds to Ghana's booming industry, I begin this chapter with a discussion of slave-castle tourism and the ways in which Gerima's film can be understood under the register of tourism. In this way, I consider the motivations for slave-castle tourism and the balance between authenticity and simulacra in this context. In the second part, I turn from the actual slave castles to their re-creation at a grassroots wax museum that serves as a popular site for referencing slavery and examine the potential benefits and risks of such an approach. Baltimore's National Great Blacks in Wax Museum is a location that offers a simulacrum of Middle Passage captivity as a strategy to spark historical memory. In the final part, I move from the popular sphere to a more formal venue's embodied representation of African captivity; reading Colonial Williamsburg's 1994 controversial slave-auction reenactment, I consider this struggle within the black public sphere over who is permitted to reenact slavery.

Part 1: Follow the Tour Guide

Sankofa offers Mona's transformation from spoiled fashion model to humbled yet historically aware black woman as the necessary reeducation of a flagrantly deluded black woman so disconnected from her past as to flout the sacred space of a slave castle. In the early moments of the film, Mona ignores, then mocks, the castle's self-appointed guardian, who demands that Elmina's sacred ground be respected. But before we condemn Mona too harshly for her previous behavior on the beach with the white photographer, let us consider why she is there in the first place. Presumably on assignment for a fashion magazine, Mona's job is a boon to the region's tourist trade. The Ghanaian government wants people to visit these sites, and a photo spread featuring a famous fashion model would increase traffic to the slave castles and other regional attractions. In the film, her work promotes Ghana's tourist trade. Touring slave castles is an important part of Ghana's economic development, generating approximately $386 million in the year 2000. In 1993 more than seventeen thousand tourists visited Elmina castle, which during its five hundred–year history has played many roles and now attracts a range of tourists. Dutch visitors can peruse artifacts from the Dutch rule in 1637, British tourists may seek information about Britain's control of the castle in 1872, whereas members of the Ashanti people can see where their king was imprisoned in 1896. But the issue of slavery and its representation remains contested, especially for African Americans and Ghanaians. As anthropologist Edward H. Bruner observes, "Ghanaians want the castles restored with good lights and heating, so they will be attractive to tourists; African Americans want the castles to be as they see them—a cemetery for slaves who died in the dungeons' inhumane conditions while waiting for the ships to transport them to the Americas. Ghanaians see the castles as festive places, African Americans as somber places" ("Tourism in Ghana" 293). The Ghanaian government navigates this tricky divide. In 1994, a conference on the preservation of Elmina and Cape Coast recommended that "the cultural heritage of all the different epochs and powers should be presented, but also that the area symbolizing the slave trade be given reverential treatment" (294).

Though the addition of the word *dungeons* emphasizes the traumatic element of the castle's history by naming the place where captives were held until transport, one African American tour group does more to ensure that this violent history remains central. One Africa Productions, a tour group founded by Imahkus Vienna Robinson, an African American who has relocated to Ghana, specializes in immersing African American and other black visitors in this particular origin of the diaspora. For example, while walking though a Cape Coast dungeon, the tour guide informs the group, "What you are walking on is literally centuries of calcified bones, flesh, and human waste. This is where the captured Africans ate, slept, and packed in their own filth, were sick and sometimes died. Everything happened in here" (Tyehimba, "Scarred Walls of Stone" n.p.). It appears that Robinson hopes to reproduce, through what Alison Landsberg calls "prosthetic memory," the traumatic effect she experienced during her first visit to a slave dungeon: "As I stood transfixed in the Women's Dungeon, I could feel and smell the presence of our Ancestors. From the dark, damp corners of that hell-hole I heard the whimpering and crying of tormented Mothers and Sisters being held in inhumane bondage never knowing what each new day . . . would bring" (Bruner, "Tourism in Ghana" 294).

Robinson's tour group performs a special reenactment in the castles titled *Through the Door of No Return: The Return,* which is only for black visitors. The group assembles in the dungeon, "where they hold hands, light candles, pray together, usually weep together, pour libation as an homage to the ancestors, and then pass through the door that the slaves went through to the slave ships taking them to the Americas." Once through the door, the group gathers to sing "Lift Every Voice and Sing" and "We Shall Overcome." The group then returns to the castle, "singing and dancing African songs to the beat of drums, festive songs to celebrate their joyous return to mother Africa" (296). Despite the essentialist view espoused by Robinson's group (One Africa views all blacks as linked by and descended from Africa; hence, despite the diaspora and the diversity of African history and culture, blacks constitute "one Africa"), the performance is emotionally resonant for many of its participants. It is a constructed articulation of a traumatic rupture and departure, followed by a therapeutic return.

By engendering an affective (and, for many, a genuine) response, Robinson's tour group is consonant with what some tourism scholars identify as the goal of modern touring. As Dean MacCannell observes, "Touristic consciousness is motivated by the desire for authentic experiences, and the tourist may believe that he is moving in this direction, but often it is very difficult to know for sure if the experience is in fact authentic" (*The Tourist* 101). Here, MacCannell refers to forms of cultural tourism where spectators long for the "real thing" because modernity has removed "reality and authenticity" from their own lives and placed it "elsewhere: in other historical periods and other cultures, in purer, simpler lifestyles" (3). Although this may be true for other forms of touring, diaspora blacks traveling to Ghana do not seek a more simple, less tainted lifestyle. Instead, they long for a sense of place that marks the "reality and authenticity" of slavery and, ultimately, the reason for their presence in the United States.

For many black people who engage in slave tourism, the journey is an effort to come to terms with the slave past. The slave castles are "tangible and necessary memorials, some of the very few places where physical evidence of their heritage can be seen, touched, walked through, and experienced with all their physical senses" (Finley, "The Door" pt. 6). A frequent visitor to Ghana's slave castles describes them as "a place you did not want to see, but were compelled to go in. It was traumatizing, but healing" (Mosk, "Cradle of Slavery" B1). In this way, the return (a suspicious one, for how can one "return" to a place he has never been?) to the slave castle engenders a process for many blacks to recognize, work through, accept, and ultimately claim their traumatic heritage. As Charles C. Mate-Kole, a member of the Association of Black Psychologists, which held its first international conference in Ghana in 2000, explains, "Having to reconnect can be a painful journey. . . . There is a painful past that some of us try to forget or disconnect ourselves from. But going back to see it, there's no question that it is therapeutic" (quote in ibid. B9).

If many blacks travel to Ghana's slave castles as pilgrims seeking reconnection or as brothers and sisters longing for a familial welcome or even as "patients" seeking racial identity therapy, many are disappointed to learn that, in Ghana, they are interpreted as none of these. Upon their arrival, their journey is "exposed as a mere tourist excursion," because for Ghanaians, "tourists—black and white—are *obruni*, a term that carries the double-edged meaning of both 'white man' and 'foreigner'" (Finley, "The Door" pt. 2). Some black visitors from the diaspora resent both the "tourist" label and the expectations attached to it. For instance, the slave castle's admission price, which is roughly four dollars higher for non-Ghanaian nationals, is often a source of complaint, if not protest. On one occasion, a group of West Indian tourists refused to pay the admission fee and staged a small protest at the Cape Coast castle entrance. As one protester said, "We didn't pay to leave here; why should we have to pay to return. We won't pay to enter a graveyard of our ancestors" (Tyehimba, "Scarred Walls of Stone" n.p.). This is one of many ways that the pilgrims' return is revealed to be a mediated experience rather than a natural, seamless one.

This conflict can also be explained by the two modes of slave tourism that converge in the castles: the modern tourist desire for authenticity and the postmodern tourist desire for simulacra or regulated activity. As a World Heritage Site, Ghana's slave castles attract a variety of races, cultures, and nationalities. For the most part, however, it is blacks from the diaspora who seek reconnection, validation, or prosthetic memory; other visitors may want to see the castles and dungeons, perhaps learn the history, or explore its architecture. These divergent expectations present a special challenge for Ghanaian tour guides who lead tours of mixed-raced groups. As a Ghanaian information officer for the West Africa Historical Museum at Cape Coast castle reveals, "There is a great difference when African-Americans go down in the dungeons than when Europeans go. The African-Americans you can see feel very sad for their forefathers" (Maier, "Chamber of Horrors" 68). In some cases, this sadness is expressed as anger. The logbook at Elmina castle contains the following comment by an American tourist from Connecticut: "Very impressive castle. Tour was very good. Great views toward the city, beach, and ocean. One concern—a man during the tour was distracting an[d] I felt offended by his anti-white sentiments, as he kept saying, 'white people this . . .' I couldn't understand exactly, but he should respect other people more who are trying to *follow the tour guide*" (Finley, "The Door" pt. 4; emphasis added). Although it is not possible (or even strictly necessary) to accurately determine the race of this American tourist (surely, many could be offended by "anti-white" sentiments or annoyed by an obstreperous person's mutterings during a high-price package tour), but what can be discerned is another way to tour a slave castle, a way that does not seek authenticity. This is the recreational tourism that Gerima subtly critiques in *Sankofa*. This is the mode that his coercive cinematic language subverts, installing in its place his version of an "authentic" slave-tourist experience.

The film's cinematic language presents *Sankofa* as a seamless connection to enslaved African ancestors, when actually the narrative is as framed by tourism as much as the film itself is a product of the larger tourist industry. In this way, it is ironic to note that Gerima positions himself as a perfect tour guide for both the slave castles and the symbolic return to the past as presented in his film. Though the film is overtly critical of Western commercialism (symbolized by Mona), it also capitulates to notions of tourism, becoming in effect a coercive "tour guide." Beyond the film, an allegorical reading of Mona's character suggests a more critical analysis of the tourist elements of Gerima's film.

As Mona descends into the dungeons, a white family of two young blonde girls and (presumably) their mother passes her, going in the opposite direction. The mother is wearing a Mickey Mouse T-shirt. The incongruity of the Mickey Mouse image in a slave dungeon suggests a subtle yet powerful critique of postmodern tourism. The emergence of Mickey is best explained by the term *McDisneyization,* which tourism theorists George Ritzer and Allan Liska define as "a modern grand narrative viewing the world as growing increasingly efficient, calculable, predictable, and dominated by controlling non-human technologies" ("McDisneyization" 97). The McDisney factor, they suggest, motivates forms of tourism that are marked not by the modern desire for authenticity but instead by the postmodern expectation for regularity, order, sterility, and "inauthenticity" (107).

At the level of its narrative, *Sankofa* stands in opposition to the McDisney factor. Eschewing the guided tour (Mona does not appear in the same frame as the tour guide) and its implied lack of "authenticity," the film suggests that whereas the white family (which is leaving the dungeons) can view the slave castles as just another tour, Mona (and, by extension, Westernized blacks) has a larger debt to pay, an important lesson to learn, and spirits of the dead to meet. At the level of production and promotion, Gerima invokes the ancestral spirits to hide his own version of McDisney. By invoking the spirits of slaves (as he does in the opening and closing scenes of the film) to guide and anchor his creative efforts, he also uses them to cloak his own intentions and present his conclusions as transparent and, perhaps, preordained.

In an interview, Gerima talks about the *cra,* an African belief system that is closely aligned with reincarnation: "Cra is a belief in spirits, a belief that people who have died but are not yet settled roam the village, trying to find a living body to enter, to go back into the living world to repent their crimes or avenge injustices done to them. All of this was on my mind while working on the story for *Sankofa"* (Woolford, "Filming Slavery" 103). Clearly, the relationship between Mona and Shola is influenced by the *cra:* Shola is a "spirit of the dead" waiting for the appropriate vessel to hear and, perhaps later, tell her story. The McDisney factor emerges in the implication that Gerima's film is not really his but, instead, is another receptacle for the ancestral spirits. In this way, he performs an inversion of McDisney: rather than presenting a sterile, uniform tourist experience, his tour assaults the senses and guides the viewer through a painful journey with an inevitable conclusion. Although he claims *Sankofa* is intended to "make you think," the film clearly encourages the viewer to think as he does, to follow *his* guided tour from inauthenticity (Mona's orange wig, transgressive behavior, and collaboration with a white man) to authenticity (her ordeals and eventual transformation). In Gerima's tour, Mona is posited as a representative African American in need of spiritual and racial reawakening. Much like the One Africa tours of slave castles offer the promise of reunion or closure to black Americans, so too does Gerima outline the perils of black amnesia regarding slavery and the brutal measures that might prompt memory.

Despite this manipulation, *Sankofa* remains a popular film among segments of the African American community. *Sankofa* does not have a national distributor (which is why I could never find it at Blockbuster or Hollywood Video). Yet word about the film has circulated through many black churches, community action groups, youth leadership and empowerment collectives, independent black bookstores, and black-owned media outlets. (I first saw the film at the National Black Graduate Student Conference.) When Gerima screens his film, largely for black audiences, a call-and-response interaction very much like that in the traditional black church fuels the discussion. As a scene that takes place at a theater in Philadelphia suggests, Gerima's promotion of his work generates feelings akin to a revival meeting: "'The ancestors have decreed that this film would be made!' pronounces a young woman in the audience, voicing the spirit in the room. 'We don't need Hollywood. We need him and others like him!' booms a mature voice from the rear of the room" (Rickey, "Labor of Love" E2). Instead of a bully pulpit, Gerima has

Sankofa, and his orthodoxy is a realist representational mode that chastens and urges viewers to see the light of his beliefs.

If it seems as though I have a conflicted relation to Gerima's project, it is because I do. The film is a provocative, useful, and powerful representation of the traumatic event of slavery and its effects. Its urgently representational strategy imaginatively deploys slave-narrative conventions to render them in a symbolic and literal cinematic language. But for my personal taste, the film's coercive tone, masked by an invocation of ancestral spirits, seems unduly manipulative.

Yet the film combines Toni Morrison's idea of rememory, Pierre Nora's concept of the *lieu de memoire,* and the African belief system of *cra* to urgently remind us of the importance of acknowledging the slave past. In this way, the film does what Natalie Zemon Davis says the best historical films do: "make cogent observations on historical events, relations, and processes" (*Slaves on Screen* 5). In addition, *Sankofa* is a site for the reconsideration of trauma theory in light of African American heritage and culture. The film stands in direct opposition to predominant modes of trauma theory that define trauma by its elusiveness. *Sankofa* implies that this ephemeral quality does not resonate with these African and African American venues. The Cape Coast and Elmina slave castles, like *Sankofa,* represent and directly reference slavery as a "real" and "authentic" traumatic experience of deep significance in black life. In this way, they insist that trauma is an event not ephemera. The National Great Blacks in Wax Museum makes this event more accessible for that segment of the black public unable to visit African slave castles.

Part 2: Traumatic Wax

In March 2000, the National Great Blacks in Wax Museum in Baltimore, Maryland, was the site of a controversial field trip for Montgomery County middle school students. Established in 1983, the wax museum is the first dedicated to African American history and culture. Its wax figures enshrine great black Americans and document significant moments in black life. In addition to figures of black celebrities and civic leaders, the museum features two exhibits designed to teach visitors about the painful legacies of African American life: slavery and lynching. (The lynching exhibit is housed in a restricted area of the museum, limited to viewers over the age of twelve.) The point of contention was the slavery exhibit that includes a full-scale replica of a slave ship featuring wax men, women, and children set in a variety of scenes: "A woman's wrists are tied to a whipping post, her body forms an arc with her legs hanging limp on the floor. Blood pours from thick gashes in the woman's ebony skin. Two white men force a brown pasty mixture down a black man's throat through a funnel. The severed head of a black man sits on a wooden barrel. Emaciated little boys wearing only burlap loin cloths and neck chains lie packed in cupboard-sized spaces. Many of the slaves, packed horizontally hip to hip, appear comatose or dead and lie near rats" (Hopkinson, "Waxing Educational" N51). Following complaints from several white parents, the Takoma Park Middle School removed the museum from the list of acceptable field trip destinations, which in turn provoked complaints from several black parents. The school principal, while acknowledging the important role the National Great Blacks in Wax Museum plays in expressing black history, felt compelled to give parents the ultimate choice: "They need to feel comfortable in terms of sending their children to this exhibit" (Malloy, "Slave Exhibit" B1).

Courtland Milloy, who featured the debate in his weekly column for the *Washington Post,* dismissed the objection that the slavery exhibit's violent images were detrimental to children: "Most of the students who take the trip are 12 years old. Just on children's television programming alone they can see nearly 10,000 acts of violence committed each year. The so-called family hour of prime time contains more than eight sexual incidents per hour. That's harmful. The slave ship is just history" (ibid.). But at least one white parent countered this position with the tacit assumption that television violence is different from the museum's representation of the Middle Passage. Patricia Hart Smith of Gaithersburg, Maryland, wrote: "When I signed my 11–year-old's parental consent form to visit the museum, I assumed it would be an age-appropriate trip. I also assumed that it would be an enjoyable, educational experience for them. When I picked up my children from school after the field trip, the usually boisterous girls sat quietly in the back seat. It was only after some prompting that I discovered that their day had been filled with images of nude black women about to be raped by their white captors, Klansmen attacking children and people being force-fed. Granted, these were only wax figures, but children of their age should not visit such an exhibit" ("Necessary Education?" A26).

Despite or perhaps because of such controversy, the small museum has managed to attract a large number of visitors to an area of Baltimore many tourists would overlook. Its popularity reveals its implicit participation in the debate about history and traumatic knowledge. Presenting carvings of foundational moments of African American life and culture in wax, the museum satisfies its claim to "stimulate an interest in African American history by revealing the little-known, often-neglected facts of history." Partially revising the traditional notions of wax museums as a lowbrow venture, the

National Great Blacks in Wax Museum can also be viewed as an attempt to provoke memories of the past for those living in the present.

Alison Landsberg's essay on the "radical politics of empathy" in the United States Holocaust Memorial Museum is instructive on this point. Though the National Great Blacks in Wax Museum is far less sophisticated than the United States Holocaust Memorial Museum, both venues seek to promote memory of traumatic events formative to cultural identity. Landsberg introduces a concept of "prosthetic memory" that is not based in an individual's consciousness but "circulates publicly" and can be "experienced with one's own body—by means of a wide range of cultural technologies—and as such, become part of one's own personal archive of experience, informing not only one's subjectivity, but one's relationship to the present and future tenses." The museum engages the realm of prosthetic memory as part of the effort to remember slavery and lynching. Viewers are reminded of the profound rupture of the Middle Passage and its consequences during slavery and Reconstruction and for the present day. The museum attempts to transmit traumatic knowledge in its wax figures, and its three-dimensional approach is intended to promote a visceral, emphatic connection to the slave past. As Landsberg suggests, prosthetic memories are prosthetic not because they are artificial but because "they are actually worn by the body; these are sensuous memories produced by experience" ("America" 66). The wax museum's reliance on realism as a form of what Landsberg describes as "experiential involvement" breaks the traditional expectations of museum spectatorship, for, as Kathleen Kendrick observes, "Unlike the marble and bronze bodies on pedestals that reinforced traditional social barriers and prompted a sense of detached reverence for the depicted individual, wax sculpture blurred and transgressed these boundaries by making realism and its attendant suspension of disbelief, not artistic style, its standard of success" ("'The Things Down Stairs'" 12). In the same way, visitors are encouraged to "connect" with the wax figures in the Middle Passage tableau, to think about the similarity of human form between depicted people and themselves. This careful arrangement of scenes and wax figures is consonant with what Dean MacCannell defines as "re-presentation" in museum exhibition, which "aims to provide the viewer with an authentic copy of a total situation that is supposed to be meaningful from the standpoint of the things inside the display" (*The Tourist* 79). Though this venue is a small grassroots museum, it amplifies the standard mode of perception, represented by MacCannell, by suggesting a "meaningful" perspective for the wax figures on the display and for those viewing it.

Though traumatic wax may disconcert theorists who believe that the past cannot be retrieved or represented, the National Great Blacks in Wax

Museum exhibits the verisimilitude of the traumatic past and its registration on the physical body to promote memory and provoke an empathic response. Kathleen Kendrick's observations about the turn-of-the-century wax museum also appropriately explain the museum's realist impulse that references the event and implicates the viewer: "Through its attempts [to] create a believable as well as recognizable artificial reality, where differences between the simulated and the real were effaced rather than emphasized, the wax museum placed visitors in an intimate, sensational engagement with bodies on display that the art museum as temple operated to dissuade" ("'The Things Down Stairs'" 12). The wax figures, then, are intended to foster an identification with, and proximity to, a set of individuals and their circumstances. How can the appeal of wax figures—which Kendrick describes as "the fluid and mystical circulation between reality and fantasy, emotion and intellect, death and life, flesh and wax" (13)—produce a link between viewer and object? If the wax figures are representations of a traumatic knowledge, do they then generate a traumatic effect?

The answer depends entirely on the viewer. One visitor reported: "The figures, sounds and descriptions brought history to life in a gruesome way. Except for a woman who felt compelled to snap pictures of each scene, the people standing around said little" (Forest, "The Great Blacks" H3). A museum tour guide notes, "We have had people go down in the slave ship and become just overwhelmed. They can't stop crying, and we have to go escort them out." But whereas some visitors are stunned, others "leave in a hurry, unable to face its message." The efforts to collapse the past and present are clearly not unequivocally successful. Even one of the museum's twelve-year-old docents was initially intimidated by the figures he introduced to visitors five days a week. He has since overcome his anxiety, but distance is a fundamental part of that resolve: "To me, they're friendly now. They stay on their side, and I stay on mine" (Selby, "People" G10). The young docent's self-protective attitude saves him, he says, from nightmares and is a tacitly oppositional reading of the museum. Museum cofounder Joanne Martin's comments on the lynching exhibit apply to the museum's mission as a whole: "If you can look at it objectively, then we haven't done our job" (Hastings, "From Shame to Pride" n.p.). Martin does not want the museum to be the site of passive or uninvolved spectatorship; instead, she wants to engender a form of prosthetic memory. The National Great Blacks in Wax Museum's attempt to provoke an affective response (be it fear, despair, anger, anxiety, or hope) is grounded in the desire to communicate traumatic aspects of black history in an empathic way by encouraging a connection with the actual figures represented by the wax images.

I experienced a certain degree of this connection during my visit on a summer Saturday morning. There were long lines to enter the museum (several tour buses were parked in front of the museum and in the Stop and Save parking lot across the street). The slave-ship exhibit, which is underground and accessed only by a narrow set of stairs, was crowded. After entering the small, dark space, I examined the wax figures set in a variety of tableaux: women huddled together in a small space as white men reached for them from above; a severed head on a barrel as a form of punishment; small children being gnawed on by rats. I noticed telling marks of the museum's status as a popular, rather than elite, venue: some of the chains looked as if they had recently come from a hardware store; someone had snapped the toes off a few wax children whose blistered feet were in reach of the visitor space. I was so intent on reading the exhibit, which is on the right side of the room, that I was startled, when I looked to the left, to see my own reflection. To increase the feeling of space and double the effect of the ship (so that it appears to have two sides rather than one), a mirrored wall opposite the tableaux reflects the scene. This effect places the viewer in the middle of the slave ship, implicating and temporarily sealing them within the traumatic wax.

The National Great Blacks in Wax Museum shares a mission with most history museums: to tell a story, preserve memory, and educate present-day viewers using scenes from the past. Its curious format (wax sculpture and scenarios) and unusual location (in a working-class, inner-city black neighborhood) contribute to its popularity as a black vernacular site aimed at reaching large and diverse black populations. The museum's high numbers of tour groups from churches and schools suggest that it is successful in reaching blacks who might long to know more black history and who are choosing the site as a place to gain this knowledge. Despite its small size and limited financial resources, the National Great Blacks in Wax Museum draws larger numbers of black visitors than the more formal and academic institution of Colonial Williamsburg. Why might a black person choose to visit the National Great Blacks in Wax Museum rather than Colonial Williamsburg? It could be the wax museum's location (many groups from the eastern seaboard charter buses to Baltimore and might stop in Washington, D.C.) or its affordability (the admission rate is less than Colonial Williamsburg), but the key element is that many black visitors grant this small wax museum more authority and credibility to present black history than the larger, predominantly white, institution in Williamsburg.

Part 3: Whose History Is This?

I turn now to a moment when Colonial Williamsburg's approach to black history plunged the museum into the national spotlight. The 1994 slave auction reenactment generated a vast amount of media coverage and engaged the black public sphere. Unlike the ritual reenactments described in the next chapter (which serve a specific community yet reach beyond them in a religious and socially and culturally redemptive gesture), historical reenactments typically attract few black spectators. In this case, however, black civil rights groups including the National Association for the Advancement of Colored People (NAACP) and Southern Christian Leadership Conference (SCLC) as well as some members of the black press all weighed in on the propriety of the Williamsburg event. The black popular response—especially in the context of black vernacular intellectual formations—is vital to the understanding of and possibilities for this event as an instance of vernacular trauma theory, a mode that extends the social-history ethos of living-history philosophy into the realm of healing through portrayal and reenactment. This event, perhaps more than any other Colonial Williamsburg program to date or since, tested the notion of embodied representation as a strategy for (re)visiting the slave past. As such, this reenactment provides a rich setting in which to consider the possibilities of bodily epistemology.

In October 1994, Colonial Williamsburg narrowly escaped a threat proffered by that most ubiquitous of American cultural symbols: Mickey Mouse. Less than one year earlier, the Disney Corporation announced plans to build "Disney's America" near two of Virginia's Civil War battlefields and too close for the comfort of Colonial Williamsburg. The planned attraction—composed of ten themed areas devoted to historical events including the American Revolution and Civil War and places such as Ellis Island—would essentially "do" American history Disney-style: "Disney's original proposal included a nightly Civil War battle between the Monitor and the Merrimac, a roller coaster in the Industrial Revolution section that took riders through a steel mill, and a virtual-reality setting that let children fly fighter planes in World War II" (B. Boyd, "Historians Win" A2). Colonial Williamsburg, with its own history of land-grabbing and aggressive property acquisition, was a veritable David when compared to the corporate entertainment and theme park Goliath, Walt Disney. Thanks in large part to citizens' groups and historians (public and academic) who lobbied against Disney, Colonial Williamsburg averted the competition that would have resulted from a new history theme park.

Disney's chief executive officer, Michael Eisner, promised to put the full weight of his corporation ("Our motion picture and television talent, our park imagineers, our interactive media and publishing executives as well as our sports enterprise and education executives") behind the American history theme park that would both entertain (in the park and its proposed adjacent hotels, residences, shops, and golf greens) and edify through the medium of living history. According to Bob Weis, senior vice president of Walt Disney Imagineering, the site would provide more than great rides: "The park will be a venue for people of all ages, especially the young, to debate and discuss the future of our nation and to learn more about its past by living it" ("Plans Unveiled" n.p.). Opposition came from those concerned about land use, urban sprawl, and development. Some protested the irony of destroying actual historical sites to construct a conglomeration of simulated historical sites. A group called Protect Historic America took its battle with Disney to the public, where they were joined by prominent academic historians, among them C. Vann Woodward and John Hope Franklin, and public historians such as David McCullough and Shelby Foote. Later, the National Trust for Historic Preservation would join forces with Protect Historic America, whose unofficial motto read, "Eeek! A mouse . . . Step on it."

Colonial Williamsburg took no official stance in the fray, though it was clear that Disney's $650 million project would shape its fortunes. Luckily for the established museum, acclaimed author and public historian David Mc-Cullough was in its corner. Though he agreed to advise Disney in its search for a new location, McCullough promised that it would not be near Williamsburg, which he defined as a prime historic site. In defense of Colonial Williamsburg, McCullough said, "The people who click their tongues and say, 'Well, it's just a recreation,' I have no patience for that. It is a real place in history and the restoration of it has been done with immense skill" (B. Boyd "Historians Win" A2). The impression here (and indeed the powerful motivator for advocacy on behalf of Colonial Williamsburg) is that Disney cannot "do" history in the same manner as Colonial Williamsburg. According to this rationale, these two corporations have widely divergent means and motives. Colonial Williamsburg is an educational foundation, a collection of museums housing artifacts and aiming to reanimate the past with the "living artifacts" of its character and first-person interpretations. On the other hand, Disney is, well, Disney: a behemoth corporation with interests in television, film, and publishing as well as huge entertainment complexes in Florida, California, France, and Japan. In brief, Colonial Williamsburg is Colonial Williamsburg, and Disney is Disney: one does "real history," and the other does "real entertainment"; they are separate if not exactly equal venues.

Many in the museum field were relieved to learn that there would be no Mickey Mouse history theme park. Just after Disney's announcement, Rex Ellis, founder of Colonial Williamsburg's African American Interpretive Programs department, spoke on the matter from his new position as director of museum programs for the Smithsonian Institution. Comparing Disney's plan to include golf and diversions with Colonial Williamsburg, which also has substantial golf-resort and conference-center components, Ellis observed, "I don't think Disney has enough respect for what museums do and what museums are to make that balance work. They haven't been talking to museum people." It was slavery, for Ellis, that separated the real historians from the dabblers. Though it is unclear how Disney would have addressed this aspect of American history—maybe a little satellite to the "detailed Civil War era village, which [would have been] the hub of Disney's America"—Ellis was convinced that Mickey's people could not do a good job: "Having fun at the expense of slavery, I will always be opposed to." Perhaps still smarting from Disney's snub—Ellis's offer to consult with Disney was ignored—Ellis believed that Disney's primary goal was entertainment, profitable entertainment, which was at odds with producing history: "How can a company concerned with the bottom line be concerned about telling the true story, which may be uncomfortable and unpleasant?" (ibid.). This claim is doubly significant: First, it denounces Disney—one of America's most recognizable icons—for representing a host of wrongs in the eyes of academics and cultural elites (such as contributing to the dumbing down of America, offering too easy substitution of simulacra for the "real," and promoting mindless diversion as a fundamental need). It also implies that Colonial Williamsburg does history better and refuses to shy away from uncomfortable history just to please its paying public.

I divert attention to this controversy to better contextualize another. The report I have just described—the remarks from Ellis about Disney's inability to "do" slave history—appeared on October 2, 1994. Nine days later, in another article by the same reporter in the same space, Ellis's claims concerning the determination and competence of Colonial Williamsburg to present "uncomfortable and unpleasant" history would be vigorously tested.

The depth of the conversation about Colonial Williamsburg's 1994 slave auction is masked by the broad scope of its media coverage. The announcement to reenact a slave auction prompted a media frenzy: CNN filmed a brief spot, as did NBC's *Today Show,* and National Public Radio interviewed the program's director. Local and regional black press outlets such as Norfolk's *New Journal and Guide* and Richmond's *Afro-American* and national magazines such as *Jet* and *Black Issues in Higher Education* all covered the story. The

New York Times, like other national newspapers, published stories, editorial columns, and letters to the editor about the event. Most of the coverage centered on this question: is it appropriate to reenact a slave auction? Would such an event be a sordid spectacle that trivialized the past or a vivid embodiment of past traumatic events? These complexities were reduced to an oft-repeated query: would this performance be a form of education or entertainment? This dichotomy largely structured the popular response and helped to guide the programmers and protesters. The intersections between "entertainment" and "education" went unnoticed. My purpose here is to explore the ambivalences and murky waters of the slave auction–reenactment controversy. My main concern is not the determination of whether the performance was educational, entertainment, or a mix of both. Rather, I am interested in the form of contested authority—the struggle between the AAIP department head, Christy Coleman, and the protesters from the NAACP and SCLC civil rights groups. What I have observed is a battle of ideas not only about telling and showing slavery in a reembodied performance but also about who gets to decide which aspects to tell. The controversy is not as clear-cut as mainstream and other media outlets made it out to be. It was not simply a coalition of activists from the International Socialists–NAACP-SCLC versus Colonial Williamsburg. Neither was it in any sense black or white. The behind-the-scenes struggle was a black-on-black conflict in two ways: First, although the local Williamsburg chapter supported the event, chapters from neighboring cities (within an hour's radius of Williamsburg) came to protest on behalf of local blacks and NAACP members who—the activists claimed—were either brainwashed or hamstrung by Colonial Williamsburg and unable to express their true opinions for fear of reprisal. Second, the civil rights activists—those most visibly acknowledged in the media—were black men, and the slave auction's "creator" (the driving force behind the event) was a black woman.

In what follows, I explore the critical life of this reenactment controversy—including questions of the scene's propriety, authority, and historical verisimilitude. The controversy itself was marked by ambivalence, as parties from both sides were subject to the same insults: race traitor, sensationalist, exploiter, manipulator. To sidestep this cycle of blame and finger-pointing, I will instead read the slave-auction reenactment scene and controversy as a site of vernacular intellectual productivity, and try to gauge the response as part of the difficulty of reenacting traumatic or crisis scenes from the slave past. One photograph—published in *Jet* soon after the event—suggests the ambivalence of the conflict. In this image of the crowd (reporters, students, tourists—largely, but not entirely, white) assembled on the main street, a long-haired young white man holds up one-half of a large sign that reads,

"Say No to Racist Shows!" In front of this white man is another one, young with glasses and a goatee, raising his left arm in a Black Power salute. Behind his raised arm—indeed, partially obstructed by his fervent gesture—stands a black woman wearing a low-shorn afro and looking nonplussed, slightly impatient, or annoyed. Hers is the only black face "fully" visible in the photo. It is impossible to know what this woman thinks about the huge crowd or the event they have assembled to see, just as it is impossible to determine her position on the controversy. However, the picture and its effect are suggestive of the ambivalence and contested authority that brought the slave-auction program to the public's notice.

This event had the potential to enact, on a broader stage, the mission statement that guided the invention of the AAIP in the early 1980s. The charter document stresses the humanity of slave life: "The slave experience is more readily understood when slaves are seen as human beings caught in an inhuman situation. When they are shown laughing, crying, hurting, loving, hating, wondering, and struggling with the same human emotions as their captors, the institution of slavery ceases to be something separate from the human experience" (Ellis, quoted in Krutko, "Colonial Williamsburg's Slave Auction" 81). Still, whereas the creators of the program thought that the auction reenactment would emphasize the humanity of the slaves in the eighteenth-century capital, the protesters had no faith in its ability to do so. In their view, black history would be presented not with humanity or sensitivity, but rather for the amusement of the touring and vacationing public. For example, a joint statement from Virginia's state branch and national office of the NAACP charged, "Colonial Williamsburg is perpetuating the fallacies of denying the true depiction of history and glorifying the horrors and humiliations of the evils of slavery through a one-day event" (quoted in Waldron, "Staged Slave Auction" 14). Though this objection critiques the reenactment's historical accuracy (raising another thorny question of mimetic authenticity) on the rather shaky grounds that it would deny truths, revel in horror, and do so for only one day (would *more* really be better in this view?), other protesters argued that the event would turn back the clock of black progress. The Reverend Dr. Milton A. Reid reminded the gathered crowd that "this is 1994" and said reenacting these moments of slavery was anathema: "As far as we have come, to go back to this, for entertainment is despicable and disgusting. This is the kind of anguish we need not display" ("Tears and Protest" A16). Another often-quoted voice was that of Jack Gravely, NAACP's political action chairman, who said, "We don't want the history of a people who have come so far and done so much to be trivialized" (B. Boyd, "CW Auctions Slaves" A1).

The objections to the auction—on the surface—appear to come down to two issues: First, a reenactment at Colonial Williamsburg (or perhaps elsewhere) of a slave auction fell under the category of "entertainment" and was thus not a teaching tool or a way to present history vividly, but was instead a diversion for pleasure. Second, the slave auction itself referred to a grim, "negative" element of slavery specifically and black history at large. In the facile and frequently cited dichotomy of positive images versus negative images of blacks in the media (to name one example), the two extremes— positive and negative—substitute for more subtle and complex readings of black-generated cultural products. The slave auction reinforced "negative" image of blacks as powerless, as victims. At the same time, the slave auction flew in the face of the progress narrative many protesters cited as the better version of black history. Colonial Williamsburg, they claimed, might have chosen to depict freedom fighters and runaways rather than the auction block. Others argued that the slave past is best left in the past, that the auction-block performance was contrary to the preferable story of a "people who have come so far and done so much."

Other objections to the reenactment concern the type of slavery history that the slave auction represented. In part, the controversy was generated by the version of black history Colonial Williamsburg presented. Dave Harvey, a white Colonial Williamsburg employee who watched the reenactment during his lunch break, told an e-mail discursion list that he "was personally struck by the normality of the occasion. The sense that this monstrous practice of chattel slavery was just another piece of commerce." It is this normality that implies that the re-creation might have been more authentic than its critics could acknowledge.

Though some dismissed the performance as "entertainment" lacking educational merit, those who took the auction's educational claims seriously charged that the reenactment was historically inaccurate, a distortion of black history. Al Freeman, the chair of Howard University's Drama Department, told *Black Issues in Higher Education* that the reenactment and Colonial Williamsburg's black programs in general were signs of white complacency about slavery: "They are now doing it and including it as some sort of revisionist history" (Phillip, "To Reenact" n.p.). King Salim Khalfani, who maintained the auction was "designed to entertain rather that teach the truth," said that the reenactment was part of the general approach to black history: "There have been so many myths and lies and distortions in the past" (B. Boyd, "Colonial Williamsburg Plans" C2). The NAACP's lack of confidence in Colonial Williamsburg's ability as an institution capable of representing black history reflects an underlying tension between the museum and the local (and broader) black community. There has long been a complicated relationship between Colonial Williamsburg—a Rockefeller Foundation–funded site initially designed to praise early America, not critique it—and the black community, which was initially segregated from visiting the site but permitted to work there in lower-level service positions. Like most large-scale institutional employers, Colonial Williamsburg played a major role in the livelihoods of black Williamsburg residents, many of whom if they did not work there knew someone who did. In addition to the financial influence the museum wielded over many local blacks, the institution—for much of its existence—ignored black contributions to colonial history. Referring to slaves euphemistically as "servants," Colonial Williamsburg avoided studied efforts to address slavery. One report in the late 1960s even claimed that although the museum was "loathe to arouse tender feelings among [their] own Negro employees," they used these same black people as a tacit example of slavery, admitting (without apparent irony) their assumption that "the presence of Negroes on the staff (usually in subservient jobs) was sufficient to suggest that we recognized slavery as once having existed here" (quoted in Ellis, "A Decade of Change" 16). This claim is suggestive of the troubled relationship between Colonial Williamsburg as an institution and the black residents of Williamsburg. It also goes a long way to partly explain the ambivalence, suspicion, and even animosity on the part of the city's black residents. If, by its own admission, the museum's practice of hiring blacks for subservient positions is supposed to "suggest" the institution of slavery, then Colonial Williamsburg is guilty of using all black employees as "twofers": getting two labors for the price of one. The black dishwasher, groundskeeper, and cashier not only do those tasks but also—by virtue of their black skin—represent the legacy of slavery and its eighteenth-century incarnation (since these black workers are clothed in eighteenth-century garb). Colonial Williamsburg got dual duty from its black employees—who were not working as first-person or character interpreters because there were no black characters before 1980—simply because they were black.

This employment and (tacitly) interpretive practice—based as it was on racism and the expectation of white racist assumptions—could easily (and permanently) discredit Colonial Williamsburg as an institution capable of presenting black history. It is likely that Colonial Williamsburg's previous treatment of blacks as both overworked employees and underrepresented historical subjects provoked many black protesters. The conversation between Jack Gravely and Christy Coleman reflects this tension. Gravely represented the position that Colonial Williamsburg was an inappropriate steward of black history: "Colonial Williamsburg does not deal with real black history. . . . [E]verything about Colonial Williamsburg is about the oppression of my people" (Krutko, "Colonial Williamsburg's Slave Auction" 22). Coleman defended the museum from her position within an African American department that had worked for fifteen years to correct Colonial Williamsburg's lily-white, silk-pants patriot history: "The Williamsburg you think we are is no longer the Williamsburg we really are. We spend a whole lot of blood, sweat, and tears everyday making sure that the story of our ancestors is told!" (49).

Brenda Andrews, one of a few black women on record as objecting to the performance, editorialized after the auction, "Colonial Williamsburg failed in their mission to use the event as a teaching tool: Slavery is still a sore spot and the insistence by organizers that they could educate people on this sensitive subject in their arena was not fulfilled" ("Slave Auction" 1). The "sore spot" here speaks to another element of bodily epistemology in the black popular sphere. This theory—which I have offered in the context of literature and film—also pertains to living-history interpretations of slavery. As with fictional characters, those who engage slave history through the bodily performance and reenactment of living history offer their own bodies as sites of historical knowledge and cultural figuration. By embodying the slave past in their performances, these museum and historical workers both represent the past *and* offer that representation to the present-day public. It is this motivation—and belief in such performances as good teaching strategies— that causes these reenactors to see themselves as walking "in the shoes" of their ancestors, to imagine themselves as both links between past and present and references to the past that permit that lapsed time to be known today.

Bodily epistemology is also present in the accounts of protester resistance. As Brenda Andrews has claimed, slavery is still a "sore spot." I believe that this pain or vulnerability about slavery motivates some of the need to put it in its place, to keep it in the past, or more commonly to think of it only as a strategic metaphor to explain the contemporary black plight. If slavery is a sore spot on the public collective black body, then a way to protect (through the diverting of attention elsewhere) that spot is through distancing and erasure. Andrews's editorial leans toward this gesture, when she writes, "The story of slavery needs to be remembered not necessarily retold." What is the difference between remembering and retelling? In the language of bodily epistemology, remembering is a private, solitary act, one that is reflective, requiring deep thought and inner consideration. Remembering, Andrews might say, is not performed before a live audience. Retelling involves speaking again of something that has already happened. This speech or declaration brings a range of association to life that was completely past. Is reluctance to retell a denial of an unflattering part of the African American past, a preference for heritage over history? Or is it that black life continues to be sufficiently embattled in the present, to the extent that attention to long-past injustices are simply unnecessary? In her editorial, Andrews moves swiftly from the injunction to remember slavery to reminders of slavery in contemporary black life. She writes of slavery, "Its residual effects continue today in the form of institutional and economic racism in employment, housing, and equal opportunity in other areas. We still see too many African Americans whose minds are enslaved by thinking linked to second class citizenship mandated by slavery" (ibid.). Although Andrews's claims are generally accurate, she still makes a troubling move to shift the grounds of slavery from the experiential and performative plane to the discursive and self-referential level. In her dismissal of Coleman and Colonial Williamsburg's attempts to represent an aspect of eighteenth-century captivity, Andrews uses the very terms—*slavery* and *enslaved*—of the debate and significantly shifts their meaning and application. Rather than seeing "slavery" in the reenacted transaction, Andrews claims that slavery is more pressing and relevant when used as a term to explain black immobility in the contemporary moment. A disturbing element of Andrews's claim emerges from where she attributes the source for slavery. By this reading, it is not whites who keep blacks down, necessarily (though there is this too); instead, Andrews is more concerned about those blacks whose "minds are enslaved" by "thinking" that restricts them to "second class citizenship." Andrews makes, then, the familiar move to transfer slavery from an immediate lived experience and transform it into a powerful metaphor.

Slavery as a discursive reference has been used to describe all manner of inconveniences (similarly, *Nazi* has been used to describe any rude person with a bossy streak, such as *Seinfeld*'s ill-tempered food-service worker, the "the soup Nazi"). Are you caught in a cycle of despair? Then you are probably a slave to negative thinking. Shahrazad Ali, author of the sensationalistic *Blackman's Guide to Understanding the Blackwoman*, also wrote a pamphlet, *Are You Still A Slave?* complete with a self-diagnostic questionnaire. More recently, and more relevantly, Joy DeGruy-Leary has lectured on posttraumatic slave disorder: behavioral patterns of blacks that linger as an unneeded yet extant reminder of survival mechanisms under slavery. And many black thinkers have described the prison-industrial complex and its inordinate numbers of incarcerated blacks as a distant (but not too distant) relative of the convict-lease system, a kissing cousin of sharecropping and plantation slavery.

My digression here is not to dismiss entirely the use of *slavery* to describe the real challenges of black life. However, I am curious as to why certain black protesters would use slavery as a metaphor without considering the myriad conditions on which that term is based. I suggest that this move is related to the "sore spot" that slavery as a historical fact occupies on the body of black and public life: a shameful, vulnerable wound best either left alone or left in a spirit of triumph and upward rising. Slavery is the place blacks rose above; without the progress narrative to frame it, the reenactment merely brought old wounds to visible scrutiny.

Other African Americans interviewed about the program expressed approval. One black man said, "I attach a certain reverence to it. It's a period we're paying for dearly to this day" ("Tears and Protest" A16). A black woman claimed, "In order to overcome this hurt and pain, it needs to be addressed" (Lackey, "Our History" B1). Another black woman refuted the NAACP's charges of sensationalism: "It isn't something they made up to get money. Wouldn't people and the NAACP be more offended if it was left out? I know I would" (B. Boyd, "Colonial Williamsburg Plans" C2).

Perhaps it was the extreme sensitivity of slavery's wounds still remaining in the psyches of blacks or the general, if sublimated, anxiety about slavery in American popular life, but the slave-auction controversy was a moment of great visibility and conflict in many arenas. Of the many debates—which included the appropriateness of first-person interpretation, the feasibility of slave auctions as performance, the suitability of Colonial Williamsburg as a site—two issues, one overt, the other hovering behind this public debate, are important to consider in this discussion of reenactments: the first is the Disney effect; the second is the gender effect.

In the struggle over the reenactment, both sides engaged the notion of Mickey Mouse history. Both would invoke the recent vanquishing of Disney as evidence supporting their claims. Those who opposed the reenactment feared that the portrayal would be Disney-style entertainment, not "real" history but a softer version to please tourists. As an editorial following the event noted, "They acted as if it was tantamount to the Walt Disney version of American history that was the focus of bitter arguments in northern Virginia before the company dropped its plans last month ("Giving Pain" D14). Proponents of the reenactment claimed that their work was rooted in historical facts and research; to cancel the auction reenactment would be to forget important facts of history. Defending the program, Coleman told a *Virginia Gazette* reporter, "You can dance around things that are uncomfortable, but we'd be no better than Disney. . . . There has been a lot of soul-searching, but there's no turning back" (Tolbert, "Slave Auction" A1). Both sides could use Disney as a straw man against which to set their positions—neither wanted a Disney-like version of slavery to be seen on the streets of Colonial Williamsburg. Both perceived the other side as promoting this view. There was little middle ground between these positions, and, ultimately, because the program was performed as scheduled, one might say that the protesters lost the battle. But the fact that the estate-sale reenactment has yet to be repeated at Colonial Williamsburg might suggest that they won the war over one form of slavery reenactment.

Before I move to consideration of the slavery reenactment and attempt to shed light on the small common ground shared by both sides, I would like to first explore the gender dimensions of this conflict. There are several factors that contributed to the tension between the NAACP and the AAIP. One is institutional: Colonial Williamsburg as a powerful history-making force that is inattentive to black history and its black employees. The NAACP was cast in the role of defender and advocate for both black history and black people. Another factor is generational: the civil rights generation set against the soul babies of the postsoul generation. As a Norfolk reporter wrote of the scene, "Three time periods existed as one on the porch of Wetherburn's Tavern of Duke of Gloucester Street: The actors in the reenactment were dressed in the eighteenth century garb and spoke in Colonial accents; the civil rights protesters seemed out of the 1960s as they sang 'We shall overcome' and one offered to be arrested; and the tourists, crowded shoulder to shoulder, wielded video cameras and complained loudly that more than a dozen reporters were blocking their view" (Lackey, "Our History" B1). The struggle among generations could also be seen in the words of a young black man who asked one of the civil rights leaders, "Who are you to tell me what part of my history I can or cannot see?" (Krutko, "Colonial Williamsburg's Slave Auction" 22). I am choosing to focus on the conflict between the NAACP and AAIP because it is part of the larger struggle within the black public sphere about the place of slavery reenactments in museums (as opposed to ritual reenactments and remembrances that are generally supported by blacks).[1]

This conflict also encapsulates the gender dimensions of many disagreements within black communities inside and beyond the academy. As countless scholars have noted, the gender divide within black popular and academic culture is broad and seemingly unbridgeable. Within black responses to the slave auction, the gender divide was most evident in the ways in which the male NAACP leadership was at odds with Christy Coleman, leader of the AAIP. This division is not so clear-cut as I have put it here: Brenda Andrews, editor in chief and publisher of Norfolk's *New Journal and Guide,* vigorously opposed the auction in her newspaper and during an interview (with Coleman present) on *Good Morning America.* And as I mentioned earlier, a majority of the spectators (supporters and protesters) were white.

Thus, it was possible to have a black person in favor of the event, while a white person shouted, "Say no to racist shows!" The gender dimension of the disagreement between the regional and state branches of the NAACP (the local Williamsburg chapter did not oppose the auction, preferring to withhold judgment until the performance was seen) is a significant indicator of a previously unconsidered element of the struggle over slavery's use in the present. Who decides how slavery is remembered? Who has the authority to shape the public memory of slavery? How does one claim the slave past? These questions were marked by the bitter intraracial gender conflicts that have long marked black popular and intellectual life.

The gender dimension emerged as a significant element during an eleventh-hour meeting between Colonial Williamsburg officials (including its president and director of interpretive programs) and civil rights leaders. The two white men with the power to stop the auction ignored the assembled black male leaders who had appealed to them. Being shut down in this way, then Virginia NAACP leader King Salim Khalfani later said, was an example of the power of this "all white, all male group." Khalfani's recollection of this moment is suggestive: "I just really remember the crassness of the officials from Colonial Williamsburg when we tried to dialog about it. And it was like women in the feminist movement say about men—that you all just don't get it. . . . To sit across from those guys and look them in the eye and see that it didn't matter what presentation we brought—they were going to do what they were going to do. It was really a lesson in power dynamics" (ibid. 19). It is telling that Khalfani resorts to a *gender* metaphor to explain an instance of a *racial* power imbalance. The civil rights leaders (black men) are powerless to dissuade Colonial Williamsburg leaders (white men). The addition of the gender metaphor, however, adds a new dimension to what might otherwise be seen as garden-variety racism. In addition to being dismissed on racial grounds, Khalfani's words have the added value of feminizing black men. By comparing his treatment to that of women and by putting himself in a position "like women," Khalfani processes the encounter as additionally humiliating: the civil rights leaders were essentially "bitched out."

The sting of this dismissal—interpolated from racial terms to gendered terms—seems to have sharpened the civil rights leaders' resolve and raised the stakes of their battle to halt the reenactment. In my view, the NAACP leaders were acting out of paternalism. Remember, the Williamsburg chapter, though skeptical of the event, would withhold judgment until seeing the performance. Ultimately, the local chapter supported the reenactment. Other regional chapters and the state body of the organization advocated on behalf of the Williamsburg chapter members who, in their view, were powerless to protest against one of the city's major employers. Jack Gravely later claimed that the Williamsburg chapter was not actually convinced by Christy Coleman's presentation to the group but was under considerable pressure and fear of reprisal from Colonial Williamsburg. When he came to recruit support from the chapter, he realized that "many of the people that we were asking to march and be over there with us and support us couldn't. . . . I remember once in the church meeting that someone said, 'Well I work there, my wife works there. That's my son—he works there, his wife works there.' That's a whole family" (ibid. 98). This considerable influence of Colonial Williamsburg on the lives of local chapter members motivated the larger body and branches in adjacent counties to advocate on behalf of Williamsburg's black people, who were cowed into silence. Or so they believed. This course of action dismissed the possibility that some blacks in Williamsburg endorsed the idea or that any black person—other than those forced by Colonial Williamsburg— would support a reenactment of this kind. The simple formula—that only whites and "sellout" blacks supported the reenactment—fails to capture the complexity of this struggle over who owns the slave past. The struggle over the slave auction was between a handful of black male civil rights leaders and an African American female program director. Still smarting from the rebuff by the white male leadership of Colonial Williamsburg, these black men "were convinced that Coleman would be more sensitive to their position. Unaware that the AAIP had developed the program, the civil rights leaders perceived themselves as advocates for hamstrung Williamsburg blacks and as standing up for exploited or brainwashed African American employees who were being economically coerced, even forced, to degrade themselves on the auction block" (ibid. 99).

On the morning before the event, the two sides met to resolve their conflict. Christy Coleman agreed to meet with the civil rights leaders inside the Wetherburn Tavern. Jack Gravely demanded the program be canceled. Coleman refused, saying that Colonial Williamsburg had a responsibility as a museum to teach "accurate history," to which Gravely disagreed. Coleman explained that she created the slave-auction reenactment to illuminate the horrors of slavery and captivity. King Salim Khalfani disagreed, telling her, "You just want to do what white men tell you to do. Period" (ibid. 22–23). Whether this curt response was prompted by the heat of the moment is of little relevance. What is striking is the repeated emergence of the gender divide or hierarchy that frequently (and historically) plagues many facets of black life. Be it black intellectual Anna Julia Cooper being asked to serve tea to a gathering of Talented Tenth male intellectuals, Zora Neale Hurston being lambasted by Richard Wright as a race traitor, black women activists being offered the "prone" positions in the movement for civil rights, or more recent complaints that Best Actress Oscar winner Halle Berry received the unprecedented award not for an excellent acting performance but for portraying a white man's lover, the story is common and familiar: black women are expected to defer to the wishes of black men. This is not to imply that African Americans are more gender contentious than American culture more broadly. Still, black women are sometimes vulnerable to the charge of racial faithlessness if their choices do not coincide with those of black men. Khalfani's acerbic comment that Coleman would "do what white men tell [her] to do" can easily be read in its converse implication: Coleman would *not* do what these *black* men were telling her to do. Coleman's authority as the program director—and principal creator of the auction—was attacked on racial and gender grounds. This conversation, held behind the doors of the tavern, away from the public, would prefigure the criticism Coleman would later face about her choice to design and perform this reenactment. Who has the authority to make these decisions? In the eyes of the assembled black leaders, a black woman did not. Curiously, Coleman drew her authority from the success of previous programs and from a distinctly female genealogical history. Defending the program before it began, Coleman introduced herself and said, "What is happening today, I think, is a very real tragedy. However, we came here to teach the story of our mothers and grandmothers. We came here, we came here to do this voluntarily. . . . We wanted to do this so that each and every one of you never forget what happened to them" (videotape of auction). Coleman promises to use the auction—which is about to begin— to tell the story of "our mothers and grandmothers," appealing to symbolic foremothers as the source of an unimpeachable authority. The civil rights activists might argue with her academic or museological credentials (as being tainted by "whiteness"), but they could not deny that she had a black mother, nor could they expect her to "forget" or "ignore" her history. Coleman invoked this matriarchal spirit to legitimate the auction reenactment, encouraging audience members to make the (improbable) assumption that what they were about to see—a reenactment of one of slavery's horrors—was a testament to the black women who preceded them.

This strategy of relying on duty owed to maternal ancestors raises the issue of empathy in addition to authority. After the auction, though a majority of the press reported a favorable response among blacks and whites, Coleman and her department's authority remained contested. A black writer stated, "It is insufficient for a few African American staffers to solely decide that it is time to present an especially painful portion of the slave experience, being auctioned, through re-enactment." Given the preponderance of negative images of blacks, she maintained that the reenacted slave auction fed into sensationalism about blacks. She continued, "The choice to re-enact 'blacks as objects' should be a state or national African American community decision, not that of a few African Americans" (Bowers, "Slave Auction" A5). She did not describe precisely how to reach the "state or national African American community," but the need to solicit more black voices is clearly a sign of doubt about Christy Coleman and her staff, and implicitly rejects her claims to tell the story of her mother and grandmother.

Other critics attacked Coleman on the grounds of both her authority and the presumption to speak "for" someone else—generally, black mothers and grandmothers, but more specifically auctioned slave women. Oscar McCary of Keen Mountain, Virginia, was not persuaded by Coleman's explanation that the auction was presented to remind the assembled crowd of the lost slave past. He claimed that Coleman had no grounds from which to speak for slave women because she was not a slave woman. This letter, which I reproduce at length, is a valuable example of such contestation within the vernacular realm.

This letter raises the important issues of authority (who can speak for the black community and represent its interests in matters of history and culture) and empathy (the notion that projection of feeling between the self and other can be the basis for understanding another's suffering). This letter represents an extreme critique of the reenactment. Even those who disapproved—before and after the event—objected on the grounds that black history should not be presented in an "entertainment" venue, or that the auction presented slaves in a passive role, or that it reinforced the negative images of blacks as "victims" rather than survivors or fighters, or that it objectified black bodies for pleasure and profit just like any other contemporary entertainment form.

McCary's letter differs greatly from these objections. His letter reflects a mode of vernacular intellectual work (or an engagement with the vernacular modes of thought about slavery) that is critical of any form of reenactment that is based on empathy. As I will discuss later, his criticism is also significantly marked by a gender anxiety surrounding Coleman's authority to reenact the slave past. At this juncture, however, it is important to consider the letter as a vernacular intellectual position. As such, the letter departs from the dichotomy I have recognized—in this project thus far—between popular and academic intellectuals. In the main, academic intellectuals are more likely to privilege discursive and rhetorical approaches to slavery. These scholars use slave narratives, letters, journals, novels, poems, and plays as the only and best way to acquire information about slavery. They believe slavery to be an experience in the historical past that cannot be reproduced—and especially not relived—in any form, in the present. They value the texts of the past, even as they are trained to read them with care, skepticism, and nuance. Vernacular intellectuals tend to stand at a remove from their academically trained counterparts in the ways they use textual resources. An academic slavery scholar usually reads the nuance and context within slave narratives—examining tropes, trends, themes, and conventions as well as metatextual concerns such as the means of producing the narrative or interview (the influence of white editors or, in the case of Works Progress Administration narratives, white interviewers who were descendants of slave owners). Vernacular intellectuals might take the same narrative at its word, seeing it as a sacred text for which scrutiny is yet another attempt to discredit black voices, black history, and black authority. This is not to suggest that vernacular intellectuals are naive or acritical—though some academics might think so, just as popular intellectuals might perceive academics as esoteric and disconnected. Vernacular intellectuals grant more credence and less suspicion to slave narratives, reading them as unmediated bearers of the past.[2] Such thinking is in line with a mode of interpretation of Holocaust testimony that claims the testimony of the most confused survivor is worth more than that of the most esteemed scholar who was not there.

Given that the lines I have sketched between vernacular and academic scholars are permeable and shifting, it should not surprise us to learn that these two groups might hold certain ideas in common. For instance, many academics—literary critics and historians—perceive the past as a completely lapsed moment, irretrievable by any means other than imaginative ventures of representation (fiction, film, poetry) created in the past or in the present moment. W. J. T. Mitchell succinctly puts the matter of slavery in academic discourse this way, "Representation (in memory, in verbal description, in images) not only 'mediates' our knowledge (of slavery and of many other things) but also obstructs, fragments, and negates that knowledge" ("Narrative" 203). Such thinking declares that the past can be *referenced* in the present but not resurrected; texts, discourse, and language are the best means to bring the past forward. In the vernacular, texts of slavery are valued, even to the point of reverence. In this mode of thought, reading slave testimony and narratives, speaking them as embodied performances, is a viable way to bring the past to the present moment. Some vernacular intellectuals, especially those with a strong spiritual component to their impressions of slavery, see themselves as connected to ancestral spirits, as "megaphones" for those distant past voices.

The following letter to the editor represents a vernacular voice that is suspicious of strategic empathy and the notion of ancestral connections between the past and present. The views of Oscar McCary are doubly significant:

first, in their concurrence with the academic scholarly position that representation is a highly mediated venture with little or no connection to the actual or real slave past and, second, for the vigor and venom with which he personally and professionally critiques Coleman, whom he refers to as "Christy"—always in quotes, as a debunking of her authority to represent slavery through living history. The letter, published shortly after the estate-sale reenactment, is as much a critique of Coleman as it is, in McCary's own terms, a crucifixion: "But let's not crucify her for her sickening actions . . . yet." McCary first describes the approval of the event by the *Newport News Daily Press* and "Jack" Gravely (his first name also in quotes once here), who gained national attention for first opposing the auction, then tacitly approving it. In the face of this acclaim, McCary asks on behalf of blacks everywhere, "So who are we to voice a different opinion? We have no right to do such a thing, but we do have the right to ask 'Christy' for a favor before she blesses us with more of her 'this is right for the community' antics again." The tone of sarcasm and anger is unmistakable. Beneath it, however, lies a feeling of resentment and powerlessness. McCary feels that the black community was not adequately represented or even considered by those mainstream media outlets (the *Daily Press*) or the "turncoat" NAACP leader. He speaks as a disenfranchised member of the black community (something for which he criticizes Coleman and Gravely). With feigned humility, McCary (on behalf of the "rest" of the black community) reserves his venom for "Christy," which is apparent in the list of eight "favors" he asks her to perform before putting on another reenactment of slavery:

First, let her be chased, run down like a vicious animal, repeated[ly] raped and dragged to the nearest slave ship. . . .

Let her then be chained, shackled and placed in the recesses of the ship without clothing in the dead of winter. . . .

Let her then be taken ashore and be washed with buckets of cold water by the slave traders. . . .

Let her then be placed on the auction block, unclothed, before hundreds of slave buyers. . . .

Let her then be bought by the White man and taken to the plantation. . . .

Let her then be the Master's mistress and bring forth a man-child each year that will work in the master's cotton fields. . . .

Let her then be witness to vicious beatings and killings of her children by the Master just for his entertainment. . . .

Let her then escape in the dead of night in a quest for freedom while vicious killer hounds give chase. . . .

After laying out these pronouncements and requirements, McCary concludes, "Once you have walked in our ancestors' shoes 'Christy,' then you can re-enact whatever you please in Williamsburg, Virginia concerning slave auctions on the Duke of Gloucester Street" ("Walk in Their Shoes" 2).

McCary's letter represents an ardent examination of the appropriateness and feasibility of historical slavery reenactments. McCary claims that Coleman cannot and should not reenact slavery (or perhaps just this event; it is unclear) because she was not a slave. Only a slave woman can accurately or, more likely, legitimately tell the story of slavery via such an expressive performance. Because of his unrelenting faith in the actual and real experience of slavery, he is unwilling to concede the slave's authority over her story to a descendant. This is a critique of empathy as a strategy for historical knowledge—"Christy" cannot claim to represent slavery because she herself has never been enslaved. His injunction to "[walk] in our ancestors' shoes, 'Christy'" is a sign of advocacy for a radical bodily epistemology. In his view, however, the episteme's governing ethos—"go there to know there"—is not a motivation for empathetic performance or reenactment but instead becomes an impossible challenge. There is no way that "Christy" can accomplish the prerequisites McCary outlines: for instance, she cannot be "repeated[ly] raped and dragged to the nearest slave ship." Because of this lack of experience, Coleman lacks the authority to speak, perform, teach, or reenact moments from the slave past.

It is possible to read this letter only as a complex vernacular analysis of slavery that can be easily aligned with academic thought on this subject. To do so, however, would be to overlook its troubling gender dimension, a significant part of the struggle over who is authorized to reenact slavery. Before moving to these disturbing aspects, I want to pause and consider the ways in which this missive coheres with formal scholarship on trauma and slavery. As I mentioned earlier, academics are largely more comfortable with the nuances of slave experience, reading the absences and silences within, say, slave narratives; scholars are more willing to accept the obliquity of inference. McCary's claim that Coleman cannot possibly reenact a slave auction is more in line with academic studies that claim, in brief, that the past is irretrievable. His words are especially resonant with a mode of Holocaust studies that claims the Holocaust to be a unique historical catastrophe, utterly inaccessible to consciousness and highly resistant to representation.

This spirit—that slavery is a sacred, unique, and unknowable experience—appears to be part of McCary's objection to the Williamsburg slave-auction reenactment. Perhaps lingering behind his letter lies the belief that slave auctions—the most visible signs of slavery's commodification of the black body—exceed the confines of reenactment. Others who disapproved of the event, such as editor Brenda Andrews, for instance, argued that slave history should be "remembered not necessarily retold" (quoted in Waldron, "Staged Slave Auction" 14). A sound bite from the news media covering the event that prompted a flurry of discussion is also relevant here: "Would you reenact a rape?" The implied response: surely not. Rex Ellis broached this propriety question from a different vantage point when he described the emotional toll of slavery reenactments for those who perform them as akin to asking a Jew to interpret at Auschwitz.

Perhaps McCary's claim—premised on his detailed explanation of what slavery was "really" like—that Coleman has no right to reenact slavery is rooted in the idea that only those who lived in slavery can accurately reenact it. McCary's story of slavery, which he renders as the legitimate version of slavery, is one too horrible to be reduced to a single history performed by Coleman and interpreters during the reenactment.[3] He promotes an extreme form of bodily epistemology, not to motivate a more proximate connection to the past but to completely sever any ties one might make by means of reenactment. Those who did not live as slaves (even their descendants) can reference slavery only in and through discourse. This places him on more common ground with literary theorists such as Hortense Spillers, who writes, "I want a discursive 'slavery,' in part, in order to 'explain' what appears to be very rich and recurrent manifestations of neo-enslavement in the very symptoms of discursive production and sociopolitical arrangement that govern our current fictions in the United States" ("Changing the Letter" 33). Among vernacular intellectuals, slavery is unmoored from its eighteenth- and nineteenth-century experiential base and used to describe contemporary conditions in black life. One commentator in the black newspaper the *Washington Informer* approved of the reenactment as "an attempt to shed light on the truth about slavery," calling it a necessary tactic "because slavery still exists in the 'inner city' all across the country—the new plantation with violence and despair—as its products" (Dale, "Telling the Truth" 16).

Despite the considerable merits of McCary's sentiments—which include reserving access to the "real" slave past for those who lived it, articulating a subordinated view within the black community, and energetically opposing what he perceives as a misguided approach to history and pedagogy—there is another less admirable feeling that governs this battle over slave history through reenactment: the battle of the sexes. The same sentiment that characterized the fight between male civil rights leaders (who opposed the event) and Coleman (who created it) is present here, but expressed in a personal, nearly pornographic fashion.

Perhaps McCary is uncomfortable with a black woman at the helm of Colonial Williamsburg's black history department. I suspect that if Rex Ellis or another man had been at the helm of this programming effort, they too would have been targeted by McCary's fury. However, many of McCary's "let her be" fantasies are specific to Coleman and her gender. Just as in Khalfani's jibe at Coleman cast her as a pawn of white male authority, a race traitor who did the bidding of white men, Coleman is again imaginatively subjected by a black man to white male power.

I would like to step back from the debates that characterized the slave-auction reenactment—education versus entertainment, true history as distorted history—to consider the unexplored and more complicated questions of trauma in African American public history and the contemporary memory of slavery. Beneath the concerns of authority (who can tell or depict slavery) and legitimacy (Colonial Williamsburg as a poor steward of black history) lies the anxiety generated when slavery is presented at all. Not only was the controversy fueled by disagreements over accurate or inaccurate history, but the debates also centered on the auction's representation of a single painfully isolated moment. The reenactment was not troubling because it was *bad* history; it rankled and disturbed because it was *incomplete* history. One man objected to the auction reenactment but praised the TV miniseries *Roots* because "we knew it was going to end on a positive note, showing their accomplishments in the face of all the things they had to confront" (Phillip, "To Reenact" n.p.). The slave-auction reenactment was a representation of a single moment from the traumatic past unmoored from the comforting resolution offered by a narrative of progress.[4]

The slave-auction reenactment, then, in its emphasis on a historical event that was both extreme (in its crystallization of the objectification and commodification of the black body) and quotidian (auctions were common, though slave sales or transactions were frequently accomplished through other means, such as inheritance, gifts, or repossession) brought forward a form of reaction formation within the black public sphere. My use of "reaction formation" is not intended to diminish the agency of the protesters or supporters of the event, by labeling their clearly articulated and thoughtful positions as merely symptoms of an agitated psychoemotional state. Instead, positions for or against the estate sale have the added component of operating as a site in which to register—on a group and cultural level—the efforts to come to terms with (or at least begin to approach) an appreciation of slavery as an event with "literal meaning and consequence." In short, the responses from within the black public sphere, from academic and vernacular intellectuals, are part of the crucial, yet difficult, work of making the traumatic real past speak. By serving as a site of memory, this reenactment prompted a bitter yet therapeutic conversation about slavery and revealed the need to go beyond the mantle of shame or its parallel preference for black heroes and heritage over difficult and ambivalent histories.

The concept of shame was frequently mentioned in conversations about the sale. A commentator from one black newspaper explained, "We think slavery was our fault. We are ashamed of having been slaves, while at the same time, we revere our ancestors for their wisdom and endurance. . . . We don't see ourselves in the light of courage and spiritual triumph. We survived the boat ride to become slaves. What is that to be proud of?" (Dale, "Telling the Truth" n.p). Erran Owens, who reenacted Daniel during the event, said that the protest gave the appearance of "being ashamed," instead of "being proud of the triumphs of African Americans" (Phillip, "To Reenact" n.p.). A black woman who took her young daughter to see the reenactment said, "I wanted her to see it so she would know what really happened and that there's nothing to be ashamed of" (Waldron, "Staged Slave Auction" 15). Several historians noted the general sense of shame some African Americans feel about slavery. Lewis Suggs said that blacks want to avoid mention of slavery because "people, some African Americans included, are ashamed. They just want to put it behind them and move on." John Hope Franklin, when asked his opinion on the reenactment, said that slavery must be discussed and remembered, weighing in on the shame factor: "[White people] did more to themselves. They barbarized themselves. Black people should not be ashamed of slavery, and I certainly have nothing to be ashamed of." Darlene Clark Hine offered a way around the quagmire of shame when she said, "Some people feel stigmatized and ashamed about what happened, but they had nothing to do with it. No one living is responsible for the past. Our responsibility is to know the past with all its pain and glory. We must know the past, unvarnished and exhilarating as it were" (Phillip, "To Reenact" n.p.).

The controversial slave-auction reenactment used the method of bodily epistemology to teach and introduce to its assembled audience something about slavery that they would not get from books alone. This method is a cornerstone for living history but is troubling for slavery—an institution based on commodification, performance, and display. This historical reenactment was a dual site of memory and meaning making about slavery, a *lieu de memoire* that permitted a glimpse into a real experience through a fictionalized lens. It is hard to say whether the program was a "success," but most hailed it as a triumph of living history, especially when Jack Gravely expressed his feelings immediately following the program, saying, "Pain had a face. Indignity had a body. Suffering had tears" ("Tears and Protest" A16). Success might also be measured in the ways in which the reenactment prompted a national discussion of slavery, became a touchstone for the difficulties of living history and slavery, and suggested many views on the efficacy of a bodily epistemology of slavery.

5. Ritual Reenactments

Re-enacting the role of a slave or [a free] woman allows me to
pay homage to my African ancestors who were enslaved. People
often ask, "Why the role of a slave?" And my response is easy:
"My ancestors were slaves." Is there any reason why I should feel
ashamed of my heritage?
　　—Donna Woodley, volunteer reenactor, "Civil War Encampment,"
　　　　press release for Strawbery Banke Museum, June 14, 1998

The slave-auction controversy discussed in the previous chapter represents
only one facet of slavery reenactment, which is a prevalent and diverse activity that blends elements of performance with the reverence of commemoration. Despite the reticence or aversion to frank public conversation about
America's slave past, multiple forms of reenactments persist to promote a
variety of visions of American slavery. In the course of this project, I have
identified several modes of slavery reenactment: ritual, historical, and participatory. Ritual reenactments are usually performed in church or for larger
spiritual purpose. In 1995, St. Paul Community Baptist Church (SPCBC) in
Brooklyn, New York, started the *The Maafa Suite,* which now has offshoots
throughout the United States, St. Croix, and Puerto Rico. African Holocaust
Day in Chicago and another form of *Maafa* commemoration at Harambee
United Church of Christ in Pennsylvania are but two examples of ritual
remembrance. Historical reenactments range from quotidian (daily-life activities in Colonial Williamsburg's programming and Monticello's Plantation
Community Weekends) to imperiled slave life presented in scenes of auction (Colonial Williamsburg's 1994 program) or in moments of escape (the
"Jerry Rescue" reenactment in Syracuse, New York, or the "Peter" story line
in Dunmore's Proclamation Weekend at Colonial Williamsburg). There are
also participatory reenactments where individuals or groups might either
volunteer or, by their presence at a particular site, become incorporated into
a reenactment. Conner Prairie, a living-history museum in Indiana, features
a popular "Follow the North Star" program, whereas Motherland Connex-

ions, a black-owned touring company in upstate New York, incorporated immersion experiences in their heritage tours. Similarly, but for younger audiences, YMCA Camp Campbell Gard in Ohio and YMCA Camp Cosby in Alabama offer middle school students an "Underground Railroad Living History" program. Afrocentric scholar Tony Browder travels around the United States with his "The Middle Passage Experience" that blindfolds its participants for a "mental journey from the African homeland, though captivity and enslavement, to present-day struggles." The National Geographic Web site hosts a virtual participatory reenactment where visitors, given the role of a slave—"*You are a slave.* Your body, your time, your very breath belong to a farmer in 1850s Maryland"—can decide at different moments whether to accompany Harriet Tubman from Maryland to Canada.

These three reenactment categories—ritual, historical, and participatory—suggest the endurance of the slave past in the popular imagination. At the same time, these activities—despite their varied goals—are all characterized by an impulse to engage the limits of discursive representation of slavery as it appears in the academy. By this I mean that each activity, performance, or program tacitly acknowledges the printed word through which narratives and histories of the slave past reach our contemporary moment. Tour guides at Colonial Williamsburg's Dunmore's Proclamation Weekend, for example, contextualize the living-history program of performed slave characters (who speak in the first person) with the documentation and historical research on which the slave character is based. St. Paul's *Maafa Suite*'s interpretive literature (program guide and souvenir newspaper) refer to several slave narratives and a few histories from which they draft their unique liturgical practices.

Popular intellectuals are aware of the discursive priorities of academe and high culture. However, they elect not to privilege that discourse in their slavery performances. Though they recognize that their gestures are indeed performances (rather than manifestations of the actual slave past), their work is less inclined to emphasize its representational aspect. Their authority to speak, reenact, imply, or suggest the slave past is linked to the same textual and narrative sources that academic intellectuals turn to in their work. A crucial difference, and one that marks the popular as a singular form of intellectual activity, is the vernacular's willingness to suspend dependence on discourse and affix belief instead to spiritual, emotional, personal, community, and even the broadest racial group concerns. In this way, the popular or vernacular sphere of intellectual activity around slavery explores a unique possibility of and for performance that might be paraphrased, to borrow from Shakespeare, as "the play's the thing": that through their gestures (acting as a slave, re-creating a moment from the slave past), they might create a proximate space to encounter slavery, a location that is both referential and reverential.

It is easy for both academics and popular thinkers to critique this mode as naive, dangerous, or deluded. Why reenact American slavery in the late twentieth and early twenty-first centuries, especially given the volatile racial climate, the increasing disparity between blacks and whites in many avenues of American life, when our world is more multiracial than the black-white dichotomy suggests? A teenager, during a question-and-answer session following a reenactment, put the matter more bluntly, asking a Colonial Williamsburg reenactor, "Are you retarded?" To the reenactor's puzzled look, the boy continued, "You must be . . . to dress up as a slave every day." I do not know how the interpreter responded to that rather hostile question. The scenario itself, however, stresses the tensions that circulate around these performances and the emotional or spiritual grounds they seek to establish themselves. How much does a performance depend on its audience and how much on the performance itself? To whom is the greater debt or responsibility owed? Although all audiences may not be as resistant as this antagonistic (or possibly embarrassed) teenager on an educational field trip, viewers may be less willing to discard their skepticism than a reenactor would like. Do performers or contextualists aim to shape their work to a contemporary audience? How do they imagine their work: is it a job or a calling? In what follows, I will examine two of the three forms of reenactment outlined earlier: ritual and historical (reserving my comments on participatory reenactments for the concluding remarks). These activities share the impulse to generate—through their own performed reembodiment—a more proximate connection between the slave past and contemporary freedom. St. Paul's ritual is in part a form of liturgical therapy that aims for individual and community healing. The historical daily-life reenactments at Colonial Williamsburg aim to teach about eighteenth-century slave life. Though they are both addressed to the popular rather than an academic sphere, their efforts to reembody American slavery are as varied as their motives.

Ritual Reenactments; or, "Do This in Remembrance of Me"

As recorded in the Gospel according to Luke, chapter 22, verse 19, "Do this in remembrance of Me" is Christ's charge to his disciples to perform a specific ritual—Holy Communion or Eucharist—for religious or spiritual memory. This Christian responsibility haunts, structures, and informs the ritual forms of slavery reenactment. Such a connection is not surprising. There have long been literary representations that link Christ's Crucifixion and black suffering; in the nineteenth century Stowe offered Uncle Tom, whereas Margaret Fuller imagined how surprised America's Christians might be if Christ returned as a black man. In the twentieth century, a host of black literature—especially poetry—links the lynched body and the crucified Christ. On a less fatal note, John Henrik Clarke penned a short story, "The Boy Who Painted Christ Black." There is a general movement among black clergy to create and promote black images of Christ and other biblical figures.[1] The Pan African Orthodox Church, which operates several Shrine of the Black Madonna Bookstore and Cultural Centers, is but one example of the elision of Christ's image and the African diaspora. The group has produced an interactive book based on the Black Holocaust Exhibit in Atlanta, the shrine's collection of slavery artifacts. Edited by Velma Maia Thomas, the book—in what some might consider a curious blend of two religious traditions—is titled *Lest We Forget*. The title serves two purposes. One is to adopt the "never forget" stance that Jewish survivors, descendants, and Jewish people more generally have regarding the Holocaust. The second interpretation is more apparent and equally relevant, I argue, to the museum's predominantly Christian African American audience. The book's title is a clear reference to the popular Christian hymn "Lead Me to Calvary."[2] The choice to title a book about the Middle Passage, slavery, and emancipation with the same phrase as a hymn of Christ's suffering—and the duty of Christians to remember it—is part of a larger black popular trend to sacralize (to make sacred) black suffering. Such a gesture is remarkable, if only for its oppositionality. This move counters and aims to partially redress what Saidiya Hartman has described as the profound indifference to black suffering in the nineteenth century. Although one might expect such a move from an Afrocentric church dedicated to black empowerment, another black church—this one with a more traditionally Baptist format—has paved the way for ritual reenactments of slavery.

In 1995, Brooklyn, New York's St. Paul's Community Baptist Church launched its production of *The Maafa Suite . . . a Healing Journey* as a two-night presentation of slave narratives, songs, and dance.[3] Conceived as an alternative to black history as usual, *The Maafa Suite* has grown to a twice-yearly event that includes lectures, tours, and seminars over a two-week period. The performance has traveled throughout the United States and made its international debut in St. Croix in 2005. I pay special attention to the ritual reenactment at the SPCBC because of its long tenure, broad array of events, active publicity, and self-reflective documentation. As the program's executive coordinator, Monica F. Walker, claims, "No one has ever endeavored to do what we have done. We are the vanguard, the flagship. Anyone can produce a show. Black people all over the world are extremely gifted and talented. But ours is sacred psychodrama. *The Maafa Suite* is intended to provide the audience with a spiritually reflective opportunity to revisit this experience. We attempt to personify the experience of our ancestors" (Youngblood, *St. Paul* 5). Other churches and groups commemorate slavery though embodied performance; for instance, a tour of Ghana's slave castles recently incorporated a slave-raid reenactment as part of its Emancipation Day celebration ("Slave Raid" n.p.). But the example of the SPCBC is instructive in its incorporation of Christianity, particularly Christ's suffering, with the Middle Passage and slavery.

As part of his broader mission, the church's senior pastor, Johnny Ray Youngblood, aligns Christ with black ancestral suffering. This strategy is successful in part because the performance itself draws on the black congregation's expectations for a worship service. As one reviewer observed, call and response is a prominent feature: "Those in the audience most familiar and comfortable with the conventions of the African American church connect easily with it, freely calling out their approval, encouragement, and amens" (Truzzi, "Middle Passage Pageant" n.p.). On the initial level of perception, the audience responds to the *Suite* much like a traditional black church congregation would to a rousing sermon. The call-and-response modality is significant insofar as it reflects a deep connection and resonance with the moments of the slave past reenacted throughout the performance. That this same emotional energy, which is usually reserved for the sacred Word, has now been extended to encompass performed scenes of slavery is a crucial development in sacralizing the slave past.

The link between Christianity and slavery remembrance also depends on bridging two categories of experience: religious worship and personal racial history. In this way, the *Suite* aims to adapt its black congregation's already held faith in Christ and attach that belief to their own historical past. In his pastoral letter about the *Suite,* Youngblood explains:

> The Commemoration of the MAAFA is to be born again. Through these ten years, a few have facetiously inquired, "What does MAAFA have to do with Jesus?" I respond to this now to enlighten: Jesus is acquainted with tragedy, suffering and catastrophe, a holocaust. What else was Calvary? Luke 4:18 says that Jesus worked with people and through people who were under the stress and strain of oppression every day. Jesus was the product of a tradition and culture that gladly announced that their God wanted them to remember, and so Jesus passes the baton of remembrance on to us. (*St. Paul* 11)[4]

This unapologetic stance, based on a firm parallel between black suffering and Christ's, plays out in the nearly four-hour *Maafa Suite* production.

The predawn bus ride from the hotel to the sanctuary contextualized the program's energy and heightened my anticipation for the 6:00 AM performance. There was a student group from a Quaker college in North Carolina and a mother and daughter from Flint, Michigan, who have attended the performance and seminars for the past seven years. When the daughter learned that this was to be my first *Maafa Suite,* she said, "Well, you're in for a real treat." I was unsure how to take this—how could a slavery commemoration be considered a "treat"? What pleasures were possible in this scenario? Might there be joy in revisiting a brutal past?

After standing in a surprisingly long line for a 6:00 AM church service, our group was led to a large table with a large container of water-filled small cups. A church worker gave us a sheet of paper with the header "Libation: An Offering to the Ancestors" with four instructions on the African tradition. The libation ritual might be intended to serve as the first step to what Alison Landsberg calls "radical empathy," forging an impossible connection across space and time. The West African ritual also extends a possibility of proximity between the past and present. The claims of Afrocentric scholar Dona Marimba Ani—whose work introduced the term *Maafa* in 1981—are an effective way to approach the use of ritual in St. Paul's commemoration activities: "When we perform rituals as our ancestors did, we become our ancestors, and so transcend the boundaries of ordinary space and time, and the limitations of separation that they impose. When we call the spirits and they enter our bodies, we symbolize in our being the joining of, and therefore communication between, two spheres of the universe; 'heaven' and the 'earth'" (Richards, *Let the Circle* 9).

After filling a cup with water said to be "from the Atlantic Ocean, which became the graveyard for millions of our African ancestors," the participant is directed to do the following final tasks: "3. Say 'pour libation in the memory of _____' (Add the name of the honored person here.) 4. If your [*sic*] desire, pour libation in memory of those ancestors who experienced the slave ship horror" ("Libation" pt. 1). The balance between direction and choice is a telling indicator of this form of popular response to the slave past. A long line of people, looking eventually to find seats they purchased for the performance, is cued to enter the sanctuary. Given the impulse that many would have to simply be seated after a lengthy wait in line, one might think that some would skip this portion of the event. But the libation is an optional gesture that nearly everyone does. And in choosing to participate, steps 3 and 4 of the instructions tacitly link the celebrant's own departed "honored person" to unknown or anonymous ancestors on the Middle Passage. The Atlantic Ocean water used for the ceremony, the directive reminds us, represents more than a beachside diversion. It is a grave, a constant, persistent reminder of lost generations. *The Maafa Suite*, then, offers its audience an immediate, if moderate, participatory function: this is not just a play or church performance. By pouring libation, audience members invoke their personal history and connect it to their larger racial history.

The brutality of the captive racial history of the Middle Passage is vividly represented just after observing the African remembrance ritual. The entrance to the main sanctuary seating is flanked by two wooden structures that look like broad shelves, measuring approximately five feet tall and nine feet long. Black men and women reach out and call to those passing by to get to the main seating area. They are dressed in brown tattered fabric, and chains rattle as they call out in what is presumably an African language. The audience trails through the gauntlet of captives who reach out to the spectators, appeal in a non-English language, or wail loudly. The long line of audience members filters through, walking slowly ahead toward the opening space, where an usher will lead them to available seats. The illusion of containment is doubled: captives on the shelves and audience members flanked by the captives. The audience is silent, briefly stunned by the visual and verbal spectacle.

One reviewer of the *Suite*'s Seattle performance described the effect this way: "From the moment the musky earth covering the lobby floor first assaults your nose, it's clear the *Maafa Suite* won't be a conventional experience. African slaves lie chained to the railings and wail as you descend the ramp. Before white patrons, they cower. To those of their own race, they reach and cry in an African tongue. Some patrons will stop and give water, stroke them in comfort. But the most common reaction, regardless of color, is a brisk trot" (Truzzi, "Middle Passage Pageant" n.p.). In a review of a performance at St. Paul's, a reviewer from a New York City black newspaper, the *New York Beacon,* set the scene for her readers: "As we come into the dimmed sanctuary of St. Paul for the performance, we enter between two cage-like structures that suggest a slave ship hull, with moaning, crying and sometimes screaming Africans inside. We are already being prepared for what is ahead as we walk down the isles [*sic*] to our seats" (Lamb, "The MAAFA Suite" 31).

Both assessments reveal an interesting effect in the reviewers' unconscious, or at least in his and her theater reviews. Both claim to have seen African slaves as opposed to the more accurate "actors portraying African slaves." Is there a difference between the phrase *African slaves* with the inclusion of the qualifier *actors portraying*? What could it mean that these writers recognized the captives as Africans even before the play began? I suggest that this elision is in part an articulation of the intended aim of the vernacular theory of trauma that *The Maafa Suite* proposes. Part of the performance's goal is not only to resurrect the specter or ghostly image of captivity (though it does this too) but also to generate an emotional response in the spectator. In Seattle, the actors cower before white spectators and reach out for black ones. In Brooklyn, the actors represent an advanced warning, preparing this black audience "for what is ahead." These actions place audience members (who are simply trying to get to their seats) in a direct position of confrontation with an embodiment of the slave past. The depiction, in an unapologetically realist mode, is designed to generate some sort of emotional, intellectual, or physical response—pity, fear, anxiety, repulsion, incredulity (either at the spectacle itself or at the audacity of its depiction).

If this captivity reenactment was needed to set the tone for a more traditional theatrical presentation in Seattle, why use this framing technique for the more expanded church presentation? Is this a sensational rendering of an unrepeatable and unique experience? Why place this spectacle between the reverential libation and the ritualized drama that follows? The captivity reenactment is a crucial part of the vernacular intellectual theorizations of slavery and its aftermath. Though there have been captivity reenactments in wax (Baltimore's National Great Blacks in Wax Museum), statuary (Detroit's Charles H. Wright Museum of African American History), audio (the recorded wails and cries that play during the slave ship re-creations in a Hull, England, museum), and performance (slave auction in Colonial Williamsburg), St. Paul's use of an *interactive* ritual reenactment to reproduce its vision of the image and feeling of the Middle Passage is a bold stroke that has striking effects. It is a vivid inauguration into *The Maafa Suite* and its ambitious goal of cultivating memory. The emphasis on suffering might appear to stress the sensational elements over the more mundane, but equally brutal, quotidian forms of bondage. I believe, however, that the shrieks, cries, and reaches of the actors set the context and tone for the performance. The jolt of unreality, the break of expectations of the traditional church service, indeed of what usually occurs in church, is designed to unsettle and perhaps uproot one's comforting beliefs and presumed knowledge. Actors who have participated in the outbursts of emotions performed represent a key part of such drama: catharsis. Youngblood conspicuously casts the commemoration as more than theater, but as "a safe harbor for the constructive ventilation of anxiety, stress, quiet, hatred and anger." In some cases, the actors forge personal connections to their visions of the past. One actor, Fay Kevelier Fletcher, links the captivity scene to her own diagnosis of incurable rheumatoid arthritis, saying, "Arthritis is the pain my people felt in their joints as they were placed in those inhumane conditions cramped up, their limbs screaming to stretch" (Youngblood, *St. Paul* 25). Though this reflection might be seen as an example of the danger of overidentification, a form that reduces a broad experience (Middle Passage captivity) to personal pain (arthritis), the *Suite* might well cast itself as providing the opposite view: the ritual drama allows this actor the space to read through her own body to connect to a person unknown to her. Her reembodiment of slavery fostered an imagined yet real (in terms of significance) bond with the past.

Another cast member, Keir L. Nelson, de-emphasized her personal connection in favor of a larger service to black people: "Our purpose is spiritually, mental and educational for our people. It is not about me! I derived an acronym for MAAFA—My African Ancestors Finally Acknowledged. We have been out of the loop on our history for so long. We bring clear vision to the nation letting our oppressors know we have not forgotten!" Kendra A. Harris echoes this sentiment, saying that through her performances of the *Suite,* she gained "knowledge of what my ancestors went through [from the] different scenes I participated in. The majority of people need to know the story of the MAAFA because they need to see the visual. They need to hear the screams, the crying, the whole experience" (ibid.). Like Nelson, Harris's "learning experience" comes from her bodily performance. A thirteen-year-old performer in an Oakland, California, performance identified the heightened perception of the slave past that she gained: "It's not like what you read in school. . . . We get to actually show what it's about and actually live it" ("Play about Maafa" n.p.). In a theatrical version of bodily epistemology, this girl, like Fletcher and Harris, considers her performance in *The Maafa Suite* a way to refer to the traumatic slave past in the present day. Their own experience of imagined proximity to lost slave ancestors can, they imply, be passed on to audience members who still suffer from historical amnesia. They too can be converted or awakened by the ritual drama.

Other cast members take a position that acknowledges more complexity than a one-on-one connection to the past. Walter Majette describes the *Suite* as a "great learning experience. It has led me to look into a period of time in which I did not exist, learn about and explore places I've never been, imagine languages I never heard or spoke, visit ancestors I've never met before, experience emotions that were not mine, free myself of myself that I might be a vessel for God and his works" (ibid.). Nelson and Majette imagine themselves as constructing history, as active creators in the process of making meaning about slavery. This is an important move that wrests control of black history and intellectual work on the slave past from formal academic institutions or others outside the community. Majette stresses the imagined quality of his experience, implying that just because his work on the *Suite* required a projected or imagined self does not mean that his experience was disingenuous.

I divert attention to these actor responses in order to return with more force to the staged captivity reenactment. This prolonged scene is emotionally challenging to perform and difficult to observe. The point seems to be to instill shock, awe, reverence. Like most theatricals, it is a manipulation placed there, designed and choreographed to express a need and evoke a response. It is intentional. The striking effect of the scene brings to mind art scholar Marcus Wood's response to the sound track of wailing voices that accompanied the slave-ship re-creation during his visit to the Wilberforce House museum in Hull, England. After identifying the recorded voices as those of museum staff members, Wood asks, "What were they thinking when they made it, and should they have made it? Are they claiming that the sounds they made are a recreation of, or equivalent to, the suffering of Africans shipped as slaves during the 'middle passage'? How do we get close to the memory of slavery?" (Wood, *Blind Memory* 295). The reports from the actors mentioned above suggest that their reenactment of the Middle Passage *is* a way to "get close" to the slave past. They perceive themselves as paying tribute, recounting a tale America sought to erase or ignore, providing a necessary empowerment service to black America. The appropriateness of the depiction—"should they have made it?"—can be gauged by the range of responses to the reenactment: skeptic to convert.

On the skeptical end would be a woman seated near me during the opening. Perhaps because of the large crowd, the performance started late. During the approximately forty-five-minute wait to filter the audience through the captives into their seats, the noise from the simulated slave-ship hold continued unabated. The recorded sound track of splashing water and crashing waves was the backdrop for the usual conversations before a church service—children were chided, prodded to wakefulness; adults discussed who had arrived and who was on their way, trying to save seats in the increasingly crowded sanctuary. Through it all, the captive actors in the simulated ship's hold kept up a steady stream of shrieks, prayers, pleas, cries. A woman behind me said, "Those people back there are doing their job well." I was struck by this comment: a metatextual observation that was apt, evocative, and troubling. Though I did not turn to ask her to elaborate (I was not being directly addressed), the statement, even in its abbreviated or offhand style, is remarkable. Was this a defense mechanism? Does it represent a way to talk back to the program's desire to instill (however dramatically or with good intentions) a form of coercive memory? What does it mean to describe the performed spectacle of captivity as a "job"? The dissonance of the statement and the break it introduced into what organizers presented as a seamless moment (which was somehow unaffected by the audience's constant chatter) are an important part of the process of *The Maafa Suite*. Most literature about the *Suite*—like its program guide and souvenir bulletin, as well as external media coverage in the black and mainstream press—privileges the *Suite*'s sacred elements and naturalizes the ways in which the program memorializes slavery by providing a space to revere the ancestors, acknowledge the past, and confront grief about historical trauma. It is important to consider *The Maafa Suite* as a process and an event. As a process, individuals exhibit and retain control over their permeability, how much the representation is permitted to enter their consciousness. As part of a way to mediate this spectacle, this woman clearly identified the captives as performers and, in so doing, denaturalized and resisted the *Suite*'s implied goal of forcing the audience to witness scenes from the traumatic past. However, just because the event is a performed, artificial re-creation—and surely none but the smallest children or most deluded adults believed that those were actual African captives—does not mean that an emotional effect and release cannot be accomplished. The hybrid genre of the piece allows it to be appreciated on multiple levels—organizers and cast members refer to it as "sacred theater," a play, a ritual, psychodrama, and "psychosocial dramatic reenactment." And although the organizers stress the importance of community building, there is always a healthy dose of dissent or skepticism in any community. The sense I got from the overheard "doing their job well" claim—a compliment, however backhanded—was not so much jarring as slightly rustling the suspension of disbelief that the *Suite* depends on for its persuasive power. If, as I have suggested earlier, the *Suite* is borrowing from extant Christian beliefs and concomitant ritual performance of black church tradition and etiquette, then such statements go against its intended goals. In short, we all know *The Maafa Suite* is a performance, a construction (after all, the audience has paid a pretty fair price and stood in a long line, two conventions of entertainment acquisition), but it is not necessary to stress this obvious yet sublimated point. In creating itself since 1995, the Commemoration of the *Maafa* (of which *The Maafa Suite* is a central but not the only part) has become a growing, viable site for witnessing, addressing, and vernacular intellectualizing about the events and legacy of the Middle Passage and slavery. It has grown from a small event into a larger community effort in which more than three hundred volunteers coordinate "visits to the African Burial Ground, workshops, lectures on history, culture, organizing and leading undoing racism rituals, firewalks, and sea side ceremonies." Perhaps because of the fervent and sometimes messianic thrust that drives the project's development and promotion, a claim from the *Suite*'s executive coordinator can be extended to contextualize the dissonance created by the previous comment on the captives' job performance. Remarking on the unity and other collective elements of the commemoration, Monica Walker says,

"It's blasphemous to dissect the Maafa. All of these components join together to form a complete body of experiences. Whether at home or abroad, the Commemoration compels people to build community, the very thing that was stolen from us" (Youngblood, *St. Paul* 8). The word that stands out at the start of this claim brings the issue of faith or belief (suspended or not) to the fore: *blasphemous*. This serious charge—implying irreverence, profanity, or mockery of or in the face of the sacred or divine—seems launched here for an unspecified reason. Does *dissect* here mean simple questioning of the commemoration or a more probing analysis of its procedures and motives? Is this to caution viewers against tearing the play apart or celebrating one aspect (say, the fire walk or the museum tour) over another? Or could this be an unconscious expression of (or foray into) the notion that the original irretrievable experiences of the Middle Passage and slavery are not to be interpreted after such a long time has elapsed? The seriousness with which commemoration coordinators take their work leads one to elicit a resounding "no" to this last question. In using the primarily religious term to establish a boundary of propriety, the coordinator is seeking to protect *The Maafa Suite* from certain (unspecified) forms of scrutiny. Yet the label of blasphemy is one that must also be taken seriously. Although such a seemingly reflexive and self-protective gesture seems suspicious, it leads me to probe further into the constructed state of the commemoration in general and the *Maafa Suite* performance. On the one hand, the "blasphemy" mantle defends the *Suite* against criticism. On the other, the label also insulates and reifies the commemoration of *The Maafa Suite* as a black-based, community-generated, sacred ritual observance. In effect, this program demonstrates clearly and unapologetically its status as a vernacular intellectual site—one that aims to cultivate or prod memory, by force, if necessary, urging its parishioners to gaze upon their reenactment of the slave past. In this and other ways, the *Suite*'s hybrid status tacitly, if unwittingly, encourages and invokes a range of responses: from deep emotional investment to "Are we there yet?" apathy. It is easy to imagine how the executive coordinator might respond to the remark about the actors doing a good job as captives: the woman would be seen as a skeptic or, worse, a heretic. Yet the play's wide-ranging generic conventions—despite its privileging of the ritual and the sacred—leave it vulnerable to and can easily support multiple readings.

This leads me to a consideration of its many genres. What precisely is *The Maafa Suite,* and, by extension, what is the commemoration of which it is a feature? Why do the promotional literature and souvenir bulletin mark the phrases "The Maafa Suite . . . a Healing Journey," "The Way Out Is Back Through," and "Commemoration of the Maafa" by the superscripted letters

"TM"? What are they trademarking and why? Is it not antithetical or counter-intuitive to trademark a celebration or remembrance ritual about the Middle Passage and slavery given the status of captives as cargo and commodities?

This move to establish a proprietary claim to these phrases is another secular version of the "It's blasphemous to dissect the Maafa" claim discussed earlier. By putting a trademark on the key slogans of the program, the church leaders have put those who would adopt their formulas (and many have drawn from the SPCBC's work, reproducing versions in Seattle, Oakland, Puerto Rico, and St. Croix, to name only four) on notice: this is "ours." Such an investment in their work as intellectual property *does* have the adverse effect of suggesting a fetishization of the slave past as an object. However, it more positively offers this program as an intellectual intervention in both larger debates and broad-based apathy and amnesia about slavery. It is a curious genre, an amalgam of different forms rooted not in mainstream academic discourse but in the work of scholars outside the academy. In what follows, I will consider the Afrocentric roots of *The Maafa Suite* and its evolution into psychodrama and ritual.

The Maafa Suite is a deliberately constructed event with a hybridized essence. Senior pastor Youngblood's letter commemorating the tenth anniversary characterizes it as "sermonic theater. It is psychodrama for the healing of the oppressed and oppressors alike. IT IS THE TRUTH! And Jesus said, 'ye shall know it and the truth shall make you free'" (*St. Paul* 11). *The Maafa Suite* in its full, nearly four-hour form reflects its hybrid state. What sources support this vernacular intellectual site, and what interpretive strategies best illuminate it? The performance and its broader commemoration are best explained as vernacular intellectual formations that are characterized by their outsider, "institutionally nonaccredited" hybrid state. As such, these formations produce a new popular-based version of trauma theory that differs significantly from what a cultural trauma theorist might call "lay trauma theory." These vernacular sources are rooted in a range of historical and intellectual religious traditions, all of which filter through the conventions of the black church.

I would like to turn now to the three components that significantly shape how *The Maafa Suite* aims to accomplish its work of reenactment, performance, and healing. First, I consider the academic sources and scholars that influence the church's program; these scholarly resources reveal the program's relationship to the traditional academy and its construction of an alternative mode of knowing the slave past. I then take seriously the play's description as psychodrama. I work back to the formal aspects of this psychoanalytic practice to explore the ways in which this mode of therapy corresponds to the popular theorization and intended therapeutic effect of *The*

Maafa Suite. My third step is to explore the play's designation as "sermonic theater." This term, coined by Youngblood exclusively for *The Maafa Suite,* helps explain the play's religious hybridity—its mix of West African religious practices with Christianity—and its privileging of the slave past through the formal practice of liturgy and sacrament. As part of its ritual healing goals, the service meets its description of "sermonic theater" by creating new rituals and putting old (or traditional) rituals alongside them. The program's nine-part opening sequence blends traditional African American gospel with a drum-call invocation of Nommo, libations to lost ancestors with Christ as a "chief ancestor," followed by the Eucharist. The most telling invention is a new ritual called "Processional of the Images," where church elders and cast members carry representations of slave ancestors. *The Maafa Suite* is composed of a multisided approach that frustrates clear generic assignment or expectations. In this way, for its founders, actors, directors, and audience, it is all that it is claimed to be—theater, sermon, ritual, liturgy, dance, music, even "THE TRUTH."

The seriousness with which the program's organizers approach the documentation of their work is most evident in its souvenir newspaper sold for five dollars after the performance. Long used as a fund-raising tool by black sororities, fraternities, churches, and other civic groups, the souvenir booklet (also known as an "ad book") documents the event, profiles the participants, and acknowledges its support from the community. Unlike the usual hand-stapled photocopies of less sophisticated ventures, however, *The Maafa Suite* commemoration document is a large-format (eleven by seventeen inches), tabloid-style, forty-four-page newspaper. It is similar to many other ad books in its full- and half-page endorsements by local businesses (Grace Family Medical Practice), politicians (a full-page ad from Ed Towns of the First Congressional District of New York and a full-page "proclamation" from Brooklyn's borough president, Marty Markowitz, officially recognizing "10th Annual Maafa Commemoration Days in Brooklyn, NY"), churches (such as the well-known Abyssinian Baptist Church in Harlem), and other civic groups (United Way of New York City). The vast majority of the paper, however, recounts the previous nine commemorations and profiles important contributors to the *Suite,* such as its administrators, director, choreographers, deaf ministry interpreters, chorus dancers, and actors. As such, the newspaper is a valuable interpretive tool that documents the program's self-reflective process and growth. It is here that we can get a rare glimpse of the formal aspects of this vernacular intellectual activity, a structural formation of a popular mode of making and performing a theory about the slave past.

Sources of Vernacular Trauma Theory

SPCBC's program began as a small performance that involved dramatic read-ings of slave narratives and gained momentum as its founders and partici-pants read and researched. They went about the task of knowledge acquisition deliberately, yet their pursuit led to avenues different from that of traditional academe. Grant Farred's study of vernacular intellectuals reveals that this circuitous route is normal, since "the vernacular is a mobile and flexible ex-perience, accommodating different trajectories, and is a theoretically supple category: it derives from a keen understanding of and engagement with the popular, but it is neither narrow nor prescriptive in its conception" (Farred, *What's My Name?* 14). Of the many trajectories of intellectual formation within and beyond the academy, SPCBC chose to align itself with the Afro-centric view. This camp might be best described as having a more popular following than an academic one. Though there are Afrocentric African and African American studies programs at accredited U.S. institutions, Temple University's department being a prominent example, many Afrocentric thinkers operate outside such institutions. Scholars such as Frances Cress Welsing, Ivan Van Sertima, or Tony Browder are popular names in certain segments of black popular life. Yet their works are rarely held in academic libraries, nor do they make their way onto many course syllabi. In contrast, highly regarded academic historians (Eugene Genovese and John Hope Franklin) or fiction writers (Ralph Ellison and Toni Morrison) or literary critics (Deborah McDowell and Nellie McKay) are infrequently known in the black popular sphere (Cornel West is an exception). This disconnection between formal and popular spheres of knowledge is apparent in the types of intellectual work chosen for the *Suite*'s scholarly grounding. The organizers claim that the term *Maafa* is attributed to "Dr. Marimba (African-American scholar and author) and has been adopted in contemporary scholarship to define the middle passage" (*St. Paul Community Baptist Church*, program 28). This citation accurately, if incompletely, cites Dona Marimba Richards (later known as Marimba Ani) as the first to use the word *Maafa* to describe the Middle Passage, but is far less accurate about its place in contempo-rary scholarship. A 2005 computer search of academic journals, databases, monographs, reviews, and other critical studies revealed only one instance of the term *Maafa* in all the decades since records were kept. Though this cursory glance is not in-depth research, the MLA, JSTOR, and Project Muse databases are nothing if not good indicators of "contemporary scholarship." So, if *Maafa* is not mentioned there, then is SPCBC's claim of its prevalent usage in contemporary scholarship false? The answer to this question can be found in the forms of intellectual sources valued and deployed by *The Maafa Suite*. In a section of the souvenir newspaper titled "The Mission," executive coordinator Monica C. Dennis describes the evolution of the *Suite*. Before the first commemoration in 1995, "many renowned scholars and historians educated and enlightened the congregation. These included Dr. Ivan Van Sertima, Dr. Frances Cress Welsing, Dr. Naim Akbar, Dr. Patricia Newton, Eugene Redd and Clemson Brown" (Youngblood, *St. Paul* 5). The history section of the document describes "years of presentations and lectures brought to the church and community" by scholars such as

> Dr. M. Ani, Erriel Roberson, Dr. Leonard Jeffries, Dr. Na'im Akbar, Attorney Alton Maddox, Dr. Ivan Van Sertima, Dr. Edwin Nichols, Dr. Joy DeGruy-Leary, Dr. Cornel West, Rev. Dr. James Forbes, Randall Robinson, Jane Elliot, Noel Ignatiev, The People's Institute for Survival and Beyond, and a host of others. By way of new knowledge and truths shared in these sessions, coupled with Dr. Youngblood's profound preaching, the congregation was forced to see the historic struggle and survival of people of African ancestry in an unparalleled and empowering light. (11)

Though this intellectual group is diverse, from Roberson to Robinson to Ignatiev, the Afrocentric mode of thought is predominant. These are the scholars for whom *Maafa* supplements or replaces terms such as *middle passage* or *transatlantic slave trade*. For example, Erriel Roberson's 1995 book, *The Maafa and Beyond: Remembrance, Ancestral Connections, and National Building for the African Global Community,* insists on this term (or an alternative he coined, *Great Suffering*) because the names commonly used are "inadequate for the remembrance and memorialization of our great tragedy" (5). He goes on to explain that there is a moral imperative to change the term: "It is blasphemous to regard human suffering and death as selling commodities or doing business. Perhaps this was the degrading attitude of slavers, and even some of those who write on the subject today, but we must REFUSE to cast it in such a callous and disrespectful light. [The term *Atlantic slave trade* denies] the horrific and uniquely significant event that it was. It would be akin to calling the Jewish Holocaust something as crass and inappropriate as 'the Great European Cleansing Project'" (5–6).

Roberson's work bears the essential hallmarks of the vernacular intellectual. As Grant Farred explains, the discourse of popular thinkers is "overburdened by structural lack (historic absence of material resources and access to capital) ... politicized as much by its content, though that may be superimposed, as by the absence of formal political channels of redress of representation" (Farred, *What's My Name?* 17). Also, Roberson's tone—part jeremiad, part self-reflexive—reflects the vernacular that is "counterposed to (and is less valued than) the formal—or 'proper'—speech of the colonizers or the metropolitanized discourse of the dominant society" (18). My point here is not to position formal academe in a hegemonic position, especially given the struggle of black academics to gain a foothold in their ascent up the ivory tower. Much diligence was required to establish African American studies, for instance, or introduce black literary and cultural studies into fields like English, history, and sociology. Even today, academic inquiry dedicated to the African American slave experience continues to be a struggle in many quarters. Rather, my claim is that work like Roberson's is not usually part of the academic enterprise. His work operates outside these formal modes of inquiry, which value an argument's pace, balance, and poise. Therefore, claims typical of Roberson—that is, this passage on the importance of black families knowing about the *Maafa*—would be anathema to many scholars of the African American slave experience. He asks, "Can you just live in peace and try to improve yourself with a murder, a beast in your house? No! As much as you may hate blood and love life you must clear your house of the danger the beasts represents to you and your family. Strong words? Yes." The "beast" of this statement appears to be ignorance, enforced by whites who aim to cloud black clarity about the slave past. In a style slightly reminiscent of Amiri Baraka, Roberson encourages blacks (or African people) to rid themselves of this false consciousness and instead arm themselves with "truth and justice. It is swift and sharper than any two-edged sword. The beast must blink once and find us around his throat, the jugular already cut. Move on African people, move on" (100).

Despite, or perhaps in keeping with, these incendiary claims, Roberson is very clear on his prescriptions for restoring black wellness through renewed historical memory. His program for teaching "the truth" about the *Maafa* is rooted in a need to cure the ailments in black culture as he (and others) sees them. Be it crime, teen pregnancy, delinquency, poverty, or poor intragenerational or intergender relationships, all these can be traced back to the violence and rupture of captivity and slavery. The pathology, if he were to use that term, is not solely of black invention, but is the result of an unclaimed past, a form of historical amnesia. He says, "Having a memory that is whole and complete as an African person means having a complex and critical understanding of the Great Suffering, or Maafa. Just as a person with amnesia is doomed to walk around confused about who he or she is, where they have come from, where they are headed and the nature of their relationships with others, so to is the African who does not know, memorialize and understand the Great Suffering" (26). His work not only is a corrective to the usual or formal knowledge of slavery—which he claims is too impersonal or even tempered to be useful—but also aims to correct black people's self-definition and self-awareness by forging links between current troubling circumstances to a violent slave past.

The corrective element of Roberson's book may help explain the emphasis on the "horror and brutality" in his book and in *The Maafa Suite*'s performance. Roberson's corrective approach depends on rehearsing and recounting the violent bodily expressions of captivity and enslavement. Perhaps to counter such apologetic views of slavery, of plantation fiction, that have pervaded America's perception of slavery, Roberson assigns blacks two important tasks to achieve historical memory and full understanding of present conditions. Both assignments involve the *Maafa*: First, "we must have an uncompromised, unromanticized view of this seminal event in the shaping of our existence," and, second, "we need to get all of it out" (ibid.). For him, healing from the traumatic effects of slavery depends on the physical body of the enslaved. At several moments, Roberson refers to slaves being beaten and physically abused to represent the horror of the *Maafa*. He quotes passages from slave narratives—like Olaudah Equiano—that emphasize the physical costs of tortured bondage. Roberson does not take the risk of indirect interference. Why might Roberson focus on the physical at the exclusion of the more subtle costs of captivity? Is this move purely sensational or, worse, a voyeuristic interest in suffering? In the chapter titled "Our Ancestors Speak," he cites long passages from slave narratives and recollections. His strategy and motivations are clear: he sees these narratives as textual embodiments of the lost yet living past. As such, his responses to them are both predetermined and overdetermined. As Saidiya Hartman wrote of tour guides at Ghana's slave castles, these narratives and later his use of lynching imagery are meant to make black visitors (readers, in this case) cry (see "The Time of Slavery"). Roberson's use of these moments reflects a need to mourn, to force catharsis. The urgency of his mission suggests that he has neither time nor interest in subtlety or nuance. His expectations are visible in his caution to readers: "Even this brief collection of narratives may be painful to read. If it is not, perhaps we are as numb to our suffering as our oppressors are to heeping [*sic*] it upon us. These are our ancestors. Let us place ourselves in their shoes as we deal with our collective pain" (*The Maafa and Beyond* 23). He elides "us" and "them," aiming for an emotional connection that transcends time and space. We are not permitted to simply read these incidents, let alone apply the interpretive criteria that John W. Blassingame made fundamental for any serious inquiry into slave testimony. In this instance, reading is not allowed to be a distinct activity, but an act of empathy, albeit coerced. This strategy of attempting to collapse the chronological and emotional barrier between the slave past and the contemporary scene is crucial to the *Maafa* movement. This drive is not merely a naive oversimplification: it is an ardently held conception that attempts to heal a blighted community using the brutalized scenes from the traumatic past as a corrective. Unlike the authority figures discussed in "To Teach You a Lesson, Boy" these injunctions to remember do not come from above or outside the black community; they exist deeply embedded within what Ellison called "the lower frequencies."

Vernacular theories of trauma, like Roberson's, privilege the physical body as a strategy for knowing the past because of its urgent need to produce and reproduce itself. Again, this vernacular work has, to the minds of academically trained scholars, a distinctly unlettered, even raw, quality. This unrefined feature is part of its appeal to some of its adherents in the black popular sphere, who see this as a sign of passionate, emotional engagement. At the same time that Roberson emphasizes a bodily component of slavery and the need to bridge the emotional gap between today's blacks and their enslaved ancestors, he is also aware of the presence of his book as an intellectual venture that is in a larger scholarly conversation. It is important to consider the relation between Roberson's perception of his book and to link that perception to the program development of SPCBC's *Maafa Suite*.

Roberson claims high stakes for his work on the *Maafa*. Though he refers to Dona Marimba Ani's ritual use of the term, Roberson is aware that his is the first book to introduce, expand, and explicate that term and its consequences to a larger black audience. Roberson claims, "So it is clear that this book has a significance that goes far beyond that of recounting history, but reaches into our psychological processes. It is offered as a healing elixir or salve for African people" (9). His book is intended to heal black suffering by deploying a version of the slave past, using the *Maafa* or Great Suffering, to redeem a black public set adrift in America. This reclaiming is part of *The Maafa Suite* also, as one observer noted: "The Commemoration of the Maafa has been and is the redemptive ticket that has and is redeeming black life and culture from the pawn shops of America such as corporate America, the mis-educational system and systems of political injustice. It is enabling us to use our gifts and talents to restore a richness and vitality to our communities that has long since been gone" (Youngblood, *St. Paul* 17). This optimism, a belief in the transformative properties and cultural work of both *The Maafa Suite* and Roberson's book that largely influenced it, is a characteristic of the faith these vernacular intellectual sites place in the work they produce. Several comments testify to the power of *The Maafa Suite* performance to alter perceptions, even influence future life choices.

Louise Green's response is typical of this view: "Going to the MAAFA Suite is a transforming evening. Don't expect to leave the way you came in" (ibid. 5). The power of a performance to affect and effect (or, more precisely, to effect affect) is also a part of Roberson's vision of his own work: "The word Maafa frames our experience in the language and context that heals, protects and enpowers [*sic*] African people, simply by its utterance. In this respect, if you have picked up this book and only read and understood the title, it can be called a success" (*The Maafa and Beyond* 176). The writer aims for a conversion experience, one that works its persuasive power by both cosmic and magical means but also depends on discursivity to make its point. The book must be read, yet through its course of argument readers are prodded into particular emotional and intellectual responses.

Roberson's work—as a foundation for the ritual reenactment of *The Maafa Suite*—indicates the strengths and limitations of the vernacular form of trauma theorization and resolution. More committed to curing African American historical amnesia than theorizing, the book is an effort to empower, to encourage commemoration, and to heal an ailing community. Though its methods are not those of formally trained scholars and critics, the book nonetheless has influence well beyond its privately printed origins. *The Maafa Suite* has given new life to Roberson's work, validated it, and given it meaning as a script for an embodied remembrance. Roberson imagined a commemoration as follows: "Our memorialization is the erecting of monuments, the building of museums, the celebration of days of remembrance, the development of appropriate curriculum materials covering the Great Suffering, the intensive study of the Great Suffering and our increased consciousness as a people. There can be no doubt that we must elevate the Maafa to its proper position of prominence in world history, so the world's people can come to grips with it and be accountable" (19). *The Maafa Suite* sets and meets this goal, for many of its participants, viewers, and congregants. It has fulfilled its lofty aims. It is a wailing wall, a bench by the road.

The Maafa Suite as Psychodrama

It is important to take seriously the multiple generic classifications *The Maafa Suite* creators and actors give the performance. To do this, it is necessary to examine the many descriptions of the *Suite*: psychodrama, sermonic or sacred theater, ritual, and even its designation as THE TRUTH. What does this confusion of categories reveal about the performance, its goals, or its mission? These multiple strands of interpretation are part of a larger tapestry of remembrance. However, given its context and location within the already sacred space of the church, I claim that *The Maafa Suite* can be best described as a ritual reenactment that accommodates psychodrama, sermon, and sacred principles.

Psychodrama is a form of psychotherapy based in theater and performance, a therapeutic analogue to psychoanalysis. In this mode, patients work with a group and a therapist (director) to act out onstage an inner conflict or traumatic event. Patients, watching group members onstage, externalize their internal struggles and confront, resolve, or at least address them in a direct and embodied way. The founder of the psychodrama movement, J. L. Moreno, aimed to push therapy beyond its traditional dependence on a one-to-one, patient-to-therapist interaction. Perhaps to strengthen the patient's role in the therapeutic process, Moreno evolved a method that required active participation, unlike that of the traditional talking cure.

Why might *The Maafa Suite* be described as psychodrama? What leads Youngblood and others to describe it in this way? Is it simply an intuited understanding of the discipline's name—*psycho* referring to psychological or mental process and *drama* referring to onstage performance? I contend that *The Maafa Suite* indeed engages both the formal and the informal elements of this subcategory of psychoanalysis. As is typical of vernacular intellectual work, *The Maafa Suite*'s creators and participants may not be aware of the formal academic definition or history of psychodrama; nonetheless, their project implements some of its procedures. Moreover, to call *The Maafa Suite* psychodrama is to draw attention to a crucial element of the *Suite*'s goals: its desire to engender therapeutic effects. In an essay published in the mid-1990s, literary scholar Hortense Spillers surmised that the black church could act as a space and place for racial healing and sociocultural mobilization ("'All the Things'"). Though they are unlikely to know of Spillers's essay, SPCBC *Suite* organizers have fulfilled that mandate. As Minister McLaughlin says, "*The Maafa Suite* is therapy and the church is the 'black leather couch.'" Not only is the cogent observation remarkable in its regard for the *Suite*'s potential to impact the daily lives and mental health of black folks, but it also claims a key symbol of psychoanalysis: the couch. Imagined as a luxurious piece of furniture—black leather—the therapeutically significant couch (an object to which many black parishioners might lack access) is offered here as an already present part of the church (a place these parishioners already know). Given the general reluctance among the black popular sphere to engage in psychotherapy—due in part to blacks' suspicion and racial bias toward traditional psychotherapy—to offer the church as a type of treatment considered by many blacks to be a luxury of the upper classes or nonblack groups reveals the ways in which this church offers a performance that does the important therapeutic tasks of healing and resolution.

If the basic method of psychodrama involves actors representing basic conflicts within the mind of one person, how does that get expanded to represent the consciousness of a large assembly? It is here that the church environment plays a key role in unifying the large mass. Similar to the black church call-and-response mode of worship (where the congregation reifies the message and the minister delivering it), the church seals the group, encouraging its members to act or imagine themselves as one voice.[5] On the stage, the assembled black audience is encouraged to see the events unfolding in front of them and around them as scenes from an experience out of their own distinct racial past. The images of traumatic events as depicted on that stage—which is made sacred in part by its location at the heart of the church, the altar—are designed to provoke emotional, largely cathartic, responses.

Two moments in the piece reveal the play's success at producing group psychotherapy in the psychodramatic modality. Taken as a whole, *The Maafa Suite* aims to produce a positive psychological effect, inducing awareness of the lost slave past, grieving that loss, and becoming empowered in the present through the ancestral spirits and Jesus Christ. Two moments of group "solidarity" are worth noting here. The first is the conclusion to the "Into the Ships" and "Capture" performances, choreographed by Jamel Gaines. The lengthy passage begins when slave traders bearing foreign goods enter the African village. Eventually, they negotiate a trade with the chief: weapons for children. The peaceful village scenario descends into chaos as three young girls are dragged away screaming, their mothers in pursuit. Summarily, the scene of joy that opened with ritual baths, dancing, and commerce dissolves into "Into the Ships," a long line of black men and women joined together as they conduct a pushing-pulling type of dance around the sanctuary. The choreographer described his process, which he prepared for by reading Tom Feeling's *Middle Passage* and Velma Maia Thomas's *Lest We Forget,* of creating "a journey from capture to chains, to cargo to auction, to plantation, underscored by our mental enslavement." The audience, Gaines explains, has a crucial role: "The audience, or witnesses, if you will, must be completely devastated and enveloped in the retelling of this legacy. The movement is very literal yet it symbolically captures the audience." For Gaines, the piece is a mode of recognition and healing that "fully acquaints the audience with not only the physical, psychological, emotional and spiritual anguish of our ancestors, but also permits the audience to tap into their own personal anguish. Tapping into that pain frees one of the shame and guilt surrounding enslavement and true healing and empowerment begins" (Youngblood, *St. Paul* 40). As Gaines claims, the effect of this piece is literally captivating. The huge sanctuary already packed with an audience becomes even more occupied as the line begins at stage left, on the ground level. From there, the cast of what eventually appears to be more than one hundred men and women makes its way through the center aisles, around the back and side sections of the sanctuary. This is not a stately procession: the dancers have created a human chain—the hands of one person extend out front and behind, grabbing the forearms of the person in front of them as well as behind them. The procession marches, in a dance formation that involves pushing, then pulling and bending, as drumbeats fill the church. The writhing stream of people seems interminable, as more dancers emerge from stage left to join the moving line. At the end of the scene, when the dancers move onstage, standing in multiple rows, the auction-block scene begins.

A white woman carrying an umbrella and followed by a silent black slave character strolls through the newly formed assemblage of captives. She wanders through them, feeling one man, looking down the trousers of another. She stops in front of a black woman and grabs her breasts, saying, "She'll make a good wet nurse. I must remember to tell Emily." At this point, the woman seated next to me remarked, "If black people had had any sense back then, they would have poisoned the little ones while they were nursing them." This whole scene is meant to be, I think, more symbolic than historically accurate. (The idea of a white woman perusing a slave market has been shown by historians to be unlikely, but it is perhaps less threatening to depict a white woman fondling these bodies than a white man.) However, this moment is the first voice given after the long, silent march to this auction block. The character, aptly named Miss Ann, is a focal point of capricious white dominance and newly acquired black subjection. She becomes the target of the audience's attention, a place to direct one's anger at the disregard with which black life was treated. At the same time, my pew mate didn't necessarily lash out at Miss Ann, but rather at those blacks "back then" who didn't do enough to resist. Even though the response to this scene is complex and impossible to fully quantify, I hazard the guess that for the assembled audience the specter of black captivity (performed in a grueling and relentless procession) in the face of Miss Ann's callous sexualized fondling of black bodies raised a few of the key elements that characterized the Middle Passage and American slavery.

The second moment, this time a scene of black resistance, seemed to generate a more favorable response. Following on the heels of the auction-block scene and a dramatic monologue from Willie Lynch, there is a dramatic monologue from the *Confessions of Nat Turner*.[6] The actor playing Turner discusses killing white men, women, and children as he and his followers roamed the Virginia countryside. Even the thinly veiled sexual references— like the especially striking "I stuck her repeatedly with my sword, which was too dull to kill"—were offered to counterbalance the previous scenes of black subjugation. The audience's response to this monologue was electric. Throughout the first-person performance, the audience spoke back to the Turner character in the same language used in call and response: "umhmm," "yes," "all right." The applause following the performance was thunderous. This was a much needed release, and the two moments suggest the possibilities for the performance as a psychodrama. However potent a description this therapeutic modality may be, I find *The Maafa Suite* best explained by its ritual and sermonic elements.

The Maafa Suite as Sermonic Theater: Sacralizing the Slave Body

As I have claimed earlier, *The Maafa Suite* is a deliberate and determined effort on the part of an element of the black popular sphere to create a strategy of remembrance, reverence, and reenactment of American slavery. The church actively documents its practices and produces handouts for audiences with explanations of libation, pledges to the ancestors, a special *Maafa* prayer, another prayer used by the event coordinators, and other textual documentation of their efforts.

In the performance itself, after the initial libation observance before entering the main seating area, the ritual element of the piece is established in a series of other sacralizing events. These events are listed in the program as "Nommo," "Nommo Invocation," "Processional of the Images," "Libations," and "The Eucharist." These scenes and observances frame the actual dramatic performance to follow; however, they are not separate from it. By establishing a sacred bond or at least invoking such a connection through these ritual observances, SPCBC organizers have arranged the program in such a way as to leave little doubt about the motives and intent of their sermonic theater. They blend West African traditions (libation), a Mali and Afrocentric concept (Nommo), a ritual of their own invention (Processional), and a sacrament as old as Christianity (Eucharist) to contextualize what their audience will be seeing for the next several hours. In addition, the presence of Nommo and the Holy Communion aims to transform the audience from passive receptors into an engaged community of believers.

After a recital of a poem, "Why Do I Love the Ocean?"—which ends with the line "It's not really water, in truth, it's my blood"—the lights in the church dim (and a series of African drummers enter the sanctuary). A recorded voice whispers, "Nommo," over the loudspeakers and is accompanied by the sound of a pulsing heartbeat. From the rear of the pews, three male church elders—bald, topless, and covered in a ceremonial white powder or paint—

walk slowly down the aisles. They carry a staff with a *sankofa* bird carved on it and a palm of damp sagebrush that they use to flick drops of water over the seated audience. The men move stealthily, yet stately, through the room, surprising many in the crowd who sit with their backs to the approaching elders. The men wind their way to the front of the church to wait while a recorded prayer—"Nommo Invocation" in the program—plays overhead. The three men move again, in front of a few African drummers, to complete the invocation-of-Nommo program segment.

Within the Afrocentric theoretical mode, Nommo is a powerful and popular concept of self-definition and empowerment through language, "based in the sacred, indispensable and creative nature of the Word" (Karenga, "Nommo" 8). Linguists George Yancey and Geneva Smitherman use it to frame a theory of a distinct African American language, where Nommo is conceptualized as an instrumental power to define in the name of black community (Clarke, "Talk about Talk" 318). In his 1972 study of black theater, Paul Carter Harrison links Nommo's linguistic power to other forms of activity: "Nommo, in the power of the word . . . activates all forces from their frozen state in a manner that establishes concreteness of experience . . . be they glad or sad, work or play, pleasure or pain, in a way that preserves [one's] humanity" (*The Drama of Nommo* xx). For Molefi Asante, Nommo is "the generating and sustaining power of the creative word" (*The Afrocentric Idea* 78). It is a "collective activity" or experience that creates and engenders a "communal happening" (90). The intent of Nommo, Asante claims, is to maintain community harmony (79). Afrocentric scholar Maulana Karenga also privileges the communal function of Nommo when he characterizes it as a rhetoric of communal deliberation, discourse, and action, directed toward bringing good into the community and the world ("Nommo" 5–6). Harnessing the communal principle in the realm of theater, African American drama scholar Jacqueline Wood summarizes the Afrocentric position as one that "takes Nommo as primarily centered in black ritualized texts intended to evoke the spiritual energies of a communal audience." Wood accepts and broadens this application when she claims that Nommo can be manifested not only in ritualized events but also in the signifying and politicized outcomes of radical black dramatic events, particularly as they embrace questions of social justice, unity in family, and community and cultural integrity ("Enabling Texts" 105). Though her work is concerned with nineteenth-century black experimental theater and twentieth-century revolutionary drama groups, Wood's perceptions are relevant for SPCBC's *Maafa Suite* and its invocations.

If Nommo is an Afrocentric philosophical and linguistic concept, why present that idea in an embodied form? Why use these characters to introduce the program, devoting a significant amount of time to their presence? I suggest the Nommo characters—played by three church elders—are designed to corporealize the linguistic power of the idea. They accomplish this task in two ways: first, if, as Harrison claims, any effect of Nommo is to "[activate] all forces from their frozen state," transforming them "in a manner that establishes concreteness of experience," then this portion of the program is crucial and must occur early. The invocation-of-Nommo segment, the use of the *sankofa*-bird staff, and the sprinkling of the seated audience are elements of an induction, one that hopes to bring the audience members from one state of perception to another. This is no brainwashing scheme. By having representations of Nommo walking the aisles, bestowing what appear to be gestures of blessing or preparation, audiences are encouraged to imagine themselves as located in more than a position of distanced spectatorship. They are now part of a larger collective experience, a "happening" presided over by the spirit of Nommo.

This tripartite spirit—or the three incarnated doctrines of the spirit—might prove a (necessary) inducement on another level. For those in the audience who did not know who or what Nommo represented, there might well have been those for whom the character was familiar. These men wore a costume—shaved head, shirtless, body powdered white—similar to a key figure in Haile Gerima's 1993 film *Sankofa*. This figure, called Sankofa in the film's credits, is a self-appointed guardian of the castle. He plays the drums to honor lost ancestors, and he shoos tourists away from the site, saying that it is a "holy place." To Mona, the film's protagonist, he shakes his staff and yells, "Go back! Go back to your past!" She later wanders into the castle dungeons, only to find herself trapped with Africans bound for the Middle Passage. The film leads us to assume that Mona's remand to the slave past is due in part to the Sankofa character's injunction.

His presence as protector or guardian of the deceased captive ancestors is also present at SPCBC's *Maafa Suite*. This character, so important to the film *Sankofa,* which screened in many black churches, including SPCBC, is part of the performance's larger project as sacred theater. The intention of the three Nommo guides is to incorporate, to offer a new experiential dimension to the larger piece: the guides are a way to speak the lost past into the present; they function as sites of West African ritual, and thus dually sacralize the Christian church space; and, given the transformative and punitive power of a character of similar appearance in *Sankofa,* which is familiar to SPCBC organizers and possibly many audience members, the three Nommo and the Nommo invocation encourage the audience to suspend their skepticism and disbelief and open their minds to the possibility of connecting to lost, departed slave ancestors.

Following the Nommo invocation and the summoning of its power to transform a linguistic expression into an approximate rendition of those referential experiences, the "Processional of the Images" segment is a logical follow-up. In this segment, parishioners and church leaders chosen by Youngblood proceed down the center aisles of the church carrying brown- and black-skinned rag dolls draped in African fabric. The dolls are meant to represent ancestors lost on the Middle Passage. The procession is a walking formation with the symmetry of a wedding march: men on one side, women on the other; all are wearing tattered brown garments, a suffering costume. In two sedate lines, they carry the dolls to the stage, where church ushers escort them up a small flight of stairs. After mounting the steps, they gently place the dolls on wooden shelves at the rear of the stage; they turn with their arms outstretched to receive another doll. The ceremony concludes when all the dolls are on the shelves and the stage is filled with the celebrants. Libation follows soon after.

The "Procession of the Images" is yet another example of what Youngblood describes as "church unusual." The notion of 3-D "graven" images being paraded and then prominently displayed behind the altar is anathema to Baptist church tradition. That these images are of lost Africans might make it even less appropriate in the eyes of many Baptists. Still, as a part of a commemoration that aims to both hold Christian churches accountable for their role in slavery and hold Christian liberation theology together with precepts of ancestor acknowledgment, this procession makes sense where it is positioned—before the observance of Holy Communion.

It is not necessary to spend much time discussing SPCBC's Eucharist sacrament, except to note that it is observed in the traditional manner—unleavened bread (matzo crackers) and wine (grape juice) represent the body and blood of Christ. To consume these sacred foods in this context is to connect with Christ and his sacrifice. Yet I conclude this chapter by acknowledging the close and explicit ties that *The Maafa Suite* makes between the martyred Christ and black captive ancestors lost on the Middle Passage. In this light, the refrain of the hymn sung after the sacrament—"The blood shall never lose its cleansing power"—speaks of both Christ's sacrifice and his redemptive powers as well as the the sacrifice of the ancestors. As one presiding minister said, "We are because they were. We are because Christ is."

6. Historical Reenactments

Ritual reenactments like *The Maafa Suite* differ significantly from those in the historical mode. These two forms, however, can be usefully placed in dialogue. Erriel Roberson, whose book on the *Maafa* expanded the term's application, has this to say about Colonial Williamsburg's historical reenactments of slavery: "Colonial Williamsburg is a celebration of European colonial history with enslaved Africans as an unavoidable incidental, viewed from the perspective of those celebrating the European heritage. This is not memorialization" (*The Maafa and Beyond* 19). Roberson's characterization of Colonial Williamsburg is congruent with that museum's description by some historians as a "Republican Disneyland." From its inception in the 1920s, funded by a Rockefeller Foundation grant to promote patriotism, until the late 1970s, Colonial Williamsburg paid little or no attention to the town's eighteenth-century practice of slavery. Preferring instead to promote the vision of "silk-pants patriots," the museum talked about famous Virginians such as George Washington and Thomas Jefferson who spent time in the colonial capital, and the larger struggle for America's independence. The museum is also preoccupied with and very proud of its "eighty-eight original buildings," many of which were saved and restored when the Rockefeller Foundation's museum funding arrived. This stress on the buildings as historical objects, factual remnants of a past historical moment, overdetermines the museum's approach, and visitors' response to presenting the past. Eric Gable and Richard Handler have shown the ways in which the museum's "claims to mimetic accuracy" lead visitors and staff to believe that "to tour Colonial Williamsburg is to experience 'the real thing'" ("Deep Dirt" 3).

The reality or authenticity of Colonial Williamsburg's presentation comes in large part from its buildings and the curation and structure of its artifacts. But Gable and Handler identified another important element of the town-cum-museum that is referred to as a marker of historical veracity: dirt. Colonial Williamsburg is a series of roads, houses, churches, and several businesses (taverns, milliners, tailors) that extends from the museum town's main thoroughfare, Duke of Gloucester Street. Closed to motor vehicle traffic, the most visible mode of transportation (ten dollars per person for a fifteen-minute tour) is horse-drawn carriages. These carriages roam the museum's main streets and are proffered as a source of authenticity in several ways. Coaches were the main mode of moving goods and for transporting the wealthy in and around eighteenth-century Williamsburg. Their drivers are dressed in eighteenth-century livery. More important for Gable and Handler's analysis of Colonial Williamsburg's mimetic ideal, the horses expend waste freely. And unlike Disney World, it is not retrieved, leaving the streets of Colonial Williamsburg strewn with horse dung. Tour guides, who walk the streets backward, so as to better face their audience, frequently ask someone to stand watch as the guide strolls in reverse and alert him or her to any upcoming piles of animal manure. This gesture allows the guide's charges to join in the work of guiding the tour, thereby replacing a potentially authoritarian relationship (between guide and guest) with one that is, apparently, cooperative and egalitarian (9). The guide and his or her group are further united in looking at the past—where streets are packed with horse manure and other hygienic practices seem lax by present standards—"road apples," a euphemism for horse dung, like other forms of dirt serve an overwhelming interpretive purpose: "Dirt is a symbol for that part of history which is unpleasant—conflict, class divisions, poverty in the midst of plenty, and even the exploited classes themselves: slaves, itinerants, the 'lower orders' in general. Dirt is also a symbol for the primitive and a dirty past implies a cleaner present. That is, dirt is the material through which a narrative of progress becomes experientially real" (13).

The notion of the experiential component of historical knowledge acquisition is a governing trope at most living-history museums and among many historical interpreters, both professional and amateur. The desire to present the real thing reveals the ways in which living-history practitioners are at odds with academic historians. Ann McGrath has advised her colleagues in history departments that "our concerns with the body must go beyond mere theorizing; we should explore the tangible realities of a spatial and tactile past navigated by embodied humans who experienced rich and changing emotional relations with the material and symbolic world" (review n.p.). The distinction between the positive valuation of history or experience seems to divide along the axis of academe and the popular. As Roy Rosenzweig and David Thelen observe, "To call something 'history' is to describe it as dead and irrelevant, completely useless. For professionals, however, 'history' is both alive and useful. The term is practically synonymous with our occupational identity, and we associate it with rigorous discipline and the authoritative use of the past. The word that seemed to have more meaning to our survey respondents [the hundreds of Americans interviewed]—'experience'—is dismissed by many professionals as random, private, shallow and even self-deceptive" (*The Presence* 191).

Given the tensions between reenactors, or historical interpreters (who aim for "authenticity" or re-created moments from the past), and academics (who ardently critique both the possibility and the promise of authenticity), on which side of the divide can we locate historical reenactments of slavery in the living-history field? On the one hand, black reenactors performing as slaves lend authenticity to the appearance of Williamsburg's historic district, where approximately 50 percent of the denizens were black. On the other hand, it is also true that these historical interpreters are *performing* both a role and a service. Do they lapse into what some reenactors describe as the "magic moment," where the present and presence fall away and the reenactor feels herself to be "really" in the past? Are the pleasures similar to that of the Civil War reenactors who long to experience "what it was like, to feel like one was there and feel what those men had felt" (Allred, "Catharsis" 6)?

This chapter concerns the costs or consequences of reembodying American slavery as a strategy in living history. Though Chapter 4 discussed the public controversy surrounding the 1994 slave-auction reenactment, I return to Colonial Williamsburg to consider slavery reenactments from a position more proximate to those who do this work. How do scholars working outside the traditional academy make meaning about slavery? What does it mean to be a slave character in a living-history enactment? What is the purpose of acting and working in the guise of a slave? Is this a job or a calling? What is required for this task? How does such a display articulate the multiple meanings of American slavery in the past and present? How do such performances shape the malleable concept of American slavery in American life and letters?

In what follows, I explore historical daily-life reenactments of slavery at Colonial Williamsburg. I approach this site as a midway point on the path between vernacular and academic forms of theory. Colonial Williamsburg can be described as a formal academic institution; it is funded by large endowments, has a research library as part of its facility, and offers research fellowships and sponsors studies in archaeology, history, and botany. It is also linked by location and history to the College of William and Mary. At the same time, Colonial Williamsburg is also a popular venue. Colonial Williamsburg is America's largest living-history museum and boosts its tourist image by offering several elite golf resorts and fine dining and shopping. It is an educational institution dependent on tourism. As such, it must at least consider, if not overtly cater to, the visiting audience and their expectations.

How does slavery reenacting become incorporated into this heady mix of corporate and public, education and entertainment, academic and vernacular? Just as living history museums wrestle with their identity and mission,[1] the role of slavery reenactors is conflicted and challenging. The challenges can be put into relief by briefly comparing slavery reenactments to Civil War reenactments. Only a cursory glance is necessary to delineate the disparate motives of reenactment as a form of popular historical knowledge. One Kentucky female Civil War reenactor describes her love of reenacting as a way to own the past, claiming that reenactment "preserve[s] our right to remember our history the way we want to do it . . . instead of the way some of the history books have portrayed it" (Rosenzweig and Thelen, *The Presence* 18). Upon interviewing other reenactors, scholars Rosenzweig and Thelen discovered that "by re-enacting the past, respondents cut through the intervening years to revisit people and scenes, to rekindle the range of feelings that had accompanied the experience as well as connections that had accumulated between the earlier moment and the present" (32). In addition to discovering or uncovering lost sentiments or striving for a form of transtemporal empathy, these reenactors—highly invested in the notion of mimesis in dress, artifact, decorum, and speech—see as their goal a moment of breaking through the illusion: "The best pay-off was when time ceased to exist and the illusion became real: the lines between the past and present become blurred. Or, at least, one feels as if one has traveled in time" (Allred, "Catharsis" 6). This sentiment was reinforced by another reenactor, who claimed, "It's about as close to time travel as you can get" (5).

The seductive qualities of time travel as described by many Civil War reenactors is based on a particular fantasy and nostalgic longing, largely unavailable or inapplicable to blacks who might reenact slavery. For instance, Randal Allred's 1996 essay claims that the tens of thousands (though more recent figures are closer to one million) of Civil War reenactors "may be a sign of our dissatisfaction with a culture increasingly at odds with its own sense of identity. For many, it is a search for a more meaningful paradigm of conviction and purpose in our time of fragmented self-absorption" (1). Allow me to pause for clarification: who exactly are this "we" who see the nineteenth-century antebellum days and gruesome battlefields as a "paradigm of conviction and purpose"? Who reenacts Civil War battles in an effort to return to a past defined as "before the disintegration of social structures, when history had causation, a certain logic ruled the universe, and there were principles worth having and paradigms worth trusting" (7). The mystery is cleared up a bit when Allred asks, in recounting an experience in a reenacted battle won by Union forces, "If we can re-create as near as is possible, the actual event, can we not revise the text?" (10). This is the crux of the matter. These Civil War reenactors described above long to turn back the clock to an idealized nostalgic antebellum period and either change past events or at least keep time frozen there. It is no overstatement, I believe, to claim that some of the disintegration of American culture that Allred mentions involves increased racial parity between blacks and whites. For these white reenactors, their hobby or passion is an imagined return to a day when whiteness meant something or at least meant more than it does today. It allows them—however subconsciously—to reify white supremacy in the name of historical veracity. For black reenactors, racial disparity precludes nostalgia.

The seductive power of nostalgia that lures some of the one million Civil War reenactors in the United States is largely absent for the comparatively few historical interpreters of slavery. One Colonial Williamsburg black character interpreter described the fundamental difference between the emotional effect of his performances and that of his white colleagues as stemming from the racial disparity in the eighteenth-century moment the museum sought to re-create: "The deeper they get, the better they feel; the deeper I get, the worse I feel. It's like asking a Jew to interpret at Auschwitz" (Lawson, "The Other Half" 266–67). Thus, the retreat into the past—cognitive, imagined, and artificial—nonetheless had the potential to effect adversely the emotional state of the reenactor. Unlike white reenactors of the Civil War portraying soldiers and camp followers who might long for a form of moral clarity they find absent in the complexity of today's moral universe, black reenactors who deliberately perform scenes and conditions of the slave past do not have the consolation of a less troubled existence. White interpreters portraying the elite of colonial society usually find themselves performing a social role (royal governor or rich widow) that is more affluent than that which they occupy as twenty-first-century museum employees. For black interpreters, however, a crucial shift from the context of freedom to that of assumed bondage is implicit in the chore of performing history in the first person.

Robert Watson, a twenty-year veteran of Colonial Williamsburg and site supervisor for the museum's Great Hope Plantation, an exhibit representing the lives of "the middling sort" in the presentation of a small farming family and a few slaves in the household, explains the challenges of recruiting young black actors or would-be interpreters to the living-history field. In addition to the relatively low salary, Watson says the work itself is not highly valued: "Most people look at this type of work we do as being 'slavey' and being degrading. . . . [Y]ou can't make this pretty for people. These people endured a lot, they went through a lot, and if you're going to represent their struggle, you got to stand the storm." Unlike the eighteenth-century elites at Colonial Williamsburg, the performance and work of historical reenactments of slavery are neither "glamorous" nor "glorifying." Still, Watson maintains that it is important. He even claims that an ancestral connection can aid in the challenging work: "You've got to find strength in their endurance to give you the push to stand in there and talk about them because they have just as great a presence as anyone else that you want to . . . slap 'founding fatherdom' on" (personal interview). This complex, if imaginary, connection—using the fact of slaves' endurance as a source for the difficulties of performing and retelling narratives of slavery—is telling on several fronts. First, Watson recognizes that historical interpretation of slavery for an African American interpreter is rife with internal and external perils. The storm he mentions may well be the flurry of criticism from other blacks who see black interpreters as sellouts, playing the darky for white amusement. Or it could be the winds of white supremacy borne from white visitors whose proximity to a slave character reifies their own white privilege in both the past and the present. Gable and Handler note black interpreters experience "subtle forms of racial discrimination from some of their white colleagues" (*The Presence* 794). In addition to this controversy, however, a second valuable lesson emerges: the "presence" of black slave forebears. Watson's comparison of the unnamed and unknown slaves of the eighteenth century with founding fathers of the era highlights the notion that distinctive titles are constructed and bestowed in a perhaps haphazard fashion, a label "slapped" on, whereas others remain anonymous. The work of black historical interpreters at Colonial Williamsburg is fraught with tension regarding historical value, representational techniques, and the choices regarding the best way to approach a traumatic history in a living-history museum.

From its creation in the early twentieth century until the late 1970s, Colonial Williamsburg avoided explicit discussion or representation of slavery in its re-creation of the colonial capital. The choice was congruent with its mandate to present Williamsburg as America's birthplace of liberty and site of culture and refinement, what contemporary critics call "silk-pants patriots." In the late 1960s, James Short, a program assistant, wrote a seven-point bulletin regarding the lack of black history in the museum. The first, and presumably definitive, reason was the institution's "corporate sense of embarrassment about the subject [that led to the policy of] the less said the better" (Ellis, "A Decade of Change" 16). Other reasons to not represent black history included the lack of records about slaves, potential awkwardness of the conversation among a "mixed groups of visitors," and the museum's preference for the word *servants* rather than *slaves*. The report also gives two reasons for the lack of black history that depend on Colonial Williamsburg's black employees: "We have (so we have told ourselves) been loathe to arouse tender feelings among our Negro employees and we have assumed that the presence of Negroes on the staff (usually in subservient jobs) was sufficient to suggest that we recognized slavery as once having existed here" (16). These two reasons are instructive for an examination of slavery reenactments in the historical mode. These statements rely on contemporary black employees' "tender feelings" while simultaneously implying that these employees' "usual-ly" low-status job positions sufficiently reference the museum's slave past. The document seems to suggest that by virtue of having low-paid blacks on-site, Colonial Williamsburg is somehow raising the specter of eighteenth-century slavery. That this claim is made with no irony or indication of improving the "subservient" positions available to blacks is evidence of the way in which black employees unwittingly (or perhaps not) served dual roles for museum administrators: they were cooks, dishwashers, custodial workers, and food vendors, and, if they happened to be seen by a museum visitor or put in a visible place, they could also remind guests of eighteenth-century slavery. Colonial Williamsburg, then, got two services from these black workers for one (likely meager) salary.

Black townspeople, the most apparent source for the "subservient" posi-tions necessary to keep Colonial Williamsburg operating, were distrustful of the museum (and that attitude persists, in some cases). Rex Ellis, founder of the African American Interpretive Programs and later the first African American vice president of the Historic District, grew up in Williamsburg as the museum grew. "All through my formative years, I had been warned about 'the restoration,' as my parents called it. 'That's not a place for you to go to, it only points to slavery, and we don't want to hear about that'" (18). As Colonial Williamsburg began programs devoted to black history in 1979, feelings similar to those of Ellis's parents continued to grow: rumors within the black community were so widespread, a local minister declared to his congregation that "Colonial Williamsburg was bringing back slavery times" (14). The pressure on those few employed as slavery reenactors—Rex Ellis and two colleagues—was significant. As Christy Coleman Matthews observed in an article commemorating the twentieth anniversary of black history at Colonial Williamsburg, "Many not only had to contend with colleagues who devalued their work, they also had to deal with friends and family who simply regarded what they chose to do for a living as, 'playing slaves for white folks.'" Despite challenges from within and outside their community, Matthews says, these black reenactors "remained steadfast in their desire to teach the histories of their ancestors. For this group, their word was a sacred mission and they fully invested themselves in it" ("A Colonial Williamsburg Revolution" 8). The notion of the interpretive work of slavery as a "sacred mission" is important, as is these early interpreters' choice to "fully [invest] themselves in it." Dedication and immersion are required for blacks to interpret slavery in the first person.

There are three forms of historical interpretation on the grounds of Colonial Williamsburg: character, first person, and third person. The predominant mode is third person. These are historical interpreters who dress in eighteenth-century clothing and talk with patrons in the present moment, as themselves, about the museum building, grounds, and facilities. They might sit outside a building, doing crowd flow control: counting off the number of guests entering a building for a tour, assembling and talking with patrons waiting for the next tour to begin, frequently explaining or contextualizing the performance within. These interpreters also work within the building, answering questions about objects or historical figures who may once have lived there. First-person and character interpreters both play the role of an eighteenth-century person and interact with guests as if the patron too were in the eighteenth-century moment. First-person interpreters, while also enmeshed in the illusion of the eighteenth century, assumed "different roles on different days or at different sites." These interpreters might "come out of the role in public" (Lawson, "The Other Half" 176).

Despite the different duration of the eighteenth-century illusion engulfing first-person or character interpreters, both roles required a faith in the effectiveness of embodiment as a strategy for imparting historical knowledge. In their performance, "both treat the past as if it were the present" (Barnes, "Living History" 2). Arthur Barnes, director of the museum's Character Interpretation Department in the mid-1980s, wrote that to successfully generate the eighteenth-century illusion, the interpreter "must immerse himself in the period; he must understand the society and its values so thoroughly that he can adopt them, naturally and without apparent effort, as his own." This strategy, Barnes observes, is similar to foreign-language acquisition. The interpreter is "attempting to do in an historical context what was always described to me as the ideal in the study of foreign languages—you succeed only when you begin to think as well as speak in the language you are studying" (ibid.). Becoming fluent in an eighteenth-century persona transforms an interpreter, Barnes claims, into a "living artifact." Barnes coined this term and offered it as the ultimate goal of historical reenactment. Guests depend on these figures to aid in their own transition from the contemporary scene to an eighteenth-century one. As "living artifacts," good reenactors are "sentient, mobile, articulate artifacts who can participate in their own analysis. They can speak directly to the subjective, intangible, qualitative issues that are such an important part of the eighteenth century experience. They can talk about how they feel about something, or what they hope will happen to them or to their families in the future" ("Character Interpretation" 3). Several white character interpreters have been described as so immersed in their role that they might well meet this exacting standard of living artifact. One performer who portrays Patrick Henry has been praised by visitors and other Colonial Williamsburg interpreters for the ease with which he interacts with guests, refusing to take the bait of an interlocutor who asks about radio or television, responding only with confusion. Another white interpreter, portraying the grieving widow of Speaker Randolph, informed me that it was "fun" to play the hostess who entertained guests in her bereavement.

These two brief examples are not designed to suggest that black interpreters do not find the same fulfillment in their work. However, it is important to recall that the element that makes white interpretive practice "fun" or amusing is more troubled, more difficult to come by for black interpreters. Though Barnes's vision of successful historical interpretation would transform a museum employee into a living artifact, for black employees that shift from subject to object is fraught with racial tension. Black interpreters, by virtue of their black skin, are always already perceived in racially subjugated positions in the American imagination. At Colonial Williamsburg, then, a black employee wearing eighteenth-century clothing—be he a front-line worker or a first-person or other interpreter—conjures the image of what that person is representing from the eighteenth century. Many black interpreters have commented on the difficulty of performing scenes from the historical period where blacks were enslaved. In her study of African American historical interpretation at Colonial Williamsburg, Anna Logan Lawson notes, "For the African American interpreter to 'become' a slave, was for that person to become an object in ways more complex than just being part of the museum's collection. In terms of the eighteenth century, it was to become property, even to enter a sub-human category, or, at the very least, to join the ranks of an oppressed class" ("The Other Half" 265–66). These words recall those of the black interpreter who, when comparing his work to that of his white colleagues, explained, "The deeper they get, the better they feel; the deeper I get, the worse I feel."

Though many reenactors might accept Barnes's injunction to become a living artifact as a hallmark of achieving the eighteenth-century illusion, the declaration is far more complicated for black performers, whose racial identity already objectifies them to a certain extent. This preoccupation with the artifact—using this term within a living-history context that purports to have a museological approach different from the standard view of museums that fetishize objects, displaying them in isolation or without context—reinforces the dependence on objects by extending that valuation standard to its employees.

The Black Body as Object in Historical Reenactments

In their critique of Colonial Williamsburg's mode of social history, Eric Gable, Richard Handler, and Anna Logan Lawson analyze the conflicted roles that objects play in Colonial Williamsburg. Though many interpreters are quick to stress that Colonial Williamsburg is a re-creation, an interpretive approach to an irretrievable past, there is an assumption that the museum's many objects—the most visible of which are the eighty-eight original buildings—are evidence of the vision of the past that they create. As the study suggests, the reigning epistemology of Colonial Williamsburg "enshrines objects and facts at the center of a history which, however interpretive it may be admitted to be, is ultimately measured in terms of an ostensibly objective and absolute truth" ("On the Uses" 792). Museum visitors strolling through the Governor's Palace are encouraged to admire the paintings and other luxury items assembled there. In so doing, these visitors, by walking through the "actual"—or what is implied to be the actual—place of the colony's ruling class, are offered what purports to be a glimpse into the lifestyles of the eighteenth century's Rich and Famous. At one point during a tour, the guide asked the few children in the group, "If this were your room, what would you be doing?" Though this question was likely intended to engage and distract small children who had no interest in the palace's enshrined luxury, it is important to consider this question as an invitation to imagine themselves in a certain role in this place, one that would transcend or exceed their current temporal location. The children responded with answers like "I'd be playing" or "I'd be cleaning my room." It is important to remember that this question is a large part of the draw of Colonial Williamsburg's living history. The overt question—What would you be doing?—applies to adults in a more subtle but no less strategic way. Some patrons are drawn, of course, to the museum's objects and its "preservation" of history. Others come for the patriotism; July 4 is possibly the museum's most popular attendance day. But these objects are also used to extend the promise of transporting one back to another time. In this way, Colonial Williamsburg uses objects much like traditional museums, based on an epistemology Gable, Handler, and Lawson describe this way: "Museums conserve and display objects. Objects are 'real.' They are immediate. They can be seen and in some cases touched. Objects, it is thought, do not lie. Thus, if proper care is taken to secure 'authentic' objects, the story that the museum tells with those objects will be 'true'" (794). These objects, offered either implicitly or explicitly as truth, are part of the larger vision of re-creating what Colonial Williamsburg would consider to be a part of an authentic past. That gesture is additionally complicated by the clearly striated racial hierarchy of the time to which Colonial Williamsburg longs to re-create. If visitors, in this case the kids on the palace tour, are asked to imagine themselves—however briefly—or locate themselves in the eighteenth century, then their racial designation (like their gender) would surely follow them, becoming part of their life experience then as much as it would be in the present. For white visitors, then, their imaginary placement in the eighteenth century would imply a sense of racial superiority (if not mastery), for black visitors a sense of racial inferiority based on the assumptions required in a slavocracy.

My turn to objects in the museum and the promise of imaginative relocation that these objects extend is especially relevant for an inquiry into the implications of offering the body—particularly the black body—as an object, or what Barnes called a "living artifact," by which to learn about the past. As part of its educational mission, "living history museums understand that in the encounter between museum visitor and living object there exists a potential for an access to the past in an experiential, interactive manner, formerly outside the scope of the museum exhibit" (Magelssen, "Resuscitating the Extinct" 98). Though Colonial Williamsburg, like living-history museums and exhibitions more generally, aims to disrupt conventional museology by emphasizing personal portrayals, there is a cost for this risky plan. In an examination of animal husbandry programs at such living-history museums as Connor Prairie, Scott Magelssen considers the ethical dilemmas of "back breeding" historical animals to produce livestock that bear remarkable genetic semblance to their eighteenth-century counterparts. Magelssen's project explores what might be described as the governing ethos of living history: that the living bodies in the present somehow disseminate a more "real" history than a collection of historic objects. This interpretive belief is an "example of how the body is a site of knowledge production somehow on an equal footing with, or even more powerful than, the book or the archive" (ibid.). Magelssen critiques some living-history museums' decision to pursue "authenticity" by raising genetically modified livestock. These animals—"back bred" to better refer to eighteenth-century animals—occupy a liminal, if significant, role in the living-history interpretive schema: "Not the same kind of performer as a human interpreter, yet not an artifact, the animal body is nevertheless often ascribed the status of historical object, a sign by which museum visitors may temporarily suspend their disbelief and pretend to enter a past milieu" (99).

The ethical dilemmas presented by the deliberate choice to breed animals so that they have the same genetic composition as animals from two hundred years earlier are relevant to the dilemmas of representing the mutable black body. Let me pause here to acknowledge the troubling implications of linking, in even the most circumspect and tenuous manner, the animal body and the black human body. I am well aware of the ambivalent position the black body is forced to occupy in the array of racist dichotomies in the American imagination both past and present. I also take this argumentative path knowing that chattel slavery in the nineteenth century—at least in legal parlance—aimed to reduce the black body to the same legal standing as animal property. I do not wish to unduly elide the black body with back-bred animals offered on the grounds of authenticity. Instead, Magelssen's look into this controversial position occupies the same vantage point I wish to use to examine the dilemmas presented by performing an eighteenth-century slave character in a twenty-first-century black body. The ease or unease with which these performers are received by their largely white audience is based, in part, on both the suspension of disbelief (pretending to "be" in eighteenth-century Williamsburg) and on the adoption of a new belief (that blacks occupy a legally mandated subordinate position and that whites occupy a legally mandated dominant position). The black body, as it moves through the imagined space of Colonial Williamsburg, shifting from a twenty-first-century racial environment to an eighteenth-century one, is offered as a "living artifact." The trouble remains, a nagging question—what does this body represent? In adding to the "authenticity" of a Colonial Williamsburg that was more than half black, how do these performers approach the role, especially when one's black skin is permanent?

In an effort to represent an eighteenth-century Williamsburg where nearly 51 percent of the population was black, black interpreters are crucial to the illusion of authenticity. Even one critic in 1966 who decried Colonial Williamsburg's lack of authenticity cited slavery as a necessary, but absent, element. Unlike what Colonial Williamsburg provided, the real eighteenth century "means 'smells, flies, pigs, dirt and slave quarters'" (quoted in Gable and Handler, "Deep Dirt" 5). This ordering is significant. Bringing up the risks of my use of Magelssen's back-breeding article, Walter Whitehall clearly links slave dwellings with the distasteful underside of the eighteenth century.

This is just one step removed from calling slaves "flies, pigs, dirt." Yet in some corners of America's racial imagination, the black body in our present moment is easily associated with this negative extreme. The racism endemic to American culture is part of the problem Colonial Williamsburg's black interpreters face when choosing to portray slave characters. As Anna Logan Lawson observes, only the African American interpreters were "becoming" objects in order to present objects, that is, slaves ("The Other Half" 216). White interpreters playing Patrick Henry or George Wythe are assuredly portraying icons, objects created in a particular version of an American patriotic fantasy. But for slave-character and first-person interpreters, that shift from twenty-first-century subject to eighteenth-century object is doubly complicated. Colonial Williamsburg's success is rooted in its invitation to its guests or visitors to step back in time, suspend their disbelief, and imagine themselves in a past time period. But this time travel presented a special problem for black employees at Colonial Williamsburg, many of whom said that "even when not in an 18th century outfit, they felt their color was a kind of costume, one which identified them with an 18th century black person" (332). When Colonial Williamsburg offered detailed interpretation of slave life at the now defunct Carter's Grove, an exhibit site six miles away from the Historic District, it was feared that the slave quarters had too much potential to erase important twentieth-century boundaries—both temporal and attitudinal. Speaking of one black interpreter working at the slave quarters, Lawson reports that the woman "wanted to 'speak for her ancestors,' not become one of them, but [as] an African American interpreter in her natural 'black' costume [she] felt that in the eyes of a white visitor she ran the risk of 'becoming' the slave inhabitant of the quarter" (333).

The Skin You're In

During the course of their work, it became crucial for black interpreters of slavery at Colonial Williamsburg to balance their personal core identity with the performed slave persona. In most interviews and other documentation of the development of African American history programs at Colonial Williamsburg, the interpretive strategy for performing reembodiments of American slavery involves a spiritual element as well as a temporal shift. A few interpreters see their work on slavery as paying tribute to lost or forgotten ancestors, others aim to complete or supplement the official historical record of America's past, and still others see their work as a foil to the patriotic, elite image of colonial life represented most frequently on the streets of Colonial Williamsburg.

It is on these streets, in the historic and restored homes such as the Randolph House or buildings like the Raleigh Tavern, that these first-person and character interpreters do the work of imaginatively reembodying American slavery. Rex Ellis, a native of Williamsburg and founder of Colonial Williamsburg's African American Interpretive Programs department, gives a deeply suggestive theory of performing slave characters. Much like Arthur Barnes's claim that the best historical interpreters would become "living artifacts," Ellis's explanation of his own (and his colleagues') representational mode involves a curious form of (re)animation. In describing the earliest representations of slavery and the personal toll of such depictions, Ellis wrote, "After two weeks of living 'in the skins' of these characters, something began to happen to me. It is one thing to come up with an idea or a script on paper, it is quite another to role-play a slave before a live and sometimes antagonistic audience" ("A Decade of Change" 18). Here, Ellis makes a distinction common among living-history practitioners: imagining and creating a character through language and textuality, on paper, are epistemologically opposed to—or at least significant departures from—performing that slave character through one's speech, dress, deportment, and mannerisms. When the invented slave character emerges from the page and onto the body of a historical interpreter, a curious grafting process ensues; as Ellis claims, "Putting on that costume became more of a burden as the days wore on. Walking down the street was no longer pleasurable. I began to think that all eyes were on me, that people were not interested in the characters I had created, but instead they used my character to confirm prejudices in their own minds" (18). The "burden" of "that costume" was enhanced, no doubt, by his black skin, acutely characterized earlier as another, a priori, "natural" costume. The pleasures Ellis once had on Colonial Williamsburg's restored streets became diminished in his guise of a slave. His increasing quasi paranoia—"I began to think that all eyes were on me"—suggests a racialized visual process explored so well by James Baldwin in "Notes of a Native Son." A touch of DuBoisean double-consciousness also plays a role as he imagines himself as seen in the eyes of the white spectators. In either case, Ellis—in his slave character—is what Baldwin described eloquently as "at the mercy of the reflexes the color of one's skin caused in other people" (1683). Throughout this explanation, Ellis keeps his attention trained on the slave characters he created to perform a historical, supplementary, and corrective role in Colonial Williamsburg's dominant narrative of eighteenth-century elites. Elsewhere, however, there is an important shift from character creation to ancestor acknowledgment.

In another discussion of Colonial Williamsburg's early African American programming, Ellis shifts the terrain of his previous provocative phrase describing first-person or character interpretation. An article titled "Re:living History" is the scene for this shift. I pause for a moment to consider the title's structure: "Re" followed by the colon suggests that the brief article is a reply or response to the already articulated notion of "living history." In the same vein, this article might also be (and is) simply "about" living history. The most evocative reading is revealed by ignoring the colon, reading the title instead as "Reliving," a form of temporal crossings and reanimation, even resurrection. This brief departure is important to keep in mind because each interpretation—a reply to a definition of living history, the making of general claims about it, or "living again" a past historical moment—relates to the form of historical reenactment of slavery at Colonial Williamsburg as articulated and practiced by the program's founder.

Two years after his essay describing his experience "living 'in the skins'" of characters he created, Ellis talked more about the program's troubled beginnings: "Despite best efforts of the foundation or management, the obstacles associated with living in the skin of a slave continued—no matter how accepted the mode of presentation" ("Re:living History" 23). As opposed to his previous description of his work as "living 'in the skins'" of a slave character, an important, if unintended, erasure has occurred. The move from *slave character* to *slave* is a strategy that reveals—among a host of implications—a slippage of the temporal boundary that characterizes the performative interpretive work of America's largest living-history museum. This slide away from *slave character* to *slave* continues as Ellis advises those who would plan similar forms of representational programs. Responding to the challenges that arise for black performers in the living-history environment, Ellis states, "Each situation will be different, but the best way to determine what support systems are needed is to work intimately with those who put themselves on the line each day, those who 'put on the skins of their ancestors' and meet the public" (25). The pugilistic or combative tone of this declaration is telling. Black interpreters of slavery place themselves in vulnerable positions— putting themselves on the line each day. The "line" here might well refer to the employee group Colonial Williamsburg calls "front line," those who are in highly visible positions and must put forth a positive image for patrons to better represent Colonial Williamsburg. But the "front line" is also an unmistakable warfare reference that harks back—for me—to Ellison's *Invisible Man* and the haunting advice from his grandfather that "our life is a war" (16). Part of this costume, or uniform, as it were, required for service on the front line of historical interpretation is another, the third, skin reference. This time, however, rather than a slave character's skin or a slave skin, the historical interpreter dons the skin "of their ancestors." The slave is no longer an abstract invention of a fertile mind, or a generic designation; in this instance, a black person interpreting slavery through performed embodiment is somehow wearing, through a highly speculative form of identification, her ancestor's skin. The slave, as presented in Colonial Williamsburg's historical approach, is neither creation nor anonymous but a predecessor connected to the performer.

This claim is highly complicated for several reasons. The ones I pursue here concern the limits and risks of empathy, the benefits and losses of imagining the transgression of a temporal moment. What is captured, or what is sought to be captured, in this articulation of performed slavery?

Ellis's references to skin—living in or putting on someone else's—are a key component of a representational strategy antithetical to traditional forms of museum interaction and knowledge production. In this instance, skin occupies two places at once. First, to put on the skin implies a subcutaneous transmission of (and transmission from) the past to the present. This skin transfer seems an easily accomplishable task—for if one can put on skin to "meet the public," then surely the skin can be removed when the performer retreats to her private self. The second implication is also significant: these performers are highly mediated and artificially, if in some cases reverently, constructed.

It is these two ideas held together—subcutaneous transmission and highly mediated representations—that fuel the complexity of the skin claim. How does one "put on" the skin of another person? Does this costuming imply that this skin can be taken off? What of the idea that black skin is a movable feast, providing food for racialized and racist thoughts and behaviors? This description of putting on an ancestor's skin is a move toward empathy, toward redressing lost and formerly if not unarticulated at least unrecognized black pain. Yet there are risks. To briefly consider one such risk, I turn to Saidiya Hartman's work *Scenes of Subjection,* where she discusses the limits of empathy. In her opening section, Hartman recounts the letters and tale of John Rankin, a white abolitionist who, in trying to comprehend the depths of black suffering, imagines himself and his family as slaves subjected to abuse. According to Hartman, pain is the means through which the white abolitionist sought to gain empathic connections to the enslaved person. He aims to identify himself and his family with the plight of black men and their families when he imagines them subjected to the whims of white domination. This endeavor is complicated because "this flight of imagination and slipping into the captive's body unlatches a Pandora's box" (18). The difficulty lies in the risks of the white abolitionist substituting himself for the slave body: in "making the slave's suffering his own, [the abolitionist] begins to feel for himself rather than for those whom this exercise in imagination presumably is designed to reach." Additionally, the empathic identification—or, rather, the imaginative substitution intended to create that condition—is itself based on a notion that denies agency or subjectivity to the slave body, a condition Hartman calls the "fungibility of the captive body." This material existence, premised on the exchange properties of the slave as a fungible, tradeable object, unwittingly reinforces black subjection as the white abolitionist supplant[s] the black captive in order to give expression to black suffering (19).

I turn to Hartman's work here to engage, in part, the main consideration of her project: the subjected black body and the uses to which it is put in literature and American imagination more generally. Through her readings of nineteenth-century narratives, letters, journals, and critical investigations of scenes of violence—beatings, rapes, murders, and other more public moments—Hartman is concerned with "the spectacular nature of black suffering and, conversely, the dissimulation of suffering through spectacle" (22). These concerns are also relevant to this consideration of historical reenactments of slavery. How does empathy operate in this context? Are the black interpreters who portray slave characters—which are representations of actual eighteenth-century slaves who lived in Williamsburg—doing what Hartman charges Rankin with, "supplant[ing] the black captive in order to give expression to black suffering"? Might there be a connection between Rankin imagining himself a beaten captive and thus "slipping into the captive's body" and Rex Ellis's description of slavery reenactment as "put[ting] on the skins of their ancestors"? Is the fact that their sense of self is diminished as they represent the past an example of the difficulty of empathic identification, its ambivalent character or repressive effects, that emerges in "the facile intimacy that enables identification with the other only as we 'feel ourselves into those we imagine as ourselves'"? Does historical reenactment, as a representational alternative to the traditional museum curational format, fall prey to the same perils as Rankin's substitution? Do both modes rely on empathy, a concept that "fails to expand the space of the other but merely places the self in its stead" (20)? Certainly, there are similarities between Rankin and the contemporary black reenactors of slavery at Colonial Williamsburg: the invention of characters, the imagined scenario, the desire to tell a certain story about slavery, and a fundamental distance from and difference between the actual slave and the person imagining the slave experience. However, unlike Rankin's substitution, I believe that black reenactors of slavery are aware of the artificial (in the sense of created rather than false) element of their depictions. It is this realization—that they are representing enslaved persons by creating a persona they imagine appropriate—that makes them less (but not entirely) vulnerable to the perils and risks of ambivalent empathy. Though Ellis might describe the work of Colonial Williamsburg's first-person or character interpreters of slavery as "living in" or putting on the "skin" of slave characters or even of a black interpreter's unknown enslaved forebears (ancestors), this performance is rooted in and dependent on a hierarchical institution, a museum with formal structures and codes. This work, then, is not simply a form of "facile identification" but, rather, a conscious result of deliberate research and planning. These black historical interpreters are, in fact, more aware of the constructed nature of their stories than the white interpreters. Whereas those who interpret the lives of the white elite have houses, artifacts, and "priceless" objects that they use to claim (falsely) a mimetic connection to the past, black history at Colonial Williamsburg is not grounded in such objects. In what Hander, Gable, and Lawson call Colonial Williamsburg's underlying hegemony of facts and objects that governs its epistemology, black history is seen as "conjectural" and impoverished because it lacks "material culture," and those who seek it are sent outside, to excavate "outbuildings" where they will find broken ceramics, fish bones, and the odd bead and button ("On the Uses" 796–97). In its context of Colonial Williamsburg, black history and specifically the stories of the enslaved occupy a subordinate position to the "mainstream" of the white elite; the museum gives the impression that minority history is a story (albeit a morally valid one), whereas mainstream history is an approximation of the truth (803). Though this suggests that black history might be seen as less "true" in the eyes of visitors and the museum, the "story" element is actually the more epistemologically useful model. Colonial Williamsburg encourages its patrons to see "truth" and "authenticity" (which it considers to be the same thing) in its streets, displays, homes, gardens, and other buildings. This, however, is a form of false consciousness—the assembled artifacts and narratives are not "just the facts," as the mainstream history renders itself. Instead, it is a curatorial interpretation designed to generate a particular impression. African American interpreters—free, as it were, from the hegemony of objects by having no objects—are more theoretically aware and critically sophisticated in their presentations on slave life. Unlike their mainstream counterparts, black interpreters "emphasize the conjecture in their presentations, focusing on the absence of fact, the inability to know" (801). For my purposes, this strengthens their interpretive positions rather than undermining them, for by acknowledging their work as deliberately created, interventions in and supplements of the dominant historical narrative of Colonial Williamsburg, this strategy eschews the museum's "hegemony of objects" and highlights what the museum aims to keep hidden: that the museum and its objects are not mimetic facts or truth but rather are created and assembled.

In the process of developing programs about slave life, the African American Interpretive Programs department faced the question of how to "do" slavery. There were two positions: "one who believed it better to focus on slavery in terms of individuals as survivors than on slavery as grimly oppressive and another group who felt that the spunky survivor belied the reality of slavery, and thus presented an inaccurate version of 18th century history" (Lawson, "The Other Half" 191). The early programming of the late 1970s, the heady days of the mid-1990s, and the more moderate efforts of the early twenty-first century all bear marks of the urge to balance oppression with survival. In the course of my research, I identify two distinct yet frequently intersecting modes of slavery reenactment. Veering away from the quagmire that surrounds almost all forms of black popular cultural work—the debate about "positive" or "negative" imagery—the historical reenactments at Colonial Williamsburg reflect a broader trajectory of the slave experience and the ways in which meaning and knowledge are produced from it. The first mode is the "quotidian," or daily-life, reenactment. This involves slave reenactors who work as cooks, as maids, and in other servant roles in the houses and taverns of the museum. The emphasis in these depictions is on the daily costs of enslavement, how to accomplish work, to negotiate between mastery and autonomy. For these moments, visitors might visit the Raleigh Tavern, where Will, a slave character, works, or the kitchens of the Randolph home. I will look at two women characters created in the mid-1990s, Judith and Cate, to consider this form. The second mode of slavery reenactment, and surely the more dramatic and, in some cases, controversial, is the "egregious" reenactment. These scenarios stress the major infractions that slavery delivered to an enslaved person, the "scenes of subjection" so eloquently explored by Saidiya Hartman. At Colonial Williamsburg, "egregious" reenactments take several forms, such as the dilemma of a slave character, Peter, who considers running away when offered freedom during a Dunmore's Proclamation Weekend in 2004, a beating scenario in the yearlong "Enslaving Virginia" program of 1999, and the 1994 slave auction.

Daily-Life Reenactments

Quotidian, or daily-life, historical reenactments are valuable components of Colonial Williamsburg's interpretive approach to the slave past. As many scholars of slavery have noted, the daily costs of slavery, which are registered in incremental moments, are frequently overlooked in abolitionist literature as well as in subsequent criticism. The emphasis on beatings constantly renders and maintains the slave body in an abjected state. The commonly stressed examples of slavery's wrongs or traumatic effects are those involving physical violations of the slave body, usually public, to auction-block sales or whippings. Such an emphasis, however, decreases the opportunity to consider other less egregious forms of slavery's captive scope. Rather than simply representing the extreme examples of abuse under slavery, like slave sales or physical abuse, the representations of the slave past also—and primarily— explore the daily-life choices, working conditions, and emotional cost of slavery as they might have been experienced by slaves in the eighteenth-century colonial capital.

Two characters in particular, developed in the late 1980s and performed through the early 1990s, were intended to teach Colonial Williamsburg visitors about slavery by allowing them to interact with a slave character. The Judith tour was a three-part group tour led by an interpreter portraying a figure from the past. Cate was a cook in the Whythe House who talked with museum visitors who toured the Powell home. These characters were conceptualized quite differently; Judith, a friendly guide, and Cate, a surly, grudging host. Both strategies use a first-person interpreter in an effort to teach visitors about slavery through interaction. When evaluating the programs, a Character Interpretation Department study noted a difference between the first-person and third-person format and how guests responded: "Visitors talked about slavery with more sophistication and depth after they encountered a first person interpretation of the subject than after the third person interpretation. Once the responses from all three groups were reviewed, the planning team felt confident about deciding to use first person interpretation" (Graft, "Evaluating Interpretive Programs" 3–4). First-person interpretation and the process of a group or individual guest interacting with a slave character enhanced the learning method, producing more sophisticated results. Perhaps the interactive mode invited more guest participation in the museum's story of slavery. In the Judith tour, guests walked with the character as she carried out orders from her mistress's errands around town. At the same time, Judith had an agenda of her own—a message to deliver. I suggest that the success of the program was due more to audience investment, the desire to play along, than any facile empathetic response. In addition, Judith's group was presented with an approach to the museum that encouraged them to think more critically about Colonial Williamsburg itself, to see it as a construction, a constellation of curatorial choices, rather than bare facts. This was important because, like many other African American characters who represented past persons, the story of black life, slave life, had no extant displayed objects or sites with which to document their existence. In a context where "eighty-eight original buildings" are chief among many objects presented as evidence of America's revolutionary past, the story of those deprived of objects has less veracity. White characters such as the Whythes, the Randolphs, and Patrick Henry are continually reified by the references to historical records and objects—preserved and displayed—that prove their existence. These people and their stories are valued at Colonial Williamsburg. For Judith and Cate, however, "there were no authentic slave items, articles from the eighteenth century owned by or associated directly with slaves" (Lawson, "The Other Half" 217). Using the formula of "object equals truth," Colonial Williamsburg falls prey to a condition common to other museums: by being object-oriented, "curators can make a fetish of the object itself, thereby obstructing our understanding of the relationships between individuals, objects and their roles in society" (Vanderstel, "Humanizing the Past" 20). In addition, they reproduce the definition of the traditional museum as a "sacred grove" (something that living-history museums generally oppose), with curatorial practices implying that "the prized possessions inside the secure and stable museum are more enduring, valuable, legitimate, and of higher quality than those outside it" (Jeffers, "Museum as Process" 110).

The first-person tour provides an encounter that fosters more critical thinking and attention to slavery and the ways it appears—or is obstructed—in other sites throughout the museum. Perhaps interacting with a slave character may help to accomplish a broader goal of museum spectatorship. Museum visitors, writes David G. Vanderstel, "must be *taught* to place the exhibit objects into a broader context, to analyze the objects themselves, and to uncover the mysteries contained within them" ("Humanizing the Past" 21). The two characters under consideration are but a small sampling of first-person interpretation of slavery at Colonial Williamsburg. However, they began to enact this learning process in reverse. Starting with a person, a character designed to be a "living artifact" but one who also represented a person who was an object in chattel slavery, the interpreters remarked on the disparity between the past and its historical records while encouraging visitors to see Colonial Williamsburg with a more critical eye. When walking the streets with the tour guide—who shifted from third-person contextualist to first-person performer, visitors were reminded that, despite what many museumgoers may want to believe, Colonial Williamsburg's displays and objects "are constructed with the idea of presenting stories of the past according to some administrative agenda" (Lawson, "The Other Half" 207).

The tour group, walking around the town with a black female occupying multiple roles and shifting between them to impart subtle and overt lessons about eighteenth-century slave life, was exposed to another interpretive layer. They became part of the character Judith's daily tasks and privy to her "secret"—that she was relaying a personal message unbeknownst to her mistress. They were also invisible shadows who went unnoticed by the white characters who addressed her. This visitor point of view, Lawson observes, "encourage[s] a sense of equality and alliance between the visitors and the slave character, giving them a double entry into the experience of slavery" (ibid. 210). Though Lawson might overstate the case regarding guests' introduction into an "experience" of slavery, they *were* exposed to a story, a scene of representation—an interpretation of the slave past. They were also inaugurated into a new way of approaching Colonial Williamsburg. Rather than seeing it as a group of facts and artifacts assembled by an invisible hand, they were encouraged to think about choices that were made, to consider what was included in the narrative and what was left out. At the close of the tour, the interpreter "returned" to her third-person perspective for a wrap-up session.

Explaining the impetus behind first-person and other interpretive work on black life at Colonial Williamsburg, Christy Coleman (who would later head the AAIP department and develop the controversial slave-sale reenactment in 1994) told her group, "What we're doing here is we're trying to set the picture right. We're trying to look at our past, not so much our history because the history might fool you. So you look at the past and you start trying to pull all of these pieces together because one [the white population] was just as dependent on the other [the black population]. It really was. We were very, very co-dependent on one another" (ibid. 222). Setting aside the "codependency apologia" for a brief moment (I will return to it shortly), the distinction made here between "the past" and "the history" is worth attention. What is the difference these two ideas? Coleman implies—and gets visitors to consider—that there are profound distinctions. Primarily, history "might fool you," especially when records are missing or opaque, documents only footnote black life, and objects used or owned by slaves are not displayed behind glass or velvet ropes. The past is broader, more complex, than history can address.

Critiquing Whiteness in Slavery Reenactment

The alliance between the interpreter (and the character, Judith, that she portrayed) and the museum visitors was reinforced in several ways, one of which was the audience's position of invisibility to white people speaking to Judith. This connection was first established during the third-person opening or preface to the tour, one that explained the ground rules and framed guest expectations. Third-person interpreters, speaking from the present moment, informed the group, "For the nature of this tour, you, the audience, are considered equals with her. You are equal to her. She will not recognize your racial person, ok? If she did, she wouldn't talk to most of you" (ibid. 207). This gesture—of placing the largely white audience on the same level as a slave character—is a compelling exception to the usual suspension of disbelief required or encouraged by the museum. Visitors to what has been referred to as the "Republican Disneyland" are often asked—overtly or subtly—to imagine themselves in a colonial time and place. From the much mentioned "eighty-eight original buildings" to the group seating and song in the taverns to the costumes available for rental or purchase, efforts abound that encourage an imagined chronological shift between the present day and the colonial past. One thing, however, that I believe rarely gets questioned in the imagined "time travel" is the racial composition of its majority visitors. It appears that white visitors—and perhaps all visitors—are encouraged at nearly every turn to imagine themselves as part of the elite and ruling classes that lived in Williamsburg in the eighteenth century. Strolling through the Palace Gardens or traipsing through the Randolph House, museum guests are asked to see themselves as individuals who might—had they lived in the eighteenth century—have dined or otherwise fraternized with the crème of colonial society. In a way, white skin privilege, and a tacit, silent form of white supremacy, factors in the touring experience for the majority of white visitors to Colonial Williamsburg. Significantly, it is programs on slavery, "The Other Half" tour or this tour mentioned above, that make tacit white privilege something to be noticed and critiqued. Placing white visitors (or any twentieth-century visitor on this tour) on the same social level as Judith temporarily divested visitors of white privilege if but for an imagined moment. In surrendering the claim to whiteness, in return, the guests were able to be seen by Judith and spend time with a slave character who engaged them without reservations or fear. Instead of being seen by the character as someone to avoid, as someone who required silence, white visitors became acknowledged by Judith, who joked with guests as she took her group through the back streets or side entrances of Colonial Williamsburg. Guests in possession of a white racial identity apparently suspended it for the duration of the tour. This is significant for the tour's goal of experiential learning of the slave past. However, rather than presenting scenes that affirmed the moral compass of the early revolutionary activists, many AAIP programs reminded guests of the nation's slave past—a historical reality that seemed at risk of disappearing. The guide's repeated phrase, "You are considered equals. . . . You are equal to her," recalled the Declaration of Independence's key phrase, "All men are created equal," and inverted the liberatory thrust behind the liberal democracy of the eighteenth century. It was only on African American tours that I observed white visitors being informed that only a small percentage of the Williamsburg population lived in mansions or palaces. Theirs were the only programs that complicated and challenged the easy substitution that Colonial Williamsburg offered: that visitors can and should imagine themselves among the city's elite denizens. Frequently, guides informed their charges that unless they were from families like the Randolphs, the Carters, or the Whythes, then the eighteenth century they would "return" to would feature hard work and a small house or shack with dirt floors, a life closer to that of slaves than the ruling elite. In fact, many slaves of the ruling class (the tour guide observed) might have been better clothed than regular whites in Williamsburg. That the Judith tour, studied by Lawson in the early 1990s, directly informed the guests that in this invented scenario they would be "equal" to a slave character is an example of the implied trust between the program's coordinators and the participants. The coordinators and guides aimed to set the audience at ease, taking the group under their wing, allowing them to be invisible shadows. In this way, the visitors both watched and in a small way participated in the representation of daily-life activities for a slave in the colonial capital. Judith's character eased this interaction by making guests feel included. The character of Cate, another example of the quotidian forms or effect of slavery, took a different, more combative, approach.

Reenacting the Emotional Cost of Slavery

Developed in the mid-1980s by Arthur Barnes (of the "living artifact" philosophy) and Christy Coleman, Cate, the surly and depressed slave, was created to "convey the grimness of slavery not only by telling . . . but even more by doing or being" (ibid. 261). Part of a house and outbuildings tour of the Powell property, Cate's character was the first stop on a two-part tour of the kitchens. After the group left the main house, where they interacted with interpreters portraying either Mr. or Mrs. Powell, the group went to talk with Cate, then ended the tour with another slave character, Judith, described above. Cate's character was a controversial one. Unlike the image the museum worked hard to cultivate—one where all experience and interactions were "positive"—this character would not affirm guest sensibility, nor would she put them at ease. In creating the character, Barnes and Coleman aimed to get beyond the "image of the slave as a clever, industrious survivor" because it both "failed to convey the real horror of the institution and also falsified the past." They wanted a character with more of an edge: in their view, if visitors were able to leave an encounter with a slave character feeling unmoved, or, worse, if they left feeling good, then the interpretation must have been inaccurate (262). It is important to place this interpretive strategy—to create a slave character that might make visitors uncomfortable—in the broader context of slavery's subjection and the limited vision of black sentience.

As Saidiya Hartman and other scholars have noted, slavery's overarching structure of dominance and subordination frequently objectified the slave subject, so much so that even today the slave body receives more critical attention that the slave soul, slave spirit, or other elements of the slave's emotional life. One could point to the (disastrous) fallout from Stanley Elkins's 1956 study comparing slave captivity on southern plantations and Jewish captives in Nazi concentration camps as an unfortunate consequence of a problematic attempt to explain slave psychology. In short, Elkins argued that the conditions of captivity generated adverse psychological consequences, as documented by therapists working with Holocaust survivors, treating them for an array of disorders. For the slave population, however, there was no psychologically therapeutic support or posttraumatic stress disorder diagnosis available. Rather, Elkins claimed that the stress of slave life turned black people into "Sambos." One perhaps unintended consequence of the flurry of scholarly writing that refuted Elkins's claims was the subsequent silence from historians and other academics on the topic of slave psychology. A compelling exception to this trend is Nell Irvin Painter's essay "Soul Murder and Slavery" that claims to bring back the useful dimensions of psychology and psychoanalysis to illuminate parts of Sojourner Truth's life and legend. Painter addressed "soul murder" as a destructive component that is part of the abjection that slaves faced.

In its aim to depict the psychological dimension of slavery, Cate's character is a departure from other black characters that put guests at ease, and it is noteworthy for its ambition to teach an elusive element of slave history. There are other controversies embedded here, one of which involved how the interpreter who played Cate might reflect poorly on black employees of Colonial Williamsburg and on blacks more generally. There was always the risk that instead of seeing a depressed, angry, or despondent slave character, those depicted traits would be attributed to an employee having a bad day.

For Cate's part of the tour, guests entered the first room to find her seated, and watching them silently. As the group filed in, silence loomed and continued. Cate would answer any opening questions with few words and in a tone that discouraged further conversation. "She did nothing to help the visitors out," observed Lawson. "Indeed, the longer the encounter went on, the more tense the atmosphere became. Some visitors would actually leave the room, going back outdoors and missing the continuation of the visit into the kitchen to meet Judith" (260). This emotional state of a surly or depressed slave woman was previously unseen in the streets or other buildings of Colonial Williamsburg; it was an anomaly.

To reiterate what others have noted about Colonial Williamsburg, the museum—a mix of educational institution and entertainment or tourist venue—aims to present its guests with a largely positive experience. The history that they ultimately present to and represent for the audience is tempered by this goal. History becomes "a recreational product, vilified by a friendly and sensitive sales force of frontline interpreters, and marketed by a corporation whose bottom line is economic profit" (Shaffer, "Selling the Past" 880). But packaging the product of black history, especially as it appears in the subject of slavery, requires historical reenactors in their renditions of slave daily life to run counter to the implicit mandate of a "positive" story and guest comfort.

Cate's interview with the visitors to the Powell House represented a bold stroke in the interpretive and performance-based historical work on slavery in Colonial Williamsburg. Cate's surly disposition refused to appease guests, but made them work to learn about her, a process that was frustrated and thwarted by her reluctance. Anna Logan Lawson describes the following encounter as a typical exchange between Cate and museum visitors:

Visitor: What do you think of Mr. Powell?
Cate: What do you mean?
Visitor: Is he fair?
Cate: What do you mean "fair"?
Visitor: Does he treat you well?
Cate: Depends on what you mean by "well."
Visitor: Does he beat you?
Cate: Sometimes.
Visitor: Did you deserve it?
Cate: Nobody deserves to be beaten. (261)

Cate's reticence and uncooperative attitude challenged Colonial Williamsburg's underlying goal to make history a positive commodity that is educational and entertaining, a place to which visitors come to reconnect with America's (and, in many cases, their own) story of the past. Cate's character avoided this agenda, turning away from it to show visitors an aspect of slave life unlikely to appear elsewhere in the museum. What does this dialogue suggest about Colonial Williamsburg's approach to reenacting black history and slavery? What does this verbal exchange reveal about typical perceptions of slavery, especially by those who would frequent Colonial Williamsburg?

I suggest that Cate's character, in its controversial, unapologetic, and un-accommodating stance, was an attempt to represent the inner life of slavery through a subtle representation of the emotional consequences of bondage. Before the guests reached Cate, the first step on their two-part tour of the outbuildings, their presence was loudly announced by the character of Mr. Powell, who went out and yelled at his slaves the way a hunter calls his hounds, shouting, "Someone's comin' to see you" or "I'm sendin' some folks out there." This display was one of the few times at Colonial Williamsburg that the di-chotomy between master and slave, dominant and subordinate, was so vividly displayed. The visitors were authorized by Powell to visit with Cate; she did not invite them. Also, that "Mr. Powell" sent the group to the outbuildings to "speak to our slaves" put the guests in a greater position of power than the slaves to whom they were allowed to meet (258). The guests, then, were a part of the structure of mastery, agents of the white authority figure who treated Cate as property. In a way, the idealized goal of reenactment promoted by Arthur Barnes had been met: Cate's character was a "living artifact," a slave who was subject to the authority, whims, and caprice of "Mr. Powell," another "living artifact." What Barnes failed to discern, however, was the position the visitor would occupy in relation to these artifacts that occupy the domi-nant and subordinate ends of the power spectrum. If, unlike the Judith tour mentioned earlier that placed the guests on the same social level as the slave character, the visitors to the Powell House are welcomed as peers, then they must, of necessity, be in positions of mastery over the slaves they are permitted to interview. For these guests, most of whom are white, this represents the first or only time that the implied white subject position—which all Colonial Williamsburg visitors are assumed to occupy, insofar as all guests are treated as if they are of Williamsburg's elite regardless of their race—is revealed to have a social cost: that their position of mastery does not entitle them to receive the positive or upbeat feelings of an enslaved person.

Several objections to this strategy emerged as the program was presented. One of these was that Cate would be mistaken not for an angry or despon-dent slave adversely affected by bondage but rather an example of a hostile black person who did not feel like working. This assumption reflected poorly on all Colonial Williamsburg's black workers and reinforced racism more generally. However, I would like to consider Cate's disposition not only as a challenge to the positive, upbeat story of black history usually offered at Colonial Williamsburg but, more important, as a critique of the implied whiteness attributed to Colonial Williamsburg guests and the presumed mastery implied therein.

Colonial Williamsburg's first-person and third-person interpreters, in my view, always interact with museum visitors as if the guest is an eighteenth-century white elite. This is most likely for practical—rather than purely pedagogical—reasons. If today's black, Asian, and Hispanic visitors were subjected to the same treatment they would have received in the eighteenth-century colonial capital, Colonial Williamsburg would have no repeat business from this demographic. Federal regulations and legislation—and corporate common sense—prevent the racial person of minority visitors from being acknowledged. However, by erasing these particularities, Colonial Williamsburg goes to the extreme position of having its first-person and character interpreters interact with all guests as if they are of the white ruling class. The danger of this strategy—one of many—is that whiteness becomes an invisible entitlement of this tourist experience.

So whereas most locations around the museum reinforce the positive elements of the implied racial and social states of Colonial Williamsburg patrons, Cate's character brings forth the negative aspects of the white social, rural position: that although white elites may have legal property rights to slaves, they cannot control black sentiment. Many white guests responded poorly to Cate's stark portrayal. Anna Logan Lawson, who during her research of black history at Colonial Williamsburg spent two summers at the Powell House, describes how visitors responded to Cate's conversation about beatings, mentioned earlier. When asked if she "deserved" to be beaten, Cate replied that no one deserves that type of abuse. Lawson reports:

> Most visitors would drop the subject at this point, but not always. There was the time when Cate got to "sometimes," and a man standing next to me muttered sarcastically, "I wonder why he beat her." Coleman overheard and pounced, asking him, "Why do you wonder why, sir?" He muttered something about Mr. Powell not approving of the way she was treating his guests. On another day, a woman who had heard the beating exchange left the building saying she thought Cate "had an attitude." She told me that she was from Chicago and had not come all the way to Williamsburg to see a black with an attitude. (261)

Both responses, I maintain, are the result of a historical slavery reenactment that breaks with the affirming, spunky-survivor model of slavery favored by Colonial Williamsburg. These two white visitors were offended by the visage of black anger and resentment they observed. Unlike the Powells, and even Judith, the slave character the group met after leaving Cate, this character did not aim to set them at ease or make them feel welcome. She did not extend to them the courtesy, respect, or other duty that even they had come to believe they merited as implied (and maybe internalized?) white elites in eighteenth-century Williamsburg. I wonder about the Chicago woman—who apparently had an ample supply of unfriendly black people back home—who didn't come to Colonial Williamsburg to see "a black with an attitude." What type of black person, then, did she expect to see? It is no great analytical stretch to argue that this woman seemed to have come for the "history" but a version of that history that affirmed her in multiple ways; when part of that reenacted history talked back—or, rather, refused to talk to her at all—then her trip was frustrated.

A similar response can be observed in the man who muttered—in an aside, not to be overheard by Cate—"I wonder why he beat her." It is important to note here that this white man was speaking to another person, a white woman he assumed to be another tourist. In fact, his interlocutor was Anna Logan Lawson, a graduate student studying the museum for her dissertation and other anthropological work. Lawson, a contributor to Handler and Gable's acclaimed study of Colonial Williamsburg's approach to social history, was a member of a savvy research team. To this tourist, however, she was a part of his team—the white racial identity corps recently imbued with fictional, yet powerful, status as an eighteenth-century elite. This explanation, though it may appear at first glance to be far-fetched, is a useful tactic to understand why a man would joke with a woman he did not know about beating another woman. Would not the woman feel a gender alliance, fearing that she too may be subject to male violence? For this man, Lawson was an appropriate audience for his whispered sentiment, a feeling, I might add, that could easily be completed with the phrase, "I'd beat her too." In his eyes, I speculate, Lawson and he occupied the same racial and social position as white elites in the setting of the museum. Encouraged to assume an identity that automatically imbued him with authority over the angry slave woman in his presence, he did not see or imagine that Lawson or any other (white) female tourist would align herself with the surly black woman. This particular example of reenacting the quotidian aspects of slavery is a powerful, if understated, mode of pedagogy. Under these conditions of dominance and subordination, Cate's resentment-as-resistance, in its quiet, subdued form, permeated the interactions between Cate and her audience. She had little power or control in this scene—at least on one level; that is, she did not invite the group to her, and she had to answer their questions because she was told to do so. She could neither leave nor refuse. Yet the subtle resistance she performed could be seen as a way to erect boundaries around her, a defense mechanism: she had to speak with this group, but she didn't have to like it, and she didn't have to help the audience like it, either. In fact, embedded in this discomfort lies the potential to teach the untenable aspects of slavery, to suggest a slim view of captivity's emotional costs. Were a guest to ask, "Why am I uncomfortable? Why does this person seem so reticent or hostile?" the answers might lead that person to consider the institution of slavery and the (in some cases recently acquired) white privilege bestowed upon them by the museum.

For such a thought process to occur, or even to begin, however, the visitor must not walk out in disgust or anger. This is part of the difficulty of this particular reenactment strategy and why such depictions were not more frequent. Cate's character was designed to represent part of slavery's emotional costs for the enslaved—by depicting her in a context free from her master's gaze (Powell's) yet still subject to a group gaze involving similar mastery components. This strategy deepened the complexity of slavery reenactments at Colonial Williamsburg and attested to groundbreaking academic work in history and literary studies about affect, sentiment, and subjection. At the same time, the surface impression received by those unwilling to think deeply about the motives for Cate's disposition was one of an inexplicably sullen black woman who, unlike almost every other character, first- or third-person interpreter, shopkeeper, waitress, or gatekeeper, was not solicitous or even civil.

As I mentioned earlier, Cate's character was an anomaly within Colonial Williamsburg, an institution whose motto is "Where history comes to life." At Colonial Williamsburg, however, the revived history is largely positive and affirming to those paying the admission price. The museum privileges and promotes a "mainstream" experience for its guests: "entertaining, educational and, above all, positive" (264). In addition, the mainstream view also valued the troubled and troubling concept of authenticity (and implied mimesis), offering visitors artifacts, buildings, and horse dung in the streets as proof of their commitment to reproducing a sense of eighteenth-century Virginia. In this frame, Lawson notes, "Cate's interpretation was a paradox. Because it was the more accurate portrayal of slavery, one can see it as coming closer to dovetailing with the 'mainstream' of the museum. But because it conflicted with how AAIP members needed to be seen and how the museum's 'mainstream' visitors wanted to see themselves and their past vis-à-vis African Americans, it was on the fringe" (269). The paradox of Cate's character as a historical reenactment of slavery navigates between veering toward the cutting edge of academic research on slavery (among scholars aiming to understand the emotional impact of slavery rather than its more visible physical components) and what is considered appropriate behavior for an employee of a large corporation interacting with a paying audience. That Cate's character was not frequently performed can be taken as a sign of what faction—those in favor of provocative representations or those invested in positive guest relations—eventually won out.

Let me pause here to say a bit more about the implied or imparted whiteness of Colonial Williamsburg's tourist. I must confess a slightly perverse pleasure at recounting Lawson's tale of the white woman from Chicago who walked out of the conversation with Cate. This white woman's discomfort is remarkable because, in my research and time at the museum, it is so rare. The tourists are encouraged to imagine themselves as being in the eighteenth-century colonial capital. The products for sale, from the reproduction baskets and fine china to the garments available for rental and muskets available for sale, the services available, such as a horse-drawn carriage tour costing approximately sixty dollars, or restaurant dining on the grounds of the museum all operate on the premise that if guests were to imagine themselves in the eighteenth century, they would not be serving wenches or stable boys. The implied white and elite status of all visitors to Colonial Williamsburg was the greatest source of dissonance for me as a black visitor and researcher. I suggest that any program or reenactment of slavery that chips away at that easily assumed mantle of whiteness and its privileges is valuable, and might represent the start of more serious considerations about slavery and America's past.

As one can easily imagine, most visitors to Colonial Williamsburg are white. Many upper and middle schools in Virginia bring groups of students on field trips to Colonial Williamsburg, which greatly increases the number of young people and people of color on Duke of Gloucester Street, the main drag of Colonial Williamsburg. Most visitors are white families and older couples. I was frequently the only black person on the tours and programs I attended during the course of this project (the fall of 2003 and spring and summer of 2004).

Two moments of dissonance stand out for me. The first suggests the concept of Colonial Williamsburg's interpolating all guests as white; the second shows the risks of this interpolation. Both moments occurred during the fall 2004 weekend program "Dunmore's Proclamation" at the Randolph House. I will address this program as an example of an "extreme" version (or crisis version) of a historical reenactment of slavery. In what follows, I will discuss the notion of fugitive reenactments as presented in the main story line of that weekend and in minor characters' similar situation. I pause here before going to this main point because the two moments to which I refer involve slavery reenactment tangentially but still significantly. Both moments involve white characters reenacting roles as white elite householders and slaveholders.

In the parlor of the Randolph House, the widow Randolph and a few neighbors sat and greeted the tour group, which began upstairs. The women sat and talked, the men stood near the unlit fireplaces, and another woman (pregnant) was embroidering a flower on linen in this very genteel scene. Unlike the other guests, I felt unsettled (we had just left an audience with two slave characters upstairs who experienced fear and anxiety about family separation) sitting with these blithe characters who seemed interested in their own comforts and unaware of the turmoil upstairs. When the subject drifted to slavery (only slightly mentioned, in terms of these characters being deprived of their property), I felt compelled to speak: "So the slaves are better off with you then?" Without missing a beat, the man dressed in silk pants and shiny buttons shot back, "Of course! They've come from a heathen land. We're civilizing them!"

The ease with which this character spoke these racist beliefs was shocking in its normality and in his unblinking ability to make such claims to a black woman. Perhaps, though I hesitate to speculate, this male performer harbored racial beliefs that fostered his ability to speak racist thoughts to a black person easily. This, however, is an uncharitable position, unworthy of my considerable efforts to understand reenactment work. More likely, this exchange—between a black visitor and a character interpreter who had become a "living artifact" of the eighteenth century—was predicated on the interpreter reading all visitors as white. As a result of spreading the mantle of whiteness so broadly among all patrons of Colonial Williamsburg, white privilege and the normality of whiteness were ubiquitous throughout the museum, even in programs designed to teach about slavery.

The second moment of dissonance arose in the same context—the Randolph House parlor—but on a different tour. The room was crowded during this rotation and, as was customary, the four character interpreters (two male and two female) spoke among themselves, acknowledged the visitors, then solicited questions from the assembled group. During part of the conversation about what the new widow would do with her slave property, she indicated the teen boys gathered and asked, "Do you have any queries of us? You are not far from the time when you will be masters yourselves." The boys said nothing. But a white girl, attired in colonial dress most likely purchased or rented from a museum gift shop, piped up, "Are you familiar with the Underground Railroad?" When Mrs. Randolph's character replied that she was not, Caroline, the young girl, continued, "I think it might have been in a different time period, I don't know, but it secretly helps slaves run away." As Mrs. Randolph exclaimed, "Oh, my!" the conversation continued:

> Mrs. Whythe: Well, I assure you, Miss Caroline, that if anyone should assist a runaway he should find himself in great difficulty, in great difficulty. And find themselves confined to a jail.
>
> Miss Caroline: I don't doubt it. I shall not doubt it.
>
> Miss Randolph: So if you hear of any such things, it's best that you let someone know, particularly an adult. You will make a fine mistress of your home when the time comes. Your mother has trained you well.

Most visitors greeted this exchange with titters and shy smiles at the precocity of a young girl clearly enamored with America's past. I, however, was not laughing. This moment was daunting, an example of the risks of the subtle whitening effect on the Colonial Williamsburg clientele. What does it mean that this girl essentially became a "tattletale" on fugitive slaves, warning the assembled masters and mistresses of the threat the Underground Railroad posed to their slaveholder status? What also can one make of the endorsement of the girl—who was neither an eighteenth-century child nor a (paid) reenactor of one—as a "fine mistress," trained well in the racial mores of the eighteenth century by her mother? Is this an achievement of which this girl's twenty-first-century mother should be proud?

This interaction is but one of the many examples of Colonial Williamsburg interpretive staff addressing all guests as if they hold a position of racial mastery. Given the ubiquity of this designation, I wonder if the quotidian, or daily-life, reenactment can penetrate the barrier imposed (on some) and erected (by others) on the museum's visitors. Did Judith's tour and her genial demeanor express a version of the slave past that—in its "spunky survivor" quality—rested easy with a visitor's consciousness? Can the subtleties of Cate's bitter performance do more to teach about slavery's emotional costs and disrupt the comforting elements of white (Colonial Williamsburg visitors') privilege? Stacy Roth, a living-history scholar and advocate, observes that although Cate's character made visitors uneasy, "the program planners have chosen to use discomfort as part of the learning experience." Visitors' sentiment (and the management and manipulation of it) is vital to the living-history enterprise, as Roth notes: "Visitors are more receptive to first-person interpretation when they are not threatened and uncomfortable" (*Past into Present* 177). Despite the fact that Cate was a challenging representation, Roth notes that this depiction did "have an impact on visitors, even if there is a certain discomfort involved." Roth suggests that this impact took the form of rationalizing Cate's response (as opposed to merely reacting with snide comments or marching off in a huff): "When faced with the presence of a slave character it is likely that many visitors will think 'well, this person is a SLAVE, SO OF COURSE they have a reason to be hostile, angry, and secretive" (e-mail correspondence on museum discussion list, October 10, 1994). Unhappiness is assumed. So although the visitor may feel uncomfortable, he may not necessarily feel threatened. It seems, however, that Cate's representation did little to disrupt the assumed racial privileges guests are encouraged to assume throughout the museum, a privilege they adhere to, even if it means promoting slavery. Perhaps I am overly pessimistic about the implications of Caroline, the chronologically misplaced little girl who tattled on fugitives both long ago (from a twenty-first-century point of view) and yet to arrive (from the simulated eighteenth-century view of the Randolphs' parlor). She was playacting. Given the chance to do so from a position of white racial mastery, however, indicates the difficult path that slavery reenactors tread in an attempt to teach about the history and attendant traumatic effects of slavery. Caroline's actions also suggest why many blacks might choose a more insular, ritual reenactment with which to commemorate slavery.

Conclusion

A Soul Baby Talks Back

In her compelling 1989 essay "Negotiating between Tenses: Witnessing Slavery after Freedom—*Dessa Rose*," Deborah McDowell concludes by broaching the ways in which Sherley Anne Williams's novel *Dessa Rose* addresses and incorporates laughter as an emotional release for its female slave protagonist: "We laughed so we wouldn't cry." More forcefully, Williams uses black laughter as a sign of freedom and autonomy: "I told myself this [laughter] was good, that it showed slavery didn't have no hold on us no more." McDowell is careful to insist that these passages are not a sign that slavery is a joke, "an institution to be laughed at, laughed about, laughed over" (159). Instead, laughter is deployed here in a manner that is consonant with contemporary scholarship on the slave experience, particularly those forms that emphasize "particular acts of agency within an oppressive and degrading system" (160). Recently, a provocative soul-baby response to this historiographic and literary situation has emerged, using a different approach to the comedic possibilities for representing slavery. While the neo-slave books and films explored in this book and elsewhere share a certain reverence for slavery, the work of a new black vernacular intellectual not only laughs at slavery but does so all the way to the bank.

Dave Chappelle produces comedy that treads the fine line between pain and pleasure. As he told a *Time* writer, "Some things are so painful that they seem as if they're not funny, but it's not like people will never laugh at them. A lot of times the humor doesn't come from pain exactly; it comes from things that make you anxious or afraid. It just helps you put them in perspective if you laugh at them" (Chappelle and Farley, "That's What I Call Funny" n.p.). A stand-up comedian with a lucrative sketch show on Comedy

Central in 2003 and 2004, Chappelle is the most recent in the history of black comedians who addressed slavery, however briefly, in their work (a few of the most well known being Garrett Morris and Richard Pryor in the 1970s and Eddie Murphy in the 1980s). And though slavery is not a joke, scholars suggest that it is a source for much of African American humor. "American slavery provides the backdrop of tragedy against which African Americans developed their distinct form of humor, in which the material of tragedy was converted into comedy, including the absurd. This often included self-deprecation, as the slaves themselves were often the subjects of their comic tales" (Gordon, "Humor" n.p.).

In what follows, I explore the methods Chappelle uses to deploy and provoke laughter as a technique for critical engagement with slavery, its representation, and its legacy. Curiously, the two sketches I analyze here—a parody of the *Roots* anniversary DVD and "The Time Haters"—are presented on *Chappelle's Show* as errors. The high jinks from Chappelle's version of *Roots* falls under the rubric of "bloopers," a popular subgenre of television production where fumbled dialogue, missed cues, and other mistakes caught on film are repackaged and sold as a separate product. "The Time Haters," a follow-up to the "Player Haters' Ball" sketch, is part of an episode devoted to shows that Chappelle says were unfit for his regular program. Chappelle claims that these proposed sketches failed to meet his comedic standard. The scenes might have been unduly offensive, as in the sketch of a boot camp for juvenile delinquents hosted by Nelson Mandela, or the skit could not be brought to a successful resolution, as in the sketch of an alternate reality where everyone, from the DMV to the KKK, is gay. Ironically, as with most bloopers or outtakes, these "errors" do indeed reach their intended audience (in a gesture of cinematic economy where nothing is wasted, many film credits are riddled with these abbreviated failed scenes). I am intrigued by the accidental quality of these sketches—or, to be more precise, the ways in which these sketches are presented as accidents or errors. I believe that it is there that the liminal space, between comedy and critical analysis, starts to accommodate the complex work of traumatic acknowledgment and address in the popular sphere.

Unlike the sacred responses to slavery's initial traumatic disruption of black life and the lingering effects of that institution on the contemporary scene, Chappelle's response is less reverential. This approach contrasts greatly to popular theories of posttraumatic slave disorder and posttraumatic slave syndrome as well as the Willie Lynch slave-management speech that is widely circulated within the black popular sphere. These strategies pay attention to the life conditions of the enslaved, proposing to endow their lives with not only credibility but also the authority to influence the character and emotional development of subsequent generations of blacks. The proponents of these theories, then, seem to owe a debt to their slave ancestors, one they willingly attempt to pay. The slavery sketches on *Chappelle's Show* might well reveal a reverence for the slave past, but they simultaneously separate the representations of slavery from the institution itself. Does making *Roots*—one of the earliest, most riveting, and most powerful depictions of slave life and black history—into a thing of laughter diminish it? Does the anachronistic placement of four "player haters" on a plantation mock slavery? Or does Chappelle urge us to think more critically about the uses of these representations?

Chappelle's Roots

The *Roots* bloopers sketch aired on *Chappelle's Show* concurrently with the release of the actual *Roots* twenty-fifth-anniversary DVD that compiled the original eight episodes with added cast interviews and other extra features. The critical and comedic elements of Chappelle's sketch depend on the assumption that most people are familiar with *Roots,* and know that it is not funny. The significance of *Roots* as a miniseries cannot be overstated. As one critic notes, "All or part of this record-breaking television extravaganza was seen in 85 percent of the nation's households, and thirty cities officially observed 'Roots Week'" (Bundles, "Looking Back" n.p.). Lisa Drew, the editor for Alex Haley's novel, recalls that "teachers taught *Roots* in their classrooms, and socialites gave dinner parties centered around watching it" (quoted in ibid.). By most accounts, the actors approached their work on *Roots* with seriousness and respect. "*Roots* has special meaning," says Ben Vereen, who played Kunta Kinte's grandson Chicken George. Nearly two decades after its release, Vereen claims, "What we did with history is untouchable." Georg Stanford Brown, another actor, describes his time on the set of *Roots* as more than a job: "It was the most meaningful experience, putting yourself in the position of having no self." John Amos, who portrayed the adult Kunta Kinte, describes a deeper sentiment, a more proximate connection to the slave past. During the first dress rehearsal, after putting on his costume and entering the field where a scene was to be filmed, Amos suffered a seizure: "I feel I was being visited by my ancestors," he recalls. "They wanted to be heard" ("Roots" n.p.). Ren Woods, who played Fanta, echoes Amos's thoughts: "It was almost as if I could feel the blood of my ancestors inside me" (Plath, *Roots* n.p.). In his *Roots* skit, Chappelle revises this reverential approach to the representation of slavery, emphasizing instead the jokes that might have lurked behind the original production.

I suggest that Chappelle's representation of *Roots* can be considered what Mark Anthony Neal would call a "soul baby" response. The generation of blacks born after the civil rights movement, into what Neal calls the post-soul era, has different expectations about their place in America, a greater sense of entitlement, authority, and access than their parents may have had. It is useful to read this sketch in the context of Chappelle's place within this generation. Born in 1973, and only three years old when *Roots* reached its 130 million viewers in January 1977, Chappelle may have a different, more distanced relationship to the powerful miniseries than those who watched the program as adults. This is not to say that everyone in the soul-baby or postsoul generation is as willing to laugh at *Roots* as *Chappelle's Show* indicates. Indeed, many grassroots hip-hop artists, such as Dead Prez, engage slavery and its attendant legacy of racism as source material for their music and activism; even more mainstream hip-hop and R&B musicians such as Missy Elliott ("Work It") and Whitney Houston ("Your Love Is My Love") reference slavery in a serious, if glancing, manner. In addition, Ishmael Reed and Alice Randall, two writers from two distinct generations, both play with the comedic effects possible when parodying popular conventions of slavery representations. Perhaps Chappelle's conception of *Roots* is more fluid, less limited to reading that representation as a sacred text because he is a comedian, not only a postsoul comedian. Or perhaps he is exploiting the irreverent possibilities his generation already noticed in *Roots*. For instance, a black woman who was in elementary school in the 1970s recalls that on the school days following the nights *Roots* aired, "Kunta Kinte" became another verbal weapon in the arsenal of grade school insults or the dozens ("Your momma's so black you look like Kunta Kinte").[1] Whereas *Roots* sparked serious adult conversation at dinner parties, on the playground many kids reduced it to jokes or racialized teasing by shouting "Run, Kunta, run" at each other during recess. In any event, it is important to consider Chappelle's retooling of *Roots*—which purports to expose the "gags, high jinks, and hilarious practical jokes" behind the original—as a critique of the notion that such texts should be considered sacred or classic. I do not believe that he is attempting to minimize or slight slavery, but instead turns a skeptical eye to those representations *and* critiques those who are unwilling to treat the miniseries as if it were any other television product. Some might charge that by making a joke out of *Roots,* he also mocks slavery. Such a claim, however, should direct our attention to the ways in which a simulacrum, or created referent, to slavery might come to elide or replace the original experiences of slavery it means to illuminate.

Chappelle's manufactured outtakes concern two pivotal moments from the original *Roots*. Both scenes feature Kunta Kinte. The first moment shows Kinte (played by John Amos) raising his newborn daughter to the heavens, saying, "Behold, the only thing greater than yourself." In the second clip, young Kinte (played by LeVar Burton) is refusing, under the pressure of the lash, to answer to the name "Toby": the white slave overseer whips Kinte's bare back, saying, "Your name is Toby," to which Kinte responds, "Kunta Kinte." Both of these moments were emotionally wrenching scenes when they appeared in the 1970s program. The first scene is significant for presenting the intimacy of a father-daughter relationship, maintaining African traditions, and the father's aim to instill in a newly born slave child a sense of power and self-esteem. The second moment is meaningful for bringing to public viewing what would become one of the most powerful scenes of the black body and mind being subject to capricious white authority.

Through the addition of new material, Chappelle's skit tweaks and revises these evocative scenes to produce another form of emotional affect: laughter. In his version of the scene, when Kunta Kinte holds his baby aloft to the midnight sky, blessing her in the tradition of his ancestors, a stream of liquid sprays from the baby's bottom, raining down on Kinte's upturned face. He quickly drops the baby, who falls to the ground, and the sound track changes from the sounds of chirping insects to a rousing "Keystone Cops" style of music. "Oh, I'm sorry," he says quickly, sheepishly, as someone rushes in to retrieve the fallen infant (which is actually a doll). The scene jumps back to the actor, who grins as his hands spread in explanation, "I told ya'll not to give me a real baby!" Leaning forward in laughter, he adds, "Pissing all over me and sh—."

There is a similarly abrupt shift in tone and mood in the next outtake scene. In this rendition of the evocative whipping scene, there is a focused close-up of Kunta Kinte's (Chappelle's) face and naked torso. When he is lashed with the whip, his face contorts slightly, but he maintains his dignity by not crying out or relenting in this rejection of the name Toby. The second time the whip strikes, rather than the stoic visage of previous takes, Chappelle's Kinte howls, "Ow!" steps down from the simulated whipping post, and turns to the white man holding the whip:

> "Damn! Steve! What I told you about hitting so hard, man?"
> "I'm sorry. Are you all right?"
> "All right? All right! I'm'a show you 'All right.'"

Chappelle walks over to the actor, pushes him to the ground, and proceeds to mockingly attack him. The jaunty "Keystone Cops" music marks the change from tragedy to comedy as the assembled cast (black actors representing slaves called to witness Kunta Kinte's punishment) and crew (a white sound engineer in a leisure suit) dissolves into laughter. Chappelle also laughs, pulls the white actor to his feet, and slaps him good-naturedly on the back. Saying, "Hold up, let me get back up there," Chappelle runs back to his mark, raises his arms, and resumes the grim posture of corporeal suffering. When his back turns, the audience learns that though he appears to be shirtless from the front, Chappelle's Kunta Kinte wears a protective back covering, a cross between a bulletproof vest and a turtle's shell, to spare him undue pain. This is apparently in contrast to LeVar Burton, who did not have protective covering when he depicted this scene. A reviewer reports, "Burton was so uncomfortable being lashed (even by an expert whip-handler) that he ruined the first take by flinching at every sound. It took a full day of working with the whip-handler to convince him that the pro could take a whip—where the tip moves 120 miles per hour—and wrap it gently around Burton's back, no matter how convincingly brutal it looked on-camera" (Plath, *Roots* n.p.).

The *Roots* bloopers sketch, like most blooper and outtake programs, exposes the means by which television and other seamlessly presented representations are created. Chappelle's sketch also serves as an allegory for a postsoul reading of this televised representation of slavery, urging viewers to consider what is being told and sold. Is there an appreciable difference, then, between Chappelle's version of *Roots* and the original? Why might one representation be considered sacred and the other profane? Perhaps it is a matter of tone and context. The original *Roots* did not sell or profit from slavery, did not traffic in its extremities for crass entertainment. Or did it? Perhaps it is useful to consider the similarities between the sacred *Roots* and its profane, if truncated, rendition. Both representations share an impulse to provide a form of supplementary, complementary knowledge about slavery and its representation. *Roots* revolutionized most Americans Tarzan-inspired perceptions of Africa and challenged the prevailing *Gone with the Wind* views of slavery. Chappelle's version incorporates and acknowledges the deep significance of these revisions. At the same time, he takes steps to show that *Roots* is a construction, a representation—though inspired by reverential goals and replete with meaningful implications—and, ultimately, a television product. Chappelle's emphasis on the construction of *Roots* does not diminish its meaning, but allows for the possibility to look more closely at, to think more carefully about, this representation and slavery as its source. Chappelle's work here suggests that if his *Roots* sketch *feels* irreverent toward slavery, it might be because we have attached a reverence, perhaps mistakenly, to a *representation* of slavery, erroneously eliding that depiction with slavery itself.

Chappelle's Bodily Epistemology: "The Time Haters"

Given Chappelle's comedic response to the representation of slavery in *Roots*, it should come as little surprise to learn that his version of bodily epistemology—the governing ethos of slavery representation and commemoration explored in this book—departs from the usual approach. To briefly restate my theory: bodily epistemology is a representational strategy that collapses the boundaries between past and present to permit characters in the present to develop more proximate knowledge of the past. In the words of Zora Neale Hurston's traveling heroine, these black protagonists and tourists "go there to know there." Fictional characters are remanded to the slave past for spiritual, emotional, or disciplinary reasons. In real life, tourists of certain slavery exhibits or historical reenactors make a simulated return to a re-created past to access knowledge of slavery via living history. Chappelle's representation of time travel to the slave past approaches the concept of bodily epistemology in an aggressive and confrontational way. Rather than featuring a present-day black protagonist who regards this painful history with guilt, anxiety, or fear, Chappelle presents characters that not only hate it but hate *on* it.

"The Time Haters," a sketch within a sketch, is framed within a regular-season episode devoted to failed skits. As with every *Chappelle's Show* episode, Chappelle does what is called a wraparound: he transitions to commercial breaks, introduces musical guests, and, most important, contextualizes each sketch with banter or other comedic material. In this wraparound, Chappelle's task is to explain why these shows failed to make it into the regular lineup, ironically airing them within a frame that challenges the audience to evaluate and analyze their comedic potential. "The Time Haters," a sequel to the "Player Haters' Ball" sketch in season 1, centers around four men—Silky Johnson (Chappelle), Buc Nasty (Charlie Murphy), Phyuck Yu (Yoshia Mita), and Beautiful (Donnell Rawlings)—who perform acts of verbal dueling and other stylized forms of "hating" on each other (for instance, "Buc Nasty, you are so dark that when you touch yourself, it's black-on-black crime").

In "The Time Haters," the players use a time machine, Yu's project for the Player Haters' Science Fair, to return to the antebellum period. The four Haters approach a plantation where blacks are working in the fields. Silky, the group's apparent leader, describes slavery as a system where blacks work "for the minimalist of wages: grits and tattered clothes." When Buc Nasty mocks the slaves' bare feet, Johnson chides him: "Buc Nasty, have some respect. One of these men could be your great-grandfather." The camera cuts quickly to the image of a man in a slave costume who indeed looks like Buc Nasty. The two men stare at each other in shocked recognition. Silky's demand that his colleague "have some respect" is Chappelle's depiction of slavery at its most reverent. Silky's claim that the slaves worked for "grits and tattered clothes" does not disrespect the slaves themselves. Instead, his words critique the injustice and disparities of a labor system that offered no real wages. When Buc Nasty starts down a path that is critical of slaves rather than slavery, Silky reminds him of his own ancestral connections to the people he wants to "hate" on. Slaves are not their target, but the frantically surprised slave master who charges into the scene is fair game.

> Slave master: What the hell are you nigras doing out here?
>
> Silky: We are the Time Haters. We traveled all the way back through time *(Dramatic music rises, then abruptly stops.)* to call you a "cracker."
>
> Slave master: You better watch your mouth.
>
> Buc Nasty: Actually, you better watch your mouth, white boy. Or I'll put these gaiters up your ass and show your insides some style.
>
> Slave master: That's enough! *(The slave master cracks a whip.)*
>
> Buc Nasty *(Snickering.)*: Look, Silky, he pulled out a whip.
>
> Silky *(Nonplussed.)*: Nice whip. *(Pulls out a gun.)* This here is a pistol. Reach for the sky, honky.
>
> *(The white man raises his hands, and the slaves behind him murmur, "Honky? Honky?")*
>
> Silky: *Honky* is a racial epithet, used for white people. It was made popular by a man named George Jefferson in the 1970s. *(Summarizes the premise of the sitcom "The Jeffersons.")* Convoluted story, I'll admit. But the point is this . . . that in the future, all black people will be free!

The sketch then returns to Chappelle's wraparound. There, he explains that the sketch failed because of what happened next, an action that brought the filming to an abrupt stop. He predicts, "*This* episode will come to a screeching halt, but I'll show it." The scene returns to Silky, still pointing his gun at the slave owner. A slave asks, "When we gon' be free?" Silky replies, "That's a good question, my man." Briefly pausing to consider, Silky says, "How about now-ish?" and shoots the slave master at point-blank range. The gun issues a loud "bang!" A red pool blossoms just above the white man's heart, coloring his white shirt. He groans, staggers, and falls to the ground, his hands still raised. This scene is repeated three times: the strident gun report, the man's moans, the red stain, and the backward tumble. Each time, the audience laughs, and the mirth is renewed after each repetition.

The Time Haters have not "returned" to the slave past to atone for or acknowledge the hidden brutalities of slavery; rather, they are there to do what they do best, to *hate* on the institution of slavery. Buc Nasty's threat to the slave master, like Silky's execution of him, is unlike other representations of bodily epistemology. These men (save for Robinson's character, who flees when the whip is cracked) are not intimidated by the violence used to maintain slavery, nor are they concerned that they might be vulnerable or subjected to this use of violence. The Time Haters embody the postsoul era, where their independence and verve are so natural and untroubled that Silky's lofty declaration of universal black freedom can be *proven* by the "convoluted story" of a black popular television program. They are firmly cloaked in the mantle of the postsoul era—a moment in which *The Jeffersons* is a sign, however indirect, of the black progress narrative. The postsoul accentuates their presence in the past. Traumatic history is not a nightmare from which they can never awake, nor a specter to be feared, but yet another opponent to be cleverly defeated by stylized insults, quirky banter, and even the report of a pistol.

After the slave master is shot amid a hail of laughter for the third time, the scene then jumps back to the onstage Chappelle, who stands doubled over, hands on his knees, quaking with silent laughter. He stands up, regaining his composure, and tells the audience, "Apparently, shooting a slave master isn't funny to anybody but me and Neal." After a brief pause that is filled with the rebuttal of this claim—audience laughter—Chappelle continues, "If I could, I'd do it every episode." Might Chappelle already be doing something much like this? Might the sharp-witted sketches that skewer, among other things, white privilege and its attendant forms of racism be read as "shooting a slave master" for fun and profit? The show itself is a form of resisting and protest, critique and interrogation. At the end of every episode, thumbing his nose at those who would claim to control him, Chappelle gets the last laugh, and uses references to slavery to make his point.

Chappelle's Reparations: "I'm Ree-ah-ch, Bee-ah-tch!" (I'm Rich, Bitch!)

A historic lucrative financial arrangement with Comedy Central made Chappelle one of the youngest, ultrawealthy black entertainers of recent note. The deal worth about fifty million dollars "vault[ed] Chappelle into the rarefied realm of television's top earners. The new contract is believed to not only mark a steep increase for Chappelle as star, writer, co-executive producer and co-creator of 'Chappelle's Show,' but more significantly, reward him with a hefty chunk of the series' robust DVD sales" (Wallenstein, "Chappelle Inks" n.p.). The large sum of money ("given" to a young black man who is neither an athlete nor a rapper) raised a few hackles and eyebrows. Chappelle addressed this skepticism by comedic misdirection and diffusion. For instance,

60 Minutes interviewer Bob Simon seemed intent on humiliating Chappelle by suggesting that his success was comparatively undeserved: "You're making more now than Mike Wallace. You're making more than Mike Wallace and Dan Rather put together. You're probably, even if you throw Ed Bradley into the mix, you're making more than Wallace and Rather and Bradley put together." Chappelle replied, "Wow. Off to Comedy Central. Man, being put in those kinda perspectives, wow. Get me a cup of coffee, Bob" ("Chappelle" n.p.). He told another reporter impressed by his new salary, "The deal made it very hard to say no. I'm not sure, but I believe there is a clause that gives me reparations for slavery" (Levin, "Chappelle" n.p.). But even his fans, as evidenced by blogs and chat forums, were concerned with and confused about what exactly Chappelle owed to the network.

In an online discussion of Chappelle's hiatus from filming the third season, one fan wrote, "Don't worry dave will come back after awhile, He isnt a sell out to his fans, just to the companies that own him [*sic*]" (Dirty Harry, "Evil Avatar" n.p.). Another agreed: "Comedy Central is paying big money for him. He'll return" (Ultima 13, "Evil Avatar" n.p.). The notion of Dave being owned by Comedy Central rankled one fan, who rushed to clarify that "Comedy Central does not 'own' Chappelle, slavery ended a little while ago. I know the picture at the end of the show may confuse you. Although he poses with manacled hands filled with money and you hear 'I'm rich beyaatch!' it doesn't really mean he is a slave owned by corporate masters. Glad I could clear that up for you" (Twigz'N'Berries, "Evil Avatar" n.p.).

But if the concluding image of every *Chappelle's Show* is not meant to suggest that he is a "slave," what does it mean? The closing credits issue a parting shot at fans and skeptics alike. The image of shackled Chappelle encompasses much of the show's work on slavery and is a useful indicator of the levels of critique and intellectual rigor that characterize his work. Like filmmaker Spike Lee's company, 40 Acres and a Mule, the logo for Chappelle's production company, Pilot Boy, references slavery. Chappelle's company logo is confrontational and aggressive, a difficult effect to pull off wearing shackles. I claim that his parting shot encapsulates Chappelle's work on slavery but also responds to those critics who tacitly disapprove of his rapidly accumulating wealth.

His company insignia features a shirtless, bald Chappelle with chained wrists raised, his hands holding fistfuls of cash, staring into the camera. This image is accompanied by an audio clip of a man shouting, "I'm ree-ah-ch, bee-ah-tch!" (I'm rich, bitch!). This is a combination of two sketches related to slavery in season 1. The image is the same one Chappelle uses to conclude his comedic revision of the *Roots* commemorative DVD that I discussed earlier. That sketch ends with a still shot of an image parodying the real anniversary

DVD. The cover art for the two DVDs—the original and the parody—are remarkably similar: a photo montage of significant scenes surround a central image of a young Kunta Kinte (LeVar Burton) with manacled hands raised, his hands balled into fists, staring into the camera. In his version of the DVD cover art, Chappelle occupies the same position as LeVar Burton's Kinte, and the pose is the same. For the company insignia, however, his fists are filled with cash. The audio portion is taken from the popular slavery reparations sketch, where Chappelle imagines "all hell breaking loose" if blacks were given financial payments in acknowledgment of slavery's wrongs.

In an extended sketch that takes the form of a special news report, a white woman does "man-on-the-street" interviews with blacks flush with the *jouissance* of new money. A black man (Donnell Rawlings) driving a semitrailer of Kool cigarettes stops at an intersection, and the reporter asks him if he will quit his job as a truck driver now that he has received reparations. The man replies that he is not a truck driver, but he "just bought this truck straight cash. Now my family has enough cigarettes to last the rest of our lives!" In celebratory emphasis, he shouts, "I'm ree-ah-ch, bee-ah-tch!"

Chappelle's company insignia is a compilation of multiple forms of representations that he has created about slavery. Drawing from his renditions of *Roots* and reparations, the logo inverts the customary hierarchy of dominance and subordination that frequently constrains blacks in the white-owned media sphere. The emblem also offers a space to rethink what might be gained through his unique strategy of deploying and producing laughter in the service of expanding the possibilities for framing slavery in public and black popular memory. The image and sound of his insignia represent his work and genius, acting as his personally generated reparation. His work challenges the white racist perception that is more comfortable with blacks in postures and positions of subjection—in the media, government, and other venues. Chappelle's slave image, in its diffident reminder of his status, exceeds the expectations many have for a young black man in the exploitative entertainment industry.

Chappelle's company insignia, like much of the comedic representations of slavery on *Chappelle's Show,* represents the ways in which the show offers its cultural work as a sign of black creativity, raising its value from a mere assemblage of sketch comedy to the terrain of redemptive social action and cultural critique. These scenes encourage others to think through the proffered scenes, to work for what they enjoy. His is not an offer of passive entertainment, but a more active form that has the consequence of provoking intellectual as well as emotional responses. As he told a reporter for the *Progressive,* "I'm more about promoting cultural dialogue than political dialogue. I think more good things come out of cultural dialogue" (Zaino, "Ask a Black Dude" n.p.). *Chappelle's Show* is not a sacred *lieu de memoire* for slavery, the site of memory so valued and necessary in works like *Kindred* or *Sankofa.* Instead, it is a *lieu de critique,* a place to ponder, to consider the concepts of commemoration and representation. Chappelle removes the concept of slavery's traumatic memory and history from a rarefied light and moves it into a comedic frame. By making it more subject to a different form of scrutiny and critical debate, Chappelle engenders a form of access to traumatic knowledge, a mode that begins with—rather than ending with or being reduced to—laughter.

Notes

Chapter 1: Trauma and Time Travel

1. Butler considers her depiction of slavery to be far less gruesome than the institution itself. Reading slave narratives, she realized that "I was not going to be able to come anywhere near presenting slavery as it was. I was going to have to do a somewhat cleaned-up version of slavery, or no one would be willing to read it. I think that's what most fiction writers do. They almost have to" (interview with Kenan 497).

2. Arieh Y. Shalev, in his article "Stress versus Traumatic Stress: From Acute Homeostatic Reactions to Chronic Psychopathology," defines the peritraumatic moment as the impact phase of the stressor.

3. Many scholars have formulated and identified slave-narrative conventions (see for example, Olney's "I Was Born").

Chapter 2: Touching Scars, Touching Slavery

1. King's narrative further supplements the (limited) explanatory power of her body when she tells the interviewer that slavery has given her a "false face," one that frightens babies, shocks young children, and makes adults wonder "what debbil got in an' made me born dis way" (Berlin, Favreau, and Miller, *Remembering Slavery* 21).

2. It is important to note that the novel privileges this reincarnation as a particularly female family legacy, but Perry implies that male characters might also experience it. Two men—Anthony Paul, the protagonist's love interest, and an unidentified male lover of her grandmother—are described in ways that suggest they might also reembody some form of the past. Perry does not offer a sustained treatment of this issue, but in Chapter 3 I consider two works that reveal several implications of using black males to reembody slavery.

3. My use of the phrase "material way" has a double meaning. *Material* refers to Perry's use of the body as solid evidence. *Material* is also another word for *fabric*.

4. The Hyperion hardcover edition of *Stigmata* features the story quilt on its cover.

5. Dermographism is a rare skin condition, "a form of physical urticaria (an irritated, patchy condition of the skin) whose outbreaks are provoked by a release of histamines when the skin is stroked, rubbed, or scratched." Effects may last up to forty-eight hours, but usually fade more quickly.

6. When quilts are the subject of academic literary analysis, the pieces are revered or even deified, as in Houston A. Baker Jr. and Charlotte Pierce-Baker's comment that "the quilts of Afro-America resemble the work of all those dismembered gods who transmute fragments and remainders into the light and breath of a new creation" ("Patches" 156). Margot Anne Kelley and Elaine Showalter also emphasize the fragmented element of quilts as a metaphoric strength (Kelley, "Sister's Choices"; Showalter, "Piecing and Writing").

7. Alice Walker's 1973 short story "Everyday Use" skillfully depicts this controversy.

Chapter 3: Teach You a Lesson, Boy

1. Here I pause to admit that the age of the protagonists is, perhaps intentionally, troubling: is a male teenager a man or a boy? I will use both terms.

2. For instance, 1979 studies of an Illinois deterrence program and Michigan's JOLT (Juvenile Offenders Learn Truth) program revealed little effect on deterring young participants from criminal behavior. In fact, in 1982 a scholar offered the controversial possibility of a "delinquency fulfilling prophesy" in which such programs increase rather than decrease the chances of juvenile delinquency. The prison tours may unintentionally cause the youth to idolize or emulate the prisoners, or attempts to intimidate the youth may be viewed as "a challenge to go out and prove to themselves, their peers and others that they were not scared" (Petrosino, Turpin-Petrosino, and Finckenauer, "Well-Meaning Programs" 367).

3. Released in 1991, *Brother Future* is a WonderWorks production, funded by the Corporation of Public Broadcasting and the National Endowment for the Arts. It features actors who have appeared in television and film roles before and since. Using unknown or lesser-known actors, *The Quest for Freedom* is part of a video series titled "In Search of the Heroes," which is currently owned by more than forty thousand schools and libraries. The series is geared toward restoring an interest in history among middle and high school students. Grace Products, the Texas firm that produces the series, began as a company serving the religious market with books for Christian education and grief counseling. In the early 1990s, company president Greg Vaughn launched a history-based video series designed to teach young people to value history, appreciate literacy, and make sound moral choices. Sponsored in part by History in Action, a Dallas foundation specializing in living history and reenactments, Grace Products released eleven videos between 1991 *(William B. Travis: The Cost of Freedom)* and 2001 *(The Wild West Story of Buffalo Bill Cody)*. A company executive identified three goals of the series: "encourage kids to be interested in history, to encourage them to read, [and] give them a basis for good moral character" (Rocker, telephone interview). *The Quest for Freedom: The Harriet Tubman Story*, the second film in the series and the first to garner an Emmy nomination (for Summer Selby as Harriet Tubman), perfectly suits the goals of the series. The press information for the film describes it as an "action packed video. [In it] a student from today enters a myste-

rious library and is catapulted back in time to meet Harriet Tubman. He takes a trip on the UNDERGROUND RAILROAD and gains an understanding of slave life. He is motivated to respect the freedoms he has today as well as the people who made it possible" (Grace Products press kit).

4. An example of gratitude in *The Quest for Freedom* is the video's quiz and essay portion. David King steps out of character to address the student audience. (This is in direct contrast to the quiz and essay section of other videos in the series, such as *The Susan B. Anthony Story*. There the actress remains in the character of Susan B. Anthony and asks the students questions about "her.") David King (the actor who portrays Ben) tells the students how he enjoyed his film role and how impressed he is with Harriet Tubman. He then tells the assembled students that he is "proud to say that [he's] in school right now" and encourages the audience to see school as their "ticket to freedom." Though the film makes the progressive steps of regarding slavery as an irretrievable moment not readily subject to mimetic repetition (though the film subtly relies on this idea), the film and its quiz (included with the teacher's guide that accompanies the video) retreat to ideological conservatism as the movie promotes the idea of individual responsibility and bootstrap moral reform.

5. "Watching and listening to the way teenagers behaved, talked, and thought provided me with many hours of material," writes Ann Eskridge, *Brother Future*'s story and teleplay writer. "It also made me realize how invisible African American teenagers are to the media—not only in books, but primarily in television and movies. I wanted to write stories about black youth that reflected their personalities and yet I wanted to add a mystical magical quality to the stories" ("About the Author" Web page, http://www.ehhs.cmich.edu/~annesk/author.htm).

6. A thirty-six-year-old African American woman, surveyed by Rosenzweig and Thelen, reflected the anxiety about young black male criminality when she claimed that she perceived the slave past as less dangerous than the crime-ridden present: "If I had a choice of living in slavery or living now I think I would have picked slavery. Because then there wasn't as much killing. Then you had your own little place and if anything happened it wasn't enough to kill me. *Then it was the white man doing it to you.* Back then it wasn't enough to die over. Now it's everybody killing everybody" (*The Presence* 69–70; emphasis added). For this woman, slavery is an oddly idyllic experience with slaves having their "own little place." It is plausible that this woman might just feel out of place, or perhaps fears that the crime surge is the result of so many young black males lacking their "own little place" in the postindustrial economy. The part of her remarks that carries the most explicatory power is the clarity provided by the "white man doing it to you." Here, this woman, like many, expresses deep concern (common and on the rise in the late 1980s and early 1990s) about the purported rise in black-on-black crime: young blacks shooting and killing each other to a hip-hop sound track that valorized such behavior. In the past, she claims, whites murdered blacks, but now blacks unleash violence within their own communities. The sexual innuendo of the words *doing it* is also significant, for it implies that during the antebellum days, white men took sexual advantage of black women, but in the early 1990s hip-hop's black male icons (like Tupac Shakur and Mike Tyson, to name only two) were increasingly "on trial" for their sexual abuse of black women.

Chapter 4: Slave Tourism and Rememory

1. When the NAACP and other civil rights leaders approached Colonial Williamsburg's president about halting the auction, their concerns went unheard. An account of the meeting claims that the assembled black leaders "did not speak with a unified voice" (Krutko, "Colonial Williamsburg's Slave Auction" 18). The group had a host of complaints about Colonial Williamsburg's approach to slavery. Some wanted Colonial Williamsburg to abandon slavery programs entirely; others supported slavery programming but not reenactments. For still others, the timing of this event—contained within a larger celebratory weekend program and scheduled to last for only forty-five minutes—trivialized slavery and diminished the horror of slave auctions.

2. It is important to note that this distinction is not a firm or stable dichotomy, since the boundaries between formal and popular shift frequently, as academics adopt principles from the popular and vice versa.

3. It is also important to note that McCary's objections stem from the fact that the auction was presented in isolation, as a single event, rather than as part of a larger constellation of slavery's abjection that included captivity and sexual coercion.

4. Additionally relevant here is the idea that most, if not all, American history narratives are framed within a progress narrative. Such a context would make it additionally controversial that black history, in this instance, was deprived of such a redemptive frame.

Chapter 5: Ritual Reenactments

1. Allan Dwight Callahan's 2006 study *Talking Book: African Americans and the Bible* traces the ways in which "biblical phrases and motifs have been manifest in African-American life far beyond the boundaries that moderns have marked off with the word *religion*" (xi).

2. The song features the refrain:

Lest I forget Gethsemane
Lest I forget Thine agony
Lest I forget Thy love for me
Lead me to Calvary.

Rephrased as an "if-then" statement, the song's thesis translates as "if I forget [or to prevent me from forgetting] about Christ's suffering, then take me to the physical and by extension emotional site where the event occurred." Given the cosmic transport the song promises (threatens?), it is no coincidence that this hymn is played during Holy Communion. (It was a feature of my childhood's first Sundays. The song's haunting melody wafted through the sanctuary as the church mothers prepared the Host, which for our Baptist congregation was matzo wafers and grape juice.)

3. In their promotional and commemorative literature and on their Web site, SPCBC attaches the "TM" superscript to the performance title, *The Maafa Suite . . . a Healing Journey,* and to the program's slogan, "The Way Out Is Back Through." I discuss later in the chapter the implications of this move. However, in my work, I will use the "TM" only when it is explicitly relevant.

4. The Gospel according to Luke, chapter 4, verse 18, reads: "The Spirit of the Lord is upon me, because he hath anointed me to preach the gospel to the poor; he hath sent me to heal the brokenhearted, to preach deliverance to the captives, and recovering of sight to the blind, to set at liberty them that are bruised."

5. This is not to say that everyone actually believes they are indeed the same, but the broad-based (democratic?) ideal of this religious belief, which leads parishioners to call each other brother or sister and refer to church elders as father or mother, is at work here.

6. Willie Lynch is a (most likely imagined) slaveholder from a widely circulated Internet document purported to be a speech on slave management. The speech talks about dividing the slave population and turning them against each other so that whites might more easily control them. This letter is, in my assessment, a recent invention, but an effective strategy: it critiques blacks for buying into a (self-fulfilling) prophecy made by a slave owner. See Rosenzweig, "The Road to Xanadu"; Cobb, "Willie Lynch Is Dead"; and Ruffins, "The Peculiar Institution."

Chapter 6: Historical Reenactments

1. Handler and Gable share a great anecdote about a couple who were surprised to learn that Colonial Williamsburg is a museum, the wife claiming, "I thought it was an attraction."

Conclusion

1. I am grateful to Z'etoile Imma for sharing this story.

Works Cited

Abraham, W. E. *The Mind of Africa.* Chicago: University of Chicago Press, 1962.

Ali, Shahrazad. *Are You Still a Slave?* Philadelphia: Civilized Publications, 1994.

———. *The Blackman's Guide to Understanding the Blackwoman.* Philadelphia: Civilized Publications, 1989.

Allred, Randal. "Catharsis, Revision, and Reenactment: Negotiating the Meaning of the American Civil War." *Journal of American Culture* 19.4 (1996): 1–13.

Amazon.com. "Customer Review" page for *Brother Future.* http://www.amazon.com/review/product/6304771010/ref=cm_cr_dp_all_helpful?%5Fencoding=UTF8&coliid=&showViewpoints=1&colid=&sortBy=bySubmissionDateDescending.

Andrews, Brenda. "Slave Auction in Williamsburg: Protest Gives Real Meaning to Slave Sales." *New Journal and Guide,* October 12–18, 1994, 1.

Asante, Molefi. *The Afrocentric Idea.* Rev. ed. Philadelphia: Temple University Press, 1998.

Baker, Houston A., Jr., and Charlotte Pierce-Baker. "Patches: Quilts and Community in Alice Walker's *Everyday Use.*" In *Everyday Use: Women Writers Texts and Contexts Series,* edited by Barbara T. Christian. New Brunswick: Rutgers University Press, 1994.

Baldwin, James. "Notes of a Native Son." 1955. In *The Norton Anthology of African American Literature,* edited by Henry Louis Gates and Nellie Y. McKay, 1679–94. New York: W. W. Norton, 1996.

Barnes, Arthur. "Character Interpretation at Colonial Williamsburg." *Colonial Williamsburg Interpreter* 6.3 (1985): 1–3.

———. "Living History: Its Many Forms." *Colonial Williamsburg Interpreter* 6.3 (1985): 1–2.

Barrett, Lindon. "African American Slave Narratives: Literacy, the Body, Authority." *American Literary History* 7.3 (1995): 415–42.

Barton, Robin. "Travel: Tourists Who Yield to the Lure of the Macabre." *Independent,* May 20, 2001, News, 2.

Behuniak-Long, Susan. "Preserving the Social Fabric: Quilting in a Technological World."

In *Quilt Culture: Tracing the Pattern,* edited by Cheryl B. Torsney and Judy Elsley. Columbia: University of Missouri Press, 1994.

Beizer, Janet. *Ventriloquized Bodies: Narratives of Hysteria in Nineteenth-Century France.* Ithaca: Cornell University Press, 1994.

Bellinger, Larry. "Scared Crooked: Are In-Your-Face Visits the Best We Can Do for 'Troubled' Teens?" *Sojourners Magazine* (September–October 2001). http://www.sojo.net/ index.cfm?action=magazine.article&issue=soj0109&article=010941c.

Berlin, Ira, Marc Favreau, and Steven F. Miller, eds. *Remembering Slavery: African Americans Talk about Their Personal Experiences of Slavery and Freedom.* New York: New Press, 1998.

Billingsley, Andrew. "Black Families in a Changing Society." In *The State of Black America, 1987,* 97–111. New York: National Urban League, 1987.

The Black Population in the United States, March 1989 and 1990. Washington, D.C.: U.S. Government Printing Office.

Blassingame, John W. *Slave Testimony: Two Centuries of Letters, Speeches, Interviews, and Autobiographies.* Baton Rouge: Louisiana State University Press, 1977.

Bowers, Detine L. "Slave Auction at Williamsburg." *Richmond Afro-American and the Richmond Planet,* November 2, 1994, A5.

Boyd, Bentley. "Colonial Williamsburg Plans Mock Slave Auction." *Newport News Daily Press,* October 6, 1994.

———. "CW Auctions Slaves: Re-enactment Provokes Emotional Debate." *Newport News Daily Press,* October 11, 1994.

———. "Historians Win the Battle of Manassas: Now They're Ready to Give Disney a Hand." *Newport News Daily Press,* October 2, 1994, A1–A2.

Boyd, Todd. *The New H.N.I.C. (Head Niggas in Charge): The Death of Civil Rights and the Reign of Hip-Hop.* New York: New York University Press, 2002.

"Brat Camp." ABC prime-time line-up Web page. http://abc.go.com/primetime/bratcamp/ show.html.

Brogan, Kathleen. *Cultural Haunting: Ghosts and Ethnicity in Recent American Literature.* Charlottesville: University Press of Virginia, 1998.

Brother Future. Dir. Roy Campanella II. Perf. Phill Lewis, Carl Lumbly, Vonetta McGee, Akosua Busia, Frank Converse, and Moses Gunn. Wonderworks Family Movie, 1991.

Bruner, Edward H. "Tourism in Ghana: The Representation of Slavery and the Return of the Black Diaspora." *American Anthropologist* 98.2 (1996): 290–304.

Bundles, A'Lelia. "Looking Back at the Roots Phenomenon." *Black Issues Book Review* 3.4 (2001). Available online at http://web2.infotrac.galegroup.com/itw/infomark /362/159/71143606w2/purl=rcl_ITOF_0_A76401576&dyn=14!xrn_1_0_A76401576?sw_ aep=viva_uva.

Butler, Octavia. "Black Women and the Science Fiction Genre." *Black Scholar* 17.2 (1986): 14–18.

———. Interview with Randall Kenan. *Callaloo* 14.2 (1991): 495–504.

———. Interview with Charles Rowell. *Callaloo* 20.1 (1997): 47–66.

———. *Kindred.* 1979. Reprint, Boston: Beacon, 1988.

Callahan, Allan Dwight. *Talking Book: African Americans and the Bible.* New Haven: Yale University Press, 2006.

Caruth, Cathy. *Trauma: Explorations in Memory.* Baltimore: Johns Hopkins University Press, 1995.

———. *Unclaimed Experience: Trauma, Narrative, and History.* Baltimore: Johns Hopkins University Press, 1996.

———. "Unclaimed Experience: Trauma and the Possibility of History." *Yale French Studies* 79 (1991): 181–92.

"Chappelle: 'An Act of Freedom.'" *60 Minutes,* December 29, 2004. http://www.cbsnews.com/stories/2004/10/19/60II/main650149.shtml.

Chappelle, Dave, and Christopher John Farley. "That's What I Call Funny: One of America's Hottest Comics on How He Translates Sore Points into Comic Relief." *Time* 165.3 (2005). http://web2.infotrac.galegroup.com/itw/infomark/362/159/71143606w2/purl=rcl_ITOF_0_A126833401&dyn=4!xrn_36_0_A126833401?sw_aep=viva_uva.

Chappelle's Show: Season One Uncensored! Dir. Rusty Cundieff, Andre Allen, Scott Vincent, Bill Berner, Bobcat Goldthwait, and Peter Lauer. Perf. Dave Chappelle. DVD. Comedy Central, 2004.

Chappelle's Show: Season Two Uncensored! Dir. Andre Allen et al. Perf. Dave Chappelle and Charles Q. Murphy. DVD. Comedy Central, 2005.

Clarke, Lynn. "Talk about Talk: Promises, Risks, and a Proposition Out of *Nommo.*" *Journal of Speculative Philosophy* 18.4 (2004): 317–25.

Cobb, William Jelani. "Willie Lynch Is Dead (1712?–2003)." *Afro-Netizen,* September 29, 2003. http://www.afro-netizen.com/2003/09/willie_lynch_is.html.

Cook, Monte. "Tips for Time Travel." In *Philosophers Look at Science Fiction,* edited by Nicholas D. Smith. Chicago: Nelson-Hall, 1982.

D'Aguiar, Fred. "The Last Essay about Slavery." In *The Age of Anxiety,* edited by Sarah Dunant and Roy Porter. London: Virago, 1996.

Dale, Dianne. "Telling the Truth about Slavery and Filling the Gaps in History." *Washington Informer,* February 22, 1995, 16.

Davis, Natalie Zemon. *Slaves on Screen: Film and Historical Vision.* Cambridge: Harvard University Press, 2000.

DeGruy-Leary, Joy. *Post-traumatic Slave Syndrome: America's Legacy of Enduring Injury and Healing.* Milwaukie, Ore.: Uptone Press, 2005.

Dickerson, Vanessa D. "Summoning Somebody: The Flesh Made Word in Toni Morrison's Fiction." In *Recovering the Black Female Body: Self-Representations by African American Women,* edited by Michael Bennett and Vanessa D. Dickerson. New Brunswick: Rutgers University Press, 2001.

Dirty Harry. "Evil Avatar: Daily Gaming News with Attitude." Online posting, August 12, 2005. http://www.evilavatar.com/forums/showthread.php?t=4171&page=2&pp=10&highlight=chappelle%27s+show.

Douglass, Frederick. *Narrative of the Life of Frederick Douglass, an American Slave, Written by Himself.* 1845. In *The Classic Slave Narratives,* edited by Henry Louis Gates Jr. New York: Mentor, 1987.

Eddie Murphy: Raw. Dir. Robert Townsend. Perf. Eddie Murphy. Felt Forum, N.Y., 1987.

Ellis, Rex. "A Decade of Change: Black History at Colonial Williamsburg." *Colonial Williamsburg: Journal of the Colonial Williamsburg Foundation* 12.3 (1990): 14–23.

———. "Re:living History: Bringing History into Play." *American Visions* 7.6 (1992): 22–25.

Ellison, Ralph. *Invisible Man.* 1952. New York: Vintage International Edition, 1990.

Elsley, Judy. *Quilts as Text(iles): The Semiotics of Quilting. Berkeley Insights in Linguistics and Semiotics.* Edited by Irmengard Rauch. Vol. 16. New York: Peter Lang, 1996.

Farred, Grant. *What's My Name? Black Vernacular Intellectuals.* Minneapolis: University of Minnesota Press, 2003.

Feelings, Tom. *The Middle Passage: White Ships/Black Cargo.* New York: Dial Books, 1995.

Felman, Shoshana, and Dori Laub, M.D. *Testimony: Crises of Witnessing in Literature, Psychoanalysis, and History.* New York: Routledge, 1992.

Finckenauer, James O. *Scared Straight! and the Panacea Phenomenon.* Englewood Cliffs, N.J.: Prentice-Hall, 1982.

Finley, Cheryl. "The Door of (No) Return." *Common-Place* 1.4 (2001): 6 pts. http://www.common-place.org.

Forest, Angela D. "The Great Blacks in Wax Museum Doesn't Shy Away from Examining Aspects of History Some Would Rather Forget." *Durham Herald Sun,* December 30, 2001, Getaways, H3.

Foster, Frances Smith. *Witnessing Slavery: The Development of Ante-bellum Slave Narratives.* 1979. Madison: University of Wisconsin Press, 1994.

Fountain, John W. "Church's Window on the Past, and the Future." *New York Times,* February 9, 2001, A14.

Gable, Eric, and Richard Handler. "Deep Dirt: Messing Up the Past at Colonial Williamsburg." *Social Analysis* 34 (1993): 3–16.

Gable, Eric, Richard Handler, and Anna Lawson. "On the Uses of Relativism: Fact, Conjecture, and Black and White Histories at Colonial Williamsburg." *American Ethnologist* 19.4 (1992): 791–805.

Gabriel, Teshome H. "Towards a Critical Theory of Third World Films." In *Cinemas of the Black Diaspora: Diversity, Dependence, and Oppositionality,* edited by Michael T. Martin. Detroit: Wayne State University Press, 1995.

Gaines, Jane. "White Privilege and Looking Relations: Race and Gender in Feminist Film Theory." *Cultural Critique* 4(1986): 59–79.

Gerima, Haile. *Sankofa.* Mypheduh Films, 1993.

———. "Spirit of the Dead." In *Jump Up and Say! A Collection of Black Storytelling,* edited by Linda Goss and Clay Goss. New York: Simon and Schuster, 1995.

Gibbs, Jewelle Taylor. *Young, Black, and Male in America: An Endangered Species.* Dover, Mass.: Auburn House, 1988.

Gilroy, Paul. "'After the Love Has Gone': Bio-politics and Etho-poetics in the Black Public Sphere." *Public Culture* 7 (1994): 49–76.

"Giving Pain a Human Face." *St. Louis Post-Dispatch,* October 14, 1994, Editorial, D14.

Glasgow, Donald. "The Black Underclass in Perspective." In *The State of Black America, 1987,* 129–44. New York: National Urban League, 1987.

Glucklich, Ariel. *Sacred Pain: Hurting the Body for the Sake of the Soul.* Oxford: Oxford University Press, 2001.

Gordon, Dexter B. "Humor in African American Discourse: Speaking of Oppression." *Journal of Black Studies* 29 (1998): 254–76. Available online at http://web6.

infotrac.galegroup.com/itw/infomark/333/637/70897192w6/purl=rcl_ITOF_0_ A21257394&dyn=3!xrn_1_0_A21257394?sw_aep=viva_uva.

Graft, Conny. "Evaluating Interpretive Programs." *Colonial Williamsburg Interpreter* 8.5 (1987): 3–6.

Handler, Richard, and Eric Gable. *The New History in an Old Museum: Creating the Past at Colonial Williamsburg.* Durham: Duke University Press, 1997.

Handler, Richard, and William Saxton. "Dyssimulation: Reflexivity, Narrative, and the Quest for Authenticity in 'Living History.'" *Cultural Anthropology* 3.3 (1988): 242–60.

Hansen, Ron. "Stigmata." *Image: A Journal of the Arts and Religion* 21 (1998): 60–66.

Harrison, Paul Carter. *The Drama of Nommo.* New York: Grove Press, 1972.

Hartman, Geoffrey H. "On Traumatic Knowledge and Literary Studies." *New Literary History* 26.3 (1995): 537–63.

Hartman, Saidiya V. "The Time of Slavery." *South Atlantic Quarterly* 101.4 (2002): 757–77.

———. *Scenes of Subjection: Terror, Slavery, and Self-Making in Nineteenth-Century America.* Race and American Culture. New York: Oxford University Press, 1997.

Hastings, Deborah. "From Shame to Pride: Using Lynching to Teach Life Lessons." Associated Press State and Local Wire, February 19, 2000.

Hazzard-Donald, Katrina. "Dance in Hip Hop Culture." In *Droppin' Science: Critical Essays on Rap Music and Hip Hop Culture,* edited by William Eric Perkins. Philadelphia: Temple University Press, 1996.

"Heifer Ranch Global Village." Heifer International Web site. http://www.heifer.org/site/c .edJRKQNiFiG/b.737833/k.8297/Heifer_Ranch Global_Village.htm.

Henderson, Mae G. "Toni Morrison's *Beloved:* Re-membering the Body as Historical Text." In *Comparative American Identities: Race, Sex, and Nationality in the Modern Text,* edited by Hortense J. Spillers, 62–86. New York: Routledge, 1991.

hooks, bell. "Challenging Capitalism and Patriarchy: Third World Viewpoint Interviews, bell hooks." *Z Magazine,* December 1995. http://www.zmag.org/ZMag/articles/ dec95hooks.htm.

———. *We Real Cool: Black Men and Masculinity.* New York: Routledge, 2004.

Hopkinson, Natalie. "Waxing Educational in Baltimore." *Washington Post,* October 8, 1999, Weekend, N51.

Hurston, Zora Neale. *Their Eyes Were Watching God.* 1937. Reprint, New York: Harper and Row, 1990.

Hussey, Jennie E. "Lead Me to Calvary." In *New Songs of Praise and Power,* edited by J. Lincoln Hall. Philadelphia: Hall-Mack, 1921.

Jacob, John E. "Black America, 1988: An Overview." In *The State of Black America, 1988.* New York: National Urban League, 1988.

Jacobs, Harriet A., Nellie Y. McKay, and Frances Smith Foster. *Incidents in the Life of a Slave Girl: Contexts, Criticism.* New York: W. W. Norton, 2001.

Jeffers, Carol S. "Museum as Process." *Journal of Aesthetic Education* 37.1 (2003): 107–19.

Johnson, Charles. "A Phenomenology of the Black Body." In *The Male Body: Features, Destinies, Exposures,* edited by Laurence Goldstein. Ann Arbor: University of Michigan Press, 1994.

Johnson, Walter. *Soul by Soul: Life Inside the Antebellum Slave Market.* Cambridge: Harvard University Press, 2000.

Jones, Edward P. *The Known World*. New York: HarperCollins, 2003.

Jones, Gayl. *Corregidora*. New York: Random House, 1975.

Juneteenth 2003 Third Annual Commemoration: A Celebration of Freedom. Charlottesville: Piedmont Virginia Community College, 2003.

Kande, Sylvie. "Look Homeward, Angel: Maroons and Mulattos in Haile Gerima's *Sankofa*." *Research in African Languages* 29.2 (1998): 128–46.

Karenga, Maulana. "Nommo, Kaiwad, and Communicative Practice: Bringing Good into the World." In *Understanding African American Rhetoric: Classical Origins to Contemporary Innovations,* edited by Ronald L. Jackson and Elaine B. Richardson. New York: Routledge, 2003.

Kelley, Margot Anne. "Sister's Choices: Quilting Aesthetics in Contemporary African American Women's Fiction." In *Everyday Use: Women Writers Texts and Contexts Series,* edited by Barbara T. Christian. New Brunswick: Rutgers University Press, 1994.

Kendrick, Kathleen. "'The Things Down Stairs': Containing Horror in the Nineteenth Century Wax Museum." *Nineteenth Century Studies* 12 (1998): 1–35.

Kitwana, Bakari. *The Hip Hop Generation: Young Blacks and the Crisis in African American Culture*. New York: Basic Civitas Books, 2002.

Krutko, Erin. "Colonial Williamsburg's Slave Auction Re-enactment: Controversy, African American History, and Public Memory." Master's thesis, College of William and Mary, 2003.

Kubitschek, Missy Dehn. *Claiming the Heritage: African American Women Novelists and History*. Jackson: University Press of Mississippi, 1991.

Kuhn, Annette. *Alien Zone: Cultural Theory and Contemporary Science Fiction Cinema*. London: Verso, 1990.

Lackey, Patrick K. "'Our History Must Be Told': The Re-enactment of a Slave Auction at Colonial Williamsburg Sparked Emotions and Debate." *Norfolk Virginian Pilot and Ledger-Star,* October 11, 1994, B1.

Lamb, Donna. "The MAAFA Suite a Powerful Production." *New York Beacon,* September 17, 2003, 31.

Landsberg, Alison. "America, the Holocaust, and the Mass Culture of Memory: Towards a Radical Politics of Empathy." *New German Critique* 71 (1997): 63–86.

Lanzmann, Claude, Ruth Larson, and David Rodowick. "Seminar with Claude Lanzmann, 11 April 1990." *Yale French Studies* 79 (1991): 82–99.

Lawson, Anna Logan. "The Other Half: Making African American History at Colonial Williamsburg." Ph.D. diss., University of Virginia, 1995.

Layton, Lynne. "Trauma, Gender Identity, and Sexuality: Discourses of Fragmentation." *American Imago* 52.1 (1995): 107–25.

Lemell, Anthony J., Jr. *Black Male Deviance*. Westport, Conn.: Praeger, 1995.

Lennon, J. John, and Malcolm Foley. *Dark Tourism*. London: Continuum, 2000.

Levecq, Christine. "Power and Repetition: Philosophies of (Literary) History in Octavia E. Butler's *Kindred*." *Contemporary Literature* 41.3 (2000): 523–53.

Levin, Gary. "Chappelle: Laughing All the Way to the Bank." *USA Today,* August 2, 2004. Available online at http://www.usatoday.com/life/television/news/2004-08-02-chappelle_x.htm.

"Libation: An Offering to the Ancestors." Photocopied handout from St. Paul Community

Baptist Church, Brooklyn, N.Y. Tenth Anniversary Commemoration of the MAAFA, September 7–25, 2004.

Lifton, Robert Jay. *Broken Connection: On Death and the Continuity of Life.* Washington, D.C.: American Psychiatric Press, 1996.

Lowenthal, David. *The Past Is a Foreign Country.* Cambridge: Cambridge University Press, 1985.

MacCannell, Dean. *The Tourist: A New Theory of the Leisure Class.* 1976. Reprint, Berkeley and Los Angeles: University of California Press, 1999.

Magelssen, Scott. "Resuscitating the Extinct: The Backbreeding of Historic Animals at U.S. Living History Museums." *Drama Review* 47.4 (2003): 98–109.

Maier, Karl. "Chamber of Horrors." *Africa Report* 38.3 (1993): 67–68.

Majors, Richard, and Janet Mancini Billson. *Cool Pose: The Dilemmas of Black Manhood in America.* New York: Touchstone / Simon and Schuster, 1992.

Matthews, Christy Coleman. "A Colonial Williamsburg Revolution: Twenty Years Interpreting African American History." *History News* 54.2 (1999): 6–11.

McCaffery, Larry. *Across the Wounded Galaxies: Interviews with Contemporary American Science Fiction Writers.* Urbana: University of Illinois Press, 1990.

McCary, Oscar. "Walk in Their Shoes, 'Christy.'" Letter to the editor. *New Journal and Guide,* October 26–November 1, 1994, 2.

McDowell, Deborah E. "In the First Place: Making Frederick Douglass and the Afro-American Narrative Tradition." In *Critical Essays on Frederick Douglass,* edited by William L. Andrews. Boston: G. K. Hall, 1991.

———. "Negotiating between Tenses: Witnessing Slavery after Freedom—*Dessa Rose.*" In *Slavery and the Literary Imagination,* edited by Deborah E. McDowell and Arnold Rampersad. Baltimore: Johns Hopkins University Press, 1989.

———. "Recovery Missions: Imagining the Body Ideals." In *Recovering the Black Female Body: Self-Representations by African American Women,* edited by Michael Bennett and Vanessa D. Dickerson. New Brunswick: Rutgers University Press, 2001.

McGrath, Ann. Review of *Making Representations: Museums in the Post-colonial Era,* by Moira G. Simpson. *Journal of Colonialism and Colonial History* 3.1 (2002).

Michaels, Walter Benn. "'You Who Never Was There': Slavery and the New Historicism, Deconstruction, and the Holocaust." *Narrative* 4.1 (1996): 1–16.

Milloy, Courtland. "Slave Exhibit Is Necessary Education." *Washington Post,* March 1, 2000, Metro, B1.

Mitchell, W. J. T. "Narrative, Memory, and Slavery." In *Cultural Artifacts and the Products of Meaning: The Page, the Image, and the Body,* edited by Margaret J. M. Ezell and Katherine O'Brien O'Kate, 199–223. Ann Arbor: University of Michigan Press, 1994.

Montag, Warren. "The Universalization of Whiteness." In *Whiteness: A Critical Reader,* edited by Mike Hill. New York: New York University Press, 1997.

Morrison, Toni. *Beloved.* New York: Plume, 1987.

Mosk, Matthew. "Cradle of Slavery: A Maryland Destination." *Washington Post,* October 2, 2000, Metro, B1, B9.

Neal, Mark Anthony. *Soul Babies: Black Popular Culture and the Post-soul Aesthetic.* New York: Routledge, 2002.

"Necessary Education?" *Washington Post,* March 15, 2000, Op-ed, A26.

Nora, Pierre. "Between Memory and History: Les lieux de memoire." In *History and Memory in African American Culture*, edited by Genevieve Fabre and Robert O'Meally. New York: Oxford University Press, 1994.

Olney, James. "I Was Born: Slave Narratives, Their Status as Autobiography, and as Literature," Callaloo 20 (Winter 1984): 46–73.

Painter, Nell Irvin. "Soul Murder and Slavery: Toward a Fully Loaded Cost Accounting." In *U.S. History as Women's History: New Feminist Essays*, edited by Linda K. Kerber. Chapel Hill: University of North Carolina Press, 1995.

Paulin, Diana. "De-essentializing Interracial Representations: Black and White Border-Crossings in Spike Lee's *Jungle Fever* and in Octavia Butler's *Kindred*." *Cultural Critique* (Spring 1997): 165–93.

Penley, Constance. "Time Travel, Primal Scene, and the Critical Dystopia." *Camera Obscura* 15 (1986): 67–84. Reprinted in *Alien Zone: Cultural Theory and Contemporary Science Fiction Cinema*, by Annette Kuhn. London: Verso, 1990.

Perry, Phyllis Alesia. *Stigmata*. New York: Anchor Books, 1998.

Peterson, Nancy J. *Against Amnesia: Contemporary Women Writers and the Crisis of Historical Memory*. Philadelphia: University of Pennsylvania Press, 2001.

Petrosino, Anthony, Carolyn Turpin-Petrosino, and James O. Finckenauer. "Well-Meaning Programs Can Have Harmful Effects! Lessons from Experiments of Programs Such as Scared Straight." *Crime and Delinquency* 46.3 (2000): 354–79.

Phillip, Mary-Christine. "To Reenact or Not to Reenact? For Some, Williamsburg Slave Auction Shows Discomfort of Humiliating Past." *Black Issues in Higher Education* 11.18 (November 3, 1994): 24.

"Plans Unveiled for 'Disney's America' Near Washington, D.C." Walt Disney Company, news release, November 11, 1993.

Plath, James. *Roots* (1977), Anniversary Edition. Reel.com, September 5, 2005. http://www.reel.com/movie.asp?MID=6211&buy=closed&PID=10096930&tab=reviews&CID=18#tabs.

"Play about Maafa Reconnects." *Oakland Tribune*, February 26, 2003.

Puschmann-Nalenz, Barbara. *Science Fiction and Postmodern Fiction: A Genre Study*. New York: Peter Lang, 1992.

The Quest for Freedom: The Harriet Tubman Story. Dir. Fred Holmes. Perf. David King and Summer Shelby. Grace Products Corporation, 1992.

Richards, Dona Marimba. *Let the Circle Be Unbroken: The Implications of African Spirituality in the Diaspora*. Trenton, N.J.: Red Sea Press, 1989.

Rickey, Carrie. "Labor of Love." *Philadelphia Inquirer*, August 25, 1994, Entertainment, E1–E2.

Ritzer, George, and Allan Liska. "'McDisneyization' and 'Post-tourism': Complementary Perspectives on Contemporary Tourism." In *Touring Cultures: Transformations of Travel and Theory*, edited by Chris Rojek and John Urry. London: Routledge, 1997.

Roberson, Erriel D. *The Maafa and Beyond: Remembrance, Ancestral Connections, and Nation Building for the African Global Community*. Columbia, Md.: Kujichagulia Press, 1995.

Rocker, Elton. Telephone interview. July 26, 2004.

Rody, Caroline. *The Daughter's Return: African-American and Caribbean Women's Fictions of History*. Oxford: Oxford University Press, 2001.

Rojek, Chris. *Ways of Escape: Modern Transformations in Leisure and Travel.* London: Macmillan, 1993.

Rojek, Chris, and John Urry, eds. *Touring Cultures: Transformations of Travel and Theory.* London: Routledge, 1997.

"Roots." *People Weekly,* March 7, 1994, 106. Available online at http://web6.infotrac .galegroup.com/itw/infomark/333/637/70897192w6/purl=rcl_ITOF_0_A14862400& dyn=7!xrn_1_0_A14862400?sw_aep=viva_uva.

Rose, Tricia. *Black Noise: Rap Music and Black Culture in Contemporary America.* Hanover, N.H.: Wesleyan University Press / University Press of New England, 1994.

Rosenzweig, Roy. "The Road to Xanadu: Public and Private Pathways on the History Web." *Journal of American History* 88.2 (September 2001): 548–79.

Rosenzweig, Roy, and David Thelen. *The Presence of the Past: Popular Uses of History in American Life.* New York: Columbia University Press, 1998.

Roth, Stacy Flora. *Past into Present: Effective Techniques for First-Person Historical Interpretation.* Chapel Hill: University of North Carolina Press, 1998.

Rothberg, Michael. *Traumatic Realism: The Demands of Holocaust Representation.* Minneapolis: University of Minnesota Press, 2000.

Rowell, Charles. "An Interview with Octavia E. Butler." *Callaloo* 20.1 (1997): 47–66.

Ruffins, Paul. "The Pecualiar Institution." *Black Issues in Higher Education* 24 (May 24, 2001).

Rushdy, Ashraf H. A. *Neo-slave Narratives: Studies in the Social Logic of a Literary Form.* Race and American Culture. New York: Oxford University Press, 1999.

———. *Remembering Generations: Race and Family in Contemporary African American Fiction.* Chapel Hill: University of North Carolina Press, 2001.

St. Paul Community Baptist Church, Brooklyn, N.Y. Tenth Anniversary Commemoration of the MAAFA, September 7–25, 2004. Program and schedule of activities.

Selby, Holly. "People, Passions on Exhibit: Patrons and Founders, Scholars and Ghosts; Baltimore Museums Come to Life in the Personalities on Display; Exploring the Future of Our Past; Baltimore Museums, Inside and Out." *Baltimore Sun,* August 30, 1998, Art, G10.

———. "Wax That Works: Success—Exhibit Overload Was Blamed for the Closing of the City Life Attractions, but Baltimore's Great Blacks in Wax Museum Continues to Inspire Busloads of Visitors." *Baltimore Sun,* July 30, 1997, Features, E1.

Shaffer, Marguerite S. "Selling the Past/Co-opting History: Colonial Williamsburg as Republican Disneyland." Review of *The New History in an Old Museum: Creating the Past at Colonial Williamsburg,* by Richard Handler and Eric Gable. *American Quarterly* 50.4 (1998): 875–84.

Shalev, Arieh Y. "Stress versus Traumatic Stress: From Acute Homeostatic Reactions to Chronic Psychopathology." In *Traumatic Stress: The Effects of Overwhelming Experience on Mind, Body, and Society,* edited by Bessel A. van der Kolk, Alexander C. McFarlane, and Lars Weisaeth, 77–101. New York: Guilford Press, 1996.

Showalter, Elaine. "Piecing and Writing." In *The Poetics of Gender,* edited by Nancy K. Miller. New York: Columbia University Press, 1986.

Simpson, Cameron. "Tourism Is Taking a Deadly Turn: Concentration Camps and Titanic Trips Are Gaining New Followers." *Glasgow Herald,* November 29, 2000, 4.

Skolnick, Jerome H., and James J. Fyfe. *Above the Law: Police and the Excessive Use of Force.* New York: Free Press, 1993.

Slattery, Dennis Patrick. *The Wounded Body: Remembering the Markings of the Flesh.* Albany: State University of New York Press, 2000.

"Slave Raid Enacted." GhanaHomePage, July 28, 2004. http://www.ghanaweb.com/ GhanaHomePage/entertainment/artikel.php?ID=62754.

Spillers, Hortense J. "'All the Things You Could Be by Now If Sigmund Freud's Wife Were Your Mother': Psychoanalysis and Race." In *Female Subjects in Black and White: Race, Psychoanalysis, and Feminism,* edited by Elizabeth Able, Barbara Christian, and Helene Moglen. Berkeley and Los Angeles: University of California Press, 1997.

———. "Changing the Letter: The Yokes, the Jokes of Discourse; or, Mrs. Stowe, Mr. Reed." In *Slavery and the Literary Imagination,* edited by Deborah E. McDowell and Arnold Rampersad. Baltimore: John Hopkins University Press, 1989.

Strawbery Banke Museum. "Civil War Encampment." Press release, June 14, 1998. http:// www.strawberybanke.org/1998/pressreleases/civilwar.html.

Swinton, David. "Economic Status of Blacks, 1986." In *The State of Black America, 1987,* 49–73. New York: National Urban League, 1987.

Tate, Claudia. "Freud and His 'Negro': Psychoanalysis as Ally and Enemy of African Americans." *Journal for the Psychoanalysis of Culture and Society* 1.1 (1996): 53–62.

———. *Psychoanalysis and Black Novels: Desire and the Protocols of Race.* New York: Oxford University Press, 1998.

"Tears and Protest at Mock Slave Sale." A special to the *New York Times,* October 11, 1994, A16.

"Teens Try Third World Life." *Charlottesville Daily Progress,* July 28, 2005, B1–B2.

Thomas, Velma Maia. *Lest We Forget: The Passage from Africa to Slavery and Emancipation.* New York: Crown, 1997.

Tolbert, Bill. "Slave Auction Re-enacted Amid Some Controversy." *Williamsburg Virginia Gazette,* October 8, 1994, A1.

Truzzi, Gianni. "Middle Passage Pageant Blends Heartbreak with Redemption." *Seattle Post-Intelligencer,* July 18, 2003.

Twigz'N'Berries. "Evil Avatar: Daily Gaming News with Attitude." Online posting, August 12, 2005. http://www.evilavatar.com/forums/showthread.php?t=4171&page=2&pp=10 &highlight=chappelle%27s+show.

2 Live Crew. "Face Down, Ass Up." On *Banned in the USA.* Luke Skyywalker Records, 1990.

Tyehimba, Cheo. "Scarred Walls of Stone." http://www.iveknownrivers.org/stories/scarred .htm.

Ultima 13. "Evil Avatar: Daily Gaming News with Attitude." Online posting, August 12, 2005. http://www.evilavatar.com/forums/showthread.php?t=4171&page=2&pp=10& highlight=chappelle%27s+show.

"The Underground Railroad: History of Slavery, Pictures, Information." http://www .nationalgeographic.com/railroad/j1.html.

Van der Kolk, Bessel A., and Onno Van der Hart. "The Intrusive Past: The Flexibility of Memory and the Engraving of Trauma." In *Trauma: Explorations in Memory,* edited by Cathy Caruth. Baltimore: Johns Hopkins University Press, 1995.

Vanderstel, David G. "Humanizing the Past: The Revitalization of the History Museum." *Journal of American Culture* 12.2 (1989): 19–25.

Waldron, Clarence. "Staged Slave Auction Sparks Debate on the Slavery and Racism." *Jet,* November 1994, 12–15.

Walker, Alice. "Everyday Use." In *Love and Trouble: Stories of Black Women,* edited by Cathy Caruth. New York: Harcourt Brace Jovanovich, 1973.

Wallace, Maurice O. *Constructing the Black Masculine: Identity and Ideality in African American Men's Literature and Culture, 1775–1995.* Durham: Duke University Press, 2002.

Wallenstein, Andrew. "Chappelle Inks $50 Mill Comedy Deal." *Hollywood Reporter,* August 3, 2004, 1. http://web2.infotrac.galegroup.com/itw/infomark/362/159/71143606w2/purl=rcl_ITOF_0_A120701588&dyn=6!xrn_55_0_A120701588?sw_aep=viva_uva.

Watson, Robert. Interview. July 29, 2005.

Webb, Jim. "You Won't Find Slavery Re-enactors." Letter to the editor. *St. Petersburg Times,* February 20, 2005.

West, Cornel. *Race Matters.* Boston: Beacon Press, 1993.

Wilson, William Julius. *When Work Disappears: The World of the New Urban Poor.* New York: Vintage Books, 1997.

Wood, Jacqueline. "Enabling Texts: African American Drama, Politics, Presentation in the African American Literature Classroom." *College Literature* 32.1 (2005): 103–26.

Wood, Marcus. *Blind Memory: Visual Representations of Slavery in England and America, 1780–1865.* Manchester: Manchester University Press, 2000.

Woolford, Pamela. "Filming Slavery: A Conversation with Haile Gerima." *Transition* 64 (1994): 90–104.

Youngblood, Rev. Dr. Johnny Ray, ed. *St. Paul Community Baptist Church, Brooklyn N.Y., 10th Anniversary Commemoration of the MAAFA, September 7th–25th, 2004.* Souvenir newspaper. New York: Expedi Printing, 2004.

Zaino, Nick A., III. "Ask a Black Dude: Meet Comedian Dave Chappelle." *Progressive,* November 2003. http://www.findarticles.com/p/articles/mi_m1295/is_11_67/ai_11073759.

Index

LISA WOOLFORK is an associate professor of English at the University of Virginia. She is the author of "Academic Mothers and Their Feminist Daughters: A Remix," which appeared in *African American Review* (2006).

The University of Illinois Press
is a founding member of the
Association of American University Presses.

Composed in 10.5/13 Adobe Minion Pro
by Jim Proefrock
at the University of Illinois Press
Manufactured by Sheridan Books, Inc.

University of Illinois Press
1325 South Oak Street
Champaign, IL 61820-6903
www.press.uillinois.edu